Sarah (Burk)

Own or Other Culture

D1439601

Own or Other Culture challenges those anthropologists who suggest that fieldwork in the 'West' is merely a reiteration of what is already 'known'. Revealing some pioneering articles written over a period of some years, this book questions the association of culture with bounded locations and anthropology's privileging of exoticised 'other' regions, to the neglect of its own centres of power. The creation of cultural difference is addressed, as well as reflexivity and gender. The Introduction places the work in its original context and in the light of recent developments and controversies in anthropology.

Confronting the ambiguities of doing fieldwork in her own country, Judith Okely discusses a wide range of subjects. The author's boarding school reveals a British exotica, colonial comparisons and the gendering of the body. Although Gypsies treat non-Gypsies as the 'other', Gypsy fortune-tellers are shown to be closer to a sceptical scientific tradition than their credulous and literate non-Gypsy clients. Further chapters in *Own or Other Culture* scrutinise Malinowski's diary and advance issues for feminist anthropology in a reassessment of de Beauvoir, Kaberry and popularist accounts of gender and bodily experience across cultures.

Some of the chapters have been published before and have come to be regarded as classics. Of the themes which emerge, some remain controversial while others have become central within anthropology, having formerly been marginalised within various specialisms. Highly illustrated with photographs, *Own or Other Culture* is written in an accessible and vivid style. It will be essential reading for all students and lecturers in Social Anthropology, Cultural, Gender and Ethnic studies.

Judith Okely is Professor of Social Anthropology at the University of Edinburgh.

Own or Other Culture

Judith Okely

London and New York

First published 1996
by Routledge
11 New Fetter Lane, London EC4P 4EE

Simultaneously published in the USA and Canada
by Routledge
29 West 35th Street, New York, NY 10001

Routledge is an International Thomson Publishing company

© 1996 Judith Okely

Typeset in Times by
Ponting–Green Publishing Services, Chesham, Bucks
Printed and bound in Great Britain by
Biddles Ltd, Guildford and King's Lynn

British Library Cataloguing in Publication Data

A catalogue record for this book is available from the
British Library

Library of Congress Cataloguing in Publication Data

A catalogue record for this book has been requested

ISBN 0–415–11512–4 (hbk)
ISBN 0–415–11513–2 (pbk)

Dedicated to two friends and former colleagues
at Durham University, the late:

Ruth First
and
David Brooks

They encouraged and inspired

Contents

Figures

Preface

This collection has been written over a number of years. Of the themes which emerge, some have become central within anthropology and others have continued to be controversial. Some have blossomed under alternative vocabularies devised by different scholars. A few subjects have been mistakenly regarded as relevant solely to enclosed specialisms within the discipline. The increasing compartmentalism of anthropology risks intellectual impoverishment. When exclusive or ghettoised specialisms are so defined, knowledge becomes fragmented.

The volume seeks to counter that tendency by highlighting the interconnections between several themes. The privileging of certain ethnographic territories over others and the invention of cultural difference through the belief in cultural and spatial isolates are challenged throughout. I point to the anthropologically constructed character of regions with arbitrary or political exclusions. I argue instead for the interconnectedness of areas and issues. Rather than excluding whatever has been categorised as the West in orthodox anthropology, I argue that it is no less exotic. Some chapters pursue the themes of autobiography or reflexivity. Feminism in anthropology is elaborated, as also are bodies and their gendering. I highlight the often hidden and imaginative potential in (ethno)graphic theory which uses individual quotations and specific examples to make wider illuminations. I reappraise classic texts by Malinowski, Kaberry and de Beauvoir. In the Introduction, I follow through these ideas in relation to selected aspects of the relevant chapters throughout the volume.

Whereas I was born in Malta, and have lived in Africa and travelled extensively in Asia, the Middle East and North America, all my professional anthropological research has been done in Europe; the continent to which it is said that I belong. The ethnographic grounding for this volume arises mainly from fieldwork conducted in England and France. The material includes Gypsies and their interrelations with non-Gypsies; a girls' boarding school; Parisian feminism; the quest by the Women's Movement in the West for cultural alternatives; and resistant individuals in Oxfordshire and rural Normandy.

Several chapters (1, 3, 4 and 5) draw on my fieldwork with Gypsies and their relations with outsiders. One chapter (6) examines the interest generated by the Women's Liberation Movement in alternative bodily experiences and cultures. Two chapters (7 and 8) emerge from nine years' incarceration and socialisation into a privileged section of British class and gendered culture. They are followed by an extensive chapter which develops my intellectual experience as a student in Paris and a liberation by déracinement. This sojourn, still within Europe, gave the cultural and personal detachment to re-examine my own culture as British barbarism. I returned to France years later, as an anthropologist for professionally framed fieldwork in Normandy. Here I confronted the contrast between my previous metropolitan and bookish knowledge of French high culture – its art, literature and philosophy – and the everyday cultural experience of provincial, rural life. The final two chapters of this volume use this contrasting experiential knowledge of France.

Some chapters are newly published (5 and 6). Only minor alterations have been made to those previously published. Chapter 1 originally appeared in the *Royal Anthropological Institute Newsletter (RAIN)* (1984). Chapter 2 was published in the *Journal of the Anthropology Society Oxford* (1975). Chapter 3 was published in S. Wallman (ed.) *Ethnicity at Work* (1979), Macmillan. Chapter 4 originally appeared in S. Ardener (ed.) *Perceiving Women* (1975), London: Malaby Press. Chapter 7 was published in *New Society* (1978). Chapter 8 was first published in S. Ardener (ed.) *Defining Females* (1978), London: Croom Helm, reprinted by Berg (1993). Chapter 9 first appeared as part of my extended study *Simone de Beauvoir: A Re-reading* (1986), London: Virago/New York: Pantheon. Chapter 10 is a revised version of the Phyllis Kaberry Memorial Lecture, published in *Man* (1991) 26, 1: 3–22.

I thank Sandra Brown, Helen Callaway, Leonore Davidoff, Andy Dawson, Panayotis Dendrinos, Ian Edgar, Maggie French, Robert Gibb, Heather Gibson (Senior Editor), Anne Griffiths, Anna Grimshaw, Marie Johnson, Jeremy MacClancy, Sinéad ní Shuinéar (for the index), Jan Penrose, Alison Scott, Susan Smith, Jane Szurek, Martin Walker and Joni Wilson for valuable comments. Pat Caplan, Marianne Gullestad, Kirsten Hastrup, Michael Herzfeld, David Parkin, Marilyn Strathern, Elizabeth Tonkin and Jojada Verrips have given intellectual encouragement.

A Senior Research Fellowship from the Economic and Social Science Research Council (II52427505094) enabled me to complete the manuscript. When I was a Lecturer at the University of Durham, I befriended Ruth First and David Brooks. They offered intellectual excitement, companionship, laughter and a sense for the absurd. Both have since met untimely deaths and it is to their memory that I dedicate this book.

Introduction

REGIONAL HEGEMONIES AND EXCLUSIONS

Anthropology has thrived on the dramatic within or between cultures. Anthropologists of 'exotica' may have unwittingly relied upon taken-for-granted assumptions of difference when confronted with other cultures. This is despite Malinowski's plea to look at the 'imponderabilia of everyday life' (1922) which may in turn be more extraordinary than anything already so framed. For the Western anthropologist of her or his own 'ethnographic region', it is recognised as customary rather than exceptional that other often unfamiliar ways of thinking and being coexist in the same territory. While orthodox anthropologists studying geographically distant cultures are prepared to acknowledge variety and differences within places far from their own biographical past, and while an academic industry is made of intra-regional comparisons, anthropologists may be indifferent to the heterogeneity of their own cultural spaces.

Although the study of Europe has been dismissed as 'easy' (Bloch 1988),[1] because it is studied by other disciplines and therefore 'known', indigenous anthropologists of Europe and the West contest this presumption (Pina-Cabral 1992). The justification for the exclusion of Europe from the anthropological map (Bloch 1988) and the rejection of the anthropological gaze turned in upon itself reveals the belief that an anthropologist is above all the voice of a region rather than of a theory or intellectual innovation. It also presumes that the anthropology of 'the West', whatever that shifting spatial and cultural category entails, is uninformative. The growing number of fine anthropological texts based on fieldwork in Europe and the West will ultimately make exoticist exclusions indefensible.[2] There are multiple realities or worlds within this historically power-laden portion of the globe. It is presumptuous to put a cordon sanitaire around constructed regions. The division between 'known' or 'other' culture can be defined neither by national nor geographical territory. The exotic should be displaced.

While this book draws on fieldwork in various European contexts, it implicitly questions the arbitrary divisions of the world into anthropologically specialised regions. 'Although anthropology aspires to being a general study of humankind' (Fardon 1990: 24), regionalisation is thoroughly institutionalised in the academy and is very much a part of colonial history. Often the localities selected for focus by different European countries reflect a former colonial relationship. French anthropologists have worked in areas once under French colonial rule and likewise British anthropologists. North American anthropologists' regional specialisms, e.g. American Indians and Latin America, also reflect hegemonic relations. The canonical 'literature' to which the regional specialist is encouraged to refer reflects those connections. It is often written by outsiders linked to the colonial authority and in their own language. Indigenous literature may not receive the same international attention (Watson 1992).

The historical and academic basis of selectivity of areas of the globe has not been adequately addressed. Claims to regional authority are often meaningless. For example, Alan Campbell describes how all the Amazonian peoples of Brazil could be crowded in the country's largest football stadium, yet because he has done fieldwork among one of these groups, he can be labelled a South Americanist in the West (Campbell 1989). Regional specialisms within the discipline mask great gaps and silences. Gilsenan (1990: 225) recalls the postgraduate study of anthropology at Oxford in the mid-1960s: 'Where was "The Middle East"? Interestingly enough nowhere.' It was

> not composed as part of the anthropological object. . . . To us students the southern Sudan was central, Egypt peripheral; New Guinea a vital and Lebanon a dead space.
>
> (ibid. 226–7)

Some areas, for example Iran and Afghanistan, have been identified as not having 'made a great theoretical impact on the discipline' (Street 1990: 245). Ironically, anthropologists of the most geographically remote nomads, the Inuit, also lament that such studies have so far 'stimulated few advances in anthropological theory' (Riches 1990: 71). In the search for the exotic isolate, even the study of South American peasants has been regarded with ambivalence because of their contact with European culture (Harris 1993).

It seems that specialists from almost any region believe that their own is marginalised relative to another. While 'Africanists eagerly turn to Asian and Amerindian monographs for inspiration, the reverse rarely occurs' (Parkin 1990: 184). Even Asian ethnographers 'at the time that their anthropological colleagues are generally conceding them centrality' feel themselves marginal in contrast to the funding and power of other disciplines claiming expertise and policy relevance (Fardon 1990: 219–20). Nevertheless, within the hierarchy of regions the exclusion of Europe from any traditional anthropological pedagogic map still stands as the extreme case (cf. Ulin 1991). Until recently, anthropology has privileged that which the metropolis has defined as remote (Ardener 1987). Although Fardon feels obliged to explain the absence of Amazonia from his volume, the absence of Europe merits no comment. It is no accident that the geographic space which has been obliterated or defined as the ethnographic periphery for orthodox anthropology is the very same which is occupied by a centre of academic power.

This neglect of 'the geographic self' and the reifications of some patches on the globe are compounded by academic practices. Even though it may be intellectually and contextually fruitful for the anthropologist to read everything he or she can lay hands on about the particular locality, this can become restrictive if less attention is paid to theoretically and comparatively significant work written beyond the historically and colonially constructed region. Here my example of the Gypsies destabilises the theoretical and empirical presumptions of regional territory. Conventions in terms of surrounding geographical space become irrelevant when it comes to the study of peoples like the Gypsies who are found in every continent. Similarly, now that anthropologists are currently less able to ignore the manipulation of national borders, multinationals and global communications, academic regionalism has become parochial confinement. The theoretical and ethnographic implications of globalisation have destabilised regional hegemonies as well as cultural atlases, long routinised by the institutions of anthropology. Decades ago, as both my and others' work makes clear, the example of Gypsies raised theoretical and ethnographic questions in anthropology which are relevant to all groups and contexts, whether the peoples are nomadic or sedentary.

In keeping with my concerns about compartmentalisation, the contents of this book draw not only on anthropological fieldwork in Europe, but also explicitly or implicitly on ethnographies and theories developed from localities around the globe. The same analysis could not have been made if comparisons had been limited to ethnographies within the one constructed region of Europe. Moreover, the material presented here, as elsewhere (Okely 1983), contains a deliberate tension between the application of near classical anthropological approaches and innovative ones for a European's 'own' culture(s). Knowledge about 'the other' in another place in turn makes my indigenous territory reappear as strange.

OWN OR OTHER CULTURE

A recurrent argument in this volume concerns the ambiguity of any boundary between cultures or persons in a shared geographical space (Strathern 1987). Differences may have been generated as much if not more by inter-group relations and constructions as by spatial boundaries. Different groups inhabiting the same spaces can create and shift boundaries by subtle means. The ambiguity of boundary is also to be found between the subject selected for study and the cultural identity of the anthropologist (Loizos 1981; Pina-Cabral 1992; Macdonald 1993). The ambiguity becomes apparent in most cases of participant observation, but in this instance is inflated by the fact that the anthropologist doing fieldwork in her own country cannot measure difference in terms of geographical distance. Consequently, boundaries may be constructed in unusually elusive ways. Differences can be disguised by similarities and lost in the commonplace. Alternatively, it may be the anthropologist's own culture which becomes other through time (see chapters 7 and 8).

Distance between persons need not be measured by geographical mileage. Other forms of estrangements intervene. For the Kaberry Memorial Lecture, delivered in the heart of Oxford (see chapter 10, this volume), I deliberately chose testimony I had recorded locally of a rural working-class man from the academically unconstructed ethnographic region of Oxfordshire. Afterwards, a distinguished anthropologist asked me how I had come to meet this individual. The genuine puzzlement in the question indicated that some of the inhabitants of one's own village may remain as elusive as cannibals. They are neither known nor inevitably accessible to the average middle-class academic on home territory.

As these various complexities already suggest, the very notion of culture has become problematic (Strathern 1987; Clifford 1988). It is too monolithic. There are insoluble difficulties in demarcating the boundaries of separate cultures. Place can no longer be viewed as coterminous with culture and identity (Hastrup and Fog Olwig 1994). Increasingly anthropology has had to confront the consequences of migrations, refugee dispersals and the multicultural metropolis. These dramatic displacements should not be regarded as the only rationale for scepticism about associating a culture with a fixed location. My research has concentrated on both the sedentary and the nomadic and in few instances were transformations and changes simply a result of crises or geographic movement. Disjunctions between groups, persons, contexts or cultures have been continuously invented as part of everyday practice as well as over extended periods of history. Similarly, elisions and syntheses have been created from the same space. All cultures are provisional. It is possible that all are hybrid, not just those once labelled syncretic as a consequence of migrations and invasions.

Gender perspectives on the own/other divide or intersection are confronted in my reappraisal of de Beauvoir's classic text *The Second Sex* (chapter 9). De Beauvoir charts the ideological tradition of treating 'woman' as always 'other' to man. Woman is object to man as subject, while the obverse is nonexistent. She, the woman writer, is also the 'other' writing back. In the guise of pan-culturalism, there is a culturally loaded character to her generalisations which rely mainly on Western paradigms. Even her representation of the West is selective and specific. I argue that in a text which claims to be global and cross-cultural, lurks de Beauvoir's own bourgeois and Roman Catholic, Parisian experience. Her polemic is grounded in her own culture, not that of all others.

THE WEST AS EXOTIC

The popular adage of making the exotic familiar and the familiar strange is not fulfilled if Western anthropology departments exclude or downgrade the study of the cultures within which academics are embedded. The avowed aim of anthropology to study all of humanity is spoiled if it excludes the Western 'I' while relying mainly on the Western eye/gaze upon 'others'. Paradoxically, and partly for economic and political reasons, departments of anthropology in Asia, Latin America and Africa see no problem in concentrating mainly on different cultures within their own space. They confront the unknown in their midst. Moreover, for them the West may become exotica. In Huizer and Mannheim's important collection *The Politics of Anthropology* (1978), many contributors challenged the assumptions of conventional Western anthropologists by arguing that it was essential to study the West; both in ways which have not been covered by other disciplines and by non-Western anthropologists. The geographical and political spaces where Western anthropologists have been socialised also contain areas of strangeness. The example of Bosnia (Bringa 1994) demonstrates how complacent Westerners have been about seemingly familiar territory, ethnic brutality and resurgent nationalism.

In this book, a Western anthropologist questions such complacency through the study of her own culture(s) and those of others within or alongside them. In the process it becomes clear that even though the power of the West's political economy may be global and disproportionate, the West is no homogenised and rationalised whole. Differences, indeed exoticas, are as much a part of the West, as they are created by the West for the Orient (Said 1978). Strange and romantic 'occidentals' are reinvented, inverted and synthesised.

The differences found within Europe or the West in general serve as a warning to anthropologists of the far away. The latter tend to erect a vast homogenised stereotype of 'the West' or their own West with which to contrast their micro-field study abroad, without recognising the cultural multiplicity of the places from whence they came. They are making a banal occidentalism of themselves. When anthropologists create this mythically unitary culture, I am compelled to ask whether they are unreflexively pointing to the autobiographical culture of their childhood and education. Alternatively, perhaps they are dependent on a few texts and an ensuing ideology which floats above all specificities.

The homogenising of Western scientific thought versus 'the rest' began with the study of the primitive as other. When Evans-Pritchard (1937) aimed to restore 'rationality' to the Azande, he did so nevertheless by presuming the pervasiveness of scientific thought in the West. My analysis of fortune-telling (chapter 5) reveals how 'non-rational' beliefs on a par with those of the Azande are pervasive among a whole cross-section of individuals in

Britain, despite their acquaintance with at least the elementary principles of Western science. The few studies of modern Western witchcraft and magic have concentrated on the receptivity towards these practices among distinct and often marginalised groups; for example, rural inhabitants of the French Bocage (Favret-Saada 1981) or closed associations (Luhrmann 1989). In contrast, chapter 5 in this collection highlights the receptivity to Gypsy fortune-telling among even the most privileged members of the dominant society. In my ethnography, it is the ethnically closed group which caters for the magically credulous population of the dominant rationalised society. It is a superb irony that the marginalised and non-literate Gypsies are closer to a sceptical Western scientific tradition than their literate non-Gypsy clients.

The unforeign exotic can thus be found or forged in the West, as the example of the Gypsies and their interrelations with non-Gypsies demonstrate. Chapter 3, 'Trading stereotypes', explores the selective exoticism or its denial among Gypsies in encounters with outsiders, whom they refer to as gorgios. Gypsies, in full knowledge of gorgio stereotypes, manipulate them to suit the contextual moment. Gypsies may choose to adopt the degraded stance; alternatively, they may exoticise or, in their own words, 'Gypsify' themselves. Another option is to pass as a gorgio. Thus surface similarities may hold contrary and subversive meanings. Anticipating Taussig's (1993) and others' discussion of mimesis, chapter 3 shows how the Gypsies mimic both stereotypes of themselves and those they hold of non-Gypsies (cf. Bhabhar 1994).

Other examples of potential exoticism in the West are provided in chapters 7 and 8 which explore the ethnography of a girls' boarding school in England. These chapters are an active reminder of the flexibility of the boundaries which are used to define any culture. Where Gypsy self-definition relies on a monolithic view of British hegemonic culture, the ethnography of girls' boarding schools quickly narrows and refines the definition of hegemonic. Over the years, many readers have been baffled by the cruel exoticism of such institutions which are normal to some but not to others. The fact that these readers have included those who were educated in Britain's majority state system bears testament to the fractures within all cultural constructs. At the same time, different views of these institutions highlight the importance of positionality in labelling practices as either commonplace or exotica.

ISOLATES OR INTERCONNECTIONS

In chapter 2 on Malinowski's *Diary*, I question the ethnographic construction of isolated, exotic communities. Malinowski's day-to-day experience was marked not only by the Trobriand Islanders, but also by the presence of white traders, administrators and missionaries. Their influence was ubiquitous, but they were largely laundered from the academic monographs (cf. Sanjek 1991: 613). The Trobrianders in Malinowski's public monographs are presented mainly as stone age 'savages'. For decades after him, anthropologists continued to seek isolates or in effect to construct them. We have tended to take on trust orthodox anthropologists' claims to heroic journeys into the unknown, isolated communities up the jungle and over the mountain ranges. The monographs emphasised self-containment and differences, seemingly born of isolation. Any previous scepticism has more recently been confirmed by a recognition of the long-term relations between the exotic groups and others, often Westerners. Anthropologists are waking up to the fact that seemingly isolated peoples are not only affected by new invasions and changes, but also that they had a history, which included migrations and new formations. Stephen Hugh-Jones, who studied the tropical forest Amerindians – a people whom the discipline has perceived as archetypically exotically self-contained – has noted critically in the work of Lévi-Strauss that 'although White people are often present in Amerindian myth and thought, they are largely absent from the pages of *Mythologiques*' (Hugh-Jones 1989: 54).

Now that the assumptions of 'isolated' communities can no longer be sustained in any part of the globe, anthropologists of Gypsies can be recognised as well versed in questions of inter-group boundaries and relations in the same geographical space. Right from the outset, such anthropologists have been obliged to examine the Gypsies' perceptions of gorgios or 'the other'. Since Gypsies are economically interdependent with the wider society, they have to confront gorgios on a daily basis, while at the same time resisting persecution and assimilation. Because gorgios are never erased from the picture, their difference is generated by inter-group relations and constructions rather than by forced spatial boundaries. The Gypsies' classification systems and cosmology cannot be divorced from their relations with gorgios and their perception of the latter's beliefs (Okely 1983). Chapters 3, 4 and 5 demonstrate these interconnections in economic and ritual spheres.

The fact that Gypsies cannot be pinned down to a region has meant that they provide a superb example of a people whose culture has been constructed and recreated in the midst of others. This lack of fixed regional association has also meant that anthropologists who study Gypsies have been obliged to examine them in their relationships with non-Gypsies both at local and intercontinental, if not global levels. This is something quite different from working with the accumulative body of knowledge produced by other anthropological studies of a specific geographical region. Anthropologists among Gypsies have found intellectual reward in comparing studies of Gypsies and their relations with outsiders in all continents. These anthropologists' relative freedom from regional determinism has enabled them to identify similarities alongside intriguing differences (Sutherland 1975; Kaminski 1980; Stewart 1987). They have drawn on concepts, themes and theories from around the globe. By good fortune, those anthropologists who chose to work in the blanked-out spaces on the anthropological map were free of the standardised paradigms.

Whatever the topic, a micro-study, drawing on participant observation, can raise questions and answers across any regions. This is true of the chapters (7 and 8) which deal with experiences associated with my girls' boarding school. The study of this quantitatively insignificant but qualitatively powerful segment of British educational culture has cross-cultural resonances. Through the ethnography, the West is revealed as bizarre. Besides, we are confronted with the possibility that the exotic may be no historical isolate but a colonial transplant found elsewhere. Connections may be made of the kind suggested by Comaroff and Comaroff in their linkage between Western models of domesticity and those exported to the colonies (1992: 265–94). 'Hegemony is homemade' (ibid. 1992: 294), if 'homemade' is taken as referring to Europe. Parallel regimes of the British public school were exported as essential ingredients of British colonialism and remain as a legacy for privileged indigenous elites.

After presentation or publication of my work on boarding schools, I received favourable yet anguished responses from former inmates of similar female institutions in North India, West Africa, South Africa and New Zealand. Despite the highly varied geographical and 'supra-cultural' contexts, all of these women recognised strong parallels between their experiences and those which my writing described. These texts are original for their ethnography of girls' private and exclusive education, as opposed to the more extensive and often ungendered social science literature on state schooling. At the same time, they illustrate how the definition of exotica is subjective and how the construction of cultural isolates is illusory.

The concluding chapters to the volume confront the notion of regional isolates in other ways. Chapter 10 treads on territory normally reserved for Australianists or, more precisely, anthropologists of Aborigines. Here I had no intention of giving a linear account of all the regionalist literature since Kaberry, but instead examined the internal consistency of her text and ethnography in the 1930s. In pursuing the notions of defiance and resistance, I also broke free of that continent and offered ethnographic examples from the other side of the globe: England in the 1914–18 War and France in the 1980s, each in their historical context.

AUTOBIOGRAPHY OR REFLEXIVITY

Chapter 2 ('The self and scientism') is, apart from the numerous reviews summarised in Firth (1988), one of the earliest on Malinowski's *Diary* (1967). I developed aspects which were denied or overlooked by Geertz (1974; 1988: 73–84). This chapter is also important because of a number of developments which have become central to contemporary anthropology. Written in 1974, the chapter raised questions about what has subsequently become known as reflexivity. At the time, my use of the concept 'subjectivity' was paired with the notion of objectivity. Given the latter's positivistic

associations and subsequent developments in postmodernism, I would hesit-
ate to use it now. By contrast, my notion of autobiography has blossomed
across disciplines as an established genre. Since the late 1970s, there has been
a burgeoning of autobiographical literature (cf. Marcus and Fischer 1986: 34
and Okely 1992), which my article anticipated. The autobiographical ingredients and a discussion of fieldwork as encounters and sets of relations have,
since the article was first published, become more integrated into the
discipline (Okely and Callaway 1992). The same is true of my decision to
discuss participant observation in a broader methodological context (cf.
Okely 1987 and 1994). Finally, the article highlighted taken-for-granted or
covert racism and masculinist priorities in Malinowski's research.

When first published, the *Diary* was read mainly as an embarrassing
exposé of the anthropologist's individual psychology without epistemological worth. In his second introduction, Firth came to recognise the interest
the book had for post-Malinowski generations of anthropologists who were
less interested in the personality of 'the man' and more in the alienating
experience of fieldwork. None the less, few of these anthropologists saw
much to learn in the *Diary* about connections between theory, ethnography
and methods (Firth 1988: xxvii). As in Stocking's (1968) review, my chapter
argued to the contrary.

Firth remains critical of any connections between the autobiographical
dimensions of fieldwork and the writing of texts (1988: xxviii). Nevertheless,
he makes a curious assertion in his critique of Clifford (1988) for treating
'the Diary and *Argonauts* as "a single expanded text"' (Firth 1988: xxx).
Firth uses Malinowski's marital status to argue that the texts must be treated
differently. The one, Firth emphasises, was written by a 'bachelor, in a time
of great stress' while *Argonauts* was written by a 'happily married-man, in a
time of relative tranquillity' (ibid. xxx). This argument goes against the spirit
of what I argued in this earlier article and subsequently (Okely 1992).
Malinowski's bachelor status is relevant to the extent that the Trobrianders
treated him as such. There was no necessary guarantee after marriage of a
shift in Malinowski's perception of women. Indeed, his *Sexual Life of
Savages* (1929) continues to betray a tendency to view women not as subjects
but as men's objects (see chapter 6, this volume). The presumption that
marriage changed Malinowski's outlook needs the more rigorous exploration
which others have made in relation to their own research (Kenna 1992;
Caplan 1992, 1993).

Overall, Firth now concedes:

I would no longer rank it as 'no more than a footnote to anthropological
history'. The concept of ethnography has altered and widened, and the book
has accordingly moved over to a more central place in the literature of
anthropological reflection.

(1988: xxxi)

My opening chapter 'Fieldwork in the Home Counties' is an example of the kind of autobiographical writing called for in 'The self and scientism'. Written for a celebration of Malinowski's centenary, it draws attention to the ambiguous or non-geographical boundary between own or other cultures and the special problems of doing research in one's own country.

The chapters on a girls' boarding school combine autobiography and ethnography. They are examples of the application of anthropology to a segment of the anthropologist's own (ex-)culture and an exercise in studying up (Nader 1969). The retrospective fieldwork in a setting generally disliked by the anthropologist contrasts with the usual fieldwork practice. In addition, the use of the author as main informant gives added authority. I did not have to resort to crafted devices to remind the reader that I had 'been there' (Clifford and Marcus 1986). The autobiographical authority has simultaneously invited readers, especially women, to compare and contrast the ethnography with their own experiences of education.

The texts experiment in making the once 'known' strange. When chapter 7 was first published in the weekly *New Society*, I received tempting requests from several publishers to write an entire monograph on the subject. Such fieldwork would indeed have been in a known place but would in no way have been 'easy', as the orthodox anthropologists would claim. Plans to revisit the location for an exploratory research weekend were quickly abandoned. Past memories as an inmate overwhelmed any identity I had acquired as an adult anthropologist. I could not return to what was remembered as a place of terror. Understandably, research for the proposed monograph was never undertaken.

While I have analysed de Beauvoir's explicit autobiography elsewhere (Okely 1986), the reassessment of de Beauvoir presented in this volume (chapter 9) draws attention to the hidden strength of her autobiographical ethnography concealed in *The Second Sex*. Although it appears to be a generalised theory about all women, I suggest that the text had resonance because it covertly drew upon the vivid and grounded detail of de Beauvoir's autobiographical experience, with which the female reader could compare or contrast her own.

The chapter plays on both de Beauvoir's autobiography and on those of her readers. My entire study of de Beauvoir, from which this is an extract, is also an engagement with literary and postmodern 'reader response' theories. For example, the gender, race, age and class of the reader has implications for the interpretation and meaning of the text. To emphasise the instability of the self, I have contrasted my reading of de Beauvoir's text when I was a student at the Sorbonne in the 1960s with a re-reading twenty-five years later. The ink underlinings in my first copy, together with letters home and my Paris diary, were important guides to the impact of her text at the time. The later reading was informed by the cumulative anthropological literature and feminist debates emerging from the Women's Movement.

Chapter 6, 'Women readers', also draws on autobiographical ethnography or participant observation through an examination of the demands which the 1970s Women's Movement placed on anthropology. I began the decade as a postgraduate in anthropology and finished it as a lecturer who, after some abortive attempts, succeeded in having accepted within an anthropology degree an optional course entitled 'Race and Gender'.[3]

FEMINISM AND GENDER

There is an implicit or explicit feminist grounding to most of the papers in this collection. While the Women's Liberation Movement produced a flowering of alternative perspectives, there was an astonishing complacency about the need to consider gender divisions in mainstream anthropology.[4] Even in the late 1970s the patriarchal paradigm remained complacent and uninformed in British anthropology, despite the publication of key volumes and articles in feminist anthropology (Lamphere and Rosaldo 1974; Reiter 1975 and Ardener 1975) and a cornucopia in sociology and history (Mitchell 1971; Oakley 1972 and Rowbotham 1973). For instance, at the 1978 ASA annual conference on 'The Anthropology of Work', several senior anthropologists were incredulous at the suggestion that housework could be treated as work. Yet the subject had been debated and refined by women social scientists for nearly a decade (cf. Oakley 1974; Malos 1980).

One professor declared that women had always been adequately studied because the standard monographs always contained sections on marriage and the family (cf. Oakley 1974: 16–18). His androcentric pronouncement from a position of authority thus froze the academic agenda. Similarly, the conference paper of a younger male anthropologist argued that in his ethnographic area, marked by a spatially enforced gender division of labour, the boundaries between men and women were now breaking down because the men regularly phoned home. I remarked to my sceptical contemporaries that over centuries, gender boundaries had not necessarily been undermined by a less 'high tech' communication, namely heterosexual intercourse.

GENDERED EXAMPLES WITHIN A FEMINIST ANTHROPOLOGY

Shirley Ardener first encouraged me to write about Gypsy women (chapter 4) for the weekly Oxford women's anthropology seminar. This was a co-operative, alternative gathering of mainly women postgraduates (see chapter 6). The atmosphere was quite different from the standard combative seminar as cock fight that academia seems to favour, and where many gifted women postgraduates and a few subaltern men were customarily silenced and marginalised. As chapter 6 shows, in the 1970s (and as is still usually the case in the 1990s) the majority of postgraduates and staff in anthropology were male. Men were discouraged from attending the Oxford women's seminar because we found that even when they numbered two or three, they continued to behave as if they were the majority. Some of us postgraduates had never given papers before and we felt at ease in a supportive atmosphere, away from what others would wish to define as 'the cut and (phallic) thrust of academia' *(my insertion!)*. One male lecturer even warned his female student that attendance at the seminars would be bad for her career. Given the patrilineal patronage, he was probably right at the time.

It might appear strange to admit decades later that, although I had considered myself a feminist since the age of eighteen (Okely 1986), I had not made a political connection between that and academic content until after my return from fieldwork among the Gypsies. Indeed, the majority of feminist anthropologists who published in the early 1970s had not necessarily embarked on a consciously feminist project (Caplan 1993), nor had they confined themselves exclusively to women as the new folklore-cum-orthodoxy now suggests (cf. Okely 1995). The seminar and the request to look at my material on gender, together with the London Women's Anthropology Conference, showed the interconnections between feminism in private life, academic research and the public domains.

Chapter 4, 'Gypsy women', pursues an early attempt to place a specific study of women and their relations with men in the context of ethnic contrasts and in relation to broader questions of gender and women's subordination, both within Britain and elsewhere. The general questions are presented as descriptions rather than universalist explanations. I was fascinated by de Beauvoir's question regarding the circumstances in which women might resist or subvert their conditions. Such questions about resistance subsequently entered mainstream anthropology in the work of Scott (1985), although de Beauvoir had raised significant questions years earlier in relation to gender.

Twenty years later, I consider that the extent of women's subordination in different cultures, groups or contexts continues to be a matter for theoretical, empirical and political discussion. I have yet to be presented with a convincing example of a society where there is no gender asymmetry in all the four spheres which I then identified: namely, economic, political, ideological and sexual. If this is what is meant by 'universalist', then I confess to the label, but would not be so bold as to present universal, pan-cultural causes, as de Beauvoir attempted.

Chapter 9 on de Beauvoir continues some of the debates within feminism. That women were subordinate needed to be stated in the postwar period and subsequent decades. Her text had didactic and polemical power despite or because of its dependence on largely Western philosophy and literature to which she drew attention, alongside a covert critique. De Beauvoir rejects economic and psychoanalytical explanations for women's subordination. But, I argue, her comprehension of these theories is often a caricature. Ultimately, de Beauvoir's explanation rests on the idealist universalism that woman is always regarded as 'the other'. De Beauvoir's association of women with nature and men with culture provided the basis for the feminist anthropologist Ortner's celebrated article (Ortner 1974) which acknowledges her debt to de Beauvoir and yet which few anthropologists with the exception of Harris (1980) have recognised. Both de Beauvoir and Ortner, I reveal, carry latent biologisms in their argument, despite the fact that both set out to undermine the suggestion that gender asymmetry can be explained by biology.

Chapter 10, 'Defiant moments', pursues the debate as to whether women can be judged as subordinate in other cultures. Kaberry's detailed monograph on *Aboriginal Woman* (1939) conveys conflicting messages, but has been accepted uncritically as proof of a society without gender asymmetry (Bell 1983 and Moore 1988: 32). An analysis of Kaberry's text reveals an alternative interpretation when I distinguish the notion of subservience from subordination. Having argued that Aboriginal women are subordinate yet not subservient, I explore examples of individual resistances to different types of subordination; not only gender, but also that related to class and ecological perspectives.

Feminist anthropology should, as Rosaldo (1974) suggested two decades ago, examine gender relations rather than women in isolation. Although the majority of monographs prior to the influence of feminist anthropology were implicitly about men rather than women, the construction and practices of masculinity were not foregrounded in the analysis. By pointing to this fundamental flaw in texts, feminist anthropologists were also demanding the problematisation of masculinities. My analysis of an English boarding school (chapter 8) explicitly argued in 1978 that the study of the all-female institution cannot be understood independently of the ideals and practice of parallel all-male institutions. Much has been written about the public school ethos, but few studies have made explicit that it is a masculinist ideology for male pupils who in adulthood join the 'old boy network'. An examination of the obverse feminine ideology points to the genderised character of the former.

Just as the category 'woman' has required dismantling, so should that of 'man'. My re-reading of de Beauvoir (Okely 1986 and chapter 9, this volume) highlights her romanticisation of 'men' and 'the male' whom she credits with all that is culture and the exciting projects in the world. De Beauvoir not only underplays cultural activities associated with women, but also ignores class, ethnic and cultural differences among men.

I present an example of Western masculinity and its association with military identity (chapter 10), using the testimony of a First World War deserter whom I had tape-recorded in the early 1970s. This was at the time when, according to the latest anti-hagiographies, women anthropologists, inspired by the Women's Liberation Movement, were allegedly only interested in studying women.

Paradoxically, both before and during the 1970s there were some arenas where the study of gendered relations privileged women, leaving men invisible; for example, popularist research on female prostitutes. In a 1975 review I argued 'in any study of prostitution, the focus of investigation should be shifted to the "client" . . . it would be more daring to locate the client – who is everywhere, but more elusive than a distant tribe' (Okely 1975: 440). Just that kind of anthropological research was being undertaken in Peru by Kate Arnold (1977).

There remains continuing potential for ethnographic and theoretical sophistication in the problematising of masculinities in feminist anthropology and anthropology in general (Cornwall and Lindisfarne 1994). The examples in this volume reveal how feminist anthropology from the 1970s to the 1990s has continuities and not only changes in emphases. A paradigmatic shift as dramatic as that which occurred in gendered anthropology in the 1970s may well emerge. But at present, the changes initiated two decades ago have yet to fulfil their potential in the discipline as a whole.

THE BODY OR BODIES

The short essay on girls' bodies written for the popularist *New Society* addressed the feminine genderising of the body. This is a topic in which a vast social science literature was about to emerge, although not always genderised (Blacking 1977; Polhemus 1978; Jackson 1983; Martin 1987; Jackson 1989; Synnott 1993). Along with my reading of Hertz (1909) and Mauss (1936), chapters 7 and 8 on the boarding school had been inspired by Foucault's *Discipline and Punish* (1977) and parts of Bourdieu (1977). My analysis in chapter 8 of girls' boarding schools especially is a detailed ethnographic working through of the insights of these French theorists, who inspired me into re-living the minutiae of past experience. What had been made normal through childhood and acculturation, I was to unlearn as strange and historically and culturally specific. Foucault's discussion of discipline, timetabling, the control and increasing surveillance of unruly and moving bodies in the spaces of military and pedagogical institutions from the eighteenth century in Europe helped me to place and demystify the controls and surveillance of the British public school in the late twentieth century. When I presented 'Girls and their bodies' (chapter 7) at the IAEUS Women's Intercongress in Delhi, someone remarked that my bodily composure confirmed my arguments. My body was permanently marked as the supreme visual aid.

Although both Hertz (1909) and Mauss (1936) had touched upon gender differences, a major failure in Foucault had been the somewhat arrogant indifference to gender differentiation and the gendering of the body. None the less, Foucault's discussion of European punishment, moving from the mutilation and destruction of the body to its detached surveillance in prisons, provided a useful contrast in gendered punishment. In British upper-class culture more often the boy's body is marked and caned whereas the girl's body is surveyed but untouched. Like Foucault's observations on European prisons which no longer institutionalised bodily mutilations, the girls' punishment and containment cannot be simplistically described as more benign and enlightened.

Foucault's contrast between the body as either untouched or subject to direct contact was also an organising principle which I transposed to genderised sport. My distinctions between 'masculine' and 'feminine' games have proved relevant beyond public schools, to include state schools and adult sport, both national and international. The gendering of sport has since been more thoroughly researched (Hargreaves 1994). In the 1990s a few gendered divisions in sport are beginning to break down. But club membership, funding and the media continue to privilege male-dominated sports.

In addition to gender, the chapters on the girls' body and boarding school explore how social class is embodied in deportment, manners and voice. Again, Bourdieu's stress on learning through embodiment was useful. The body is not just a passive receptacle but a moving, growing person especially vulnerable to surveillance and internalisation in a 'total institution' (Goffman 1968).

Earlier connections between the body as symbol of the social order and pollution beliefs had been developed by Douglas (1966, 1973), whose work provided theoretical stimulus to interpretations of the Gypsies' pollution beliefs and bodily practices. 'Gypsy women' (chapter 4) explores the implications of the gendered and sexualised body, including rules about its clothing. In this same chapter, there are some first steps in discussing sexuality, in addition to offering a cross-cultural contrast in the symbolic elaboration of menstruation and birth. Even today, it is extremely problematic to publish any detailed discussion of the former, given the vulnerability of Gypsies to exoticism by outsiders' publications.

De Beauvoir's pronouncements on the female and male body are confronted in chapter 9. De Beauvoir is renowned for her statement that woman is 'made not born', and by implication made 'feminine' by culture rather than by the biological body. Yet de Beauvoir undermines her own thesis by giving bodily explanations for largely Western generalisations. These slippages I expose.

Too often questions raised by feminists remain academically marginalised, but take centre stage when subsequently taken up by male authors (Mascia-Lees et al. 1989; Marcus 1992: 174; del Valle 1993: 3). The rush of interest in bodily knowledge in the 1970s had been greatly inspired by the Women's Liberation Movement. Western women were interested in alternative ways of giving birth and cross-cultural views of menstruation. Technology had provided new forms of birth control through the pill, and abortion was legalised in Britain and elsewhere. At the same time, women saw themselves increasingly commodified in a consumer culture. Eventually and thanks also to de Beauvoir, they found the vocabulary and articulated a protest against being seen as sexual objects; as bodies without autonomy, but controlled by others. De Beauvoir (chapter 9) was the earliest to articulate the recognition that women are more likely to be seen as objects than subjects.

This recognition helped stimulate the search for alternative gendered bodies in other cultures by Western women in the 1970s (chapter 6). Sadly, social anthropology was lacking the bodily and sexualised material from women's or gendered perspectives. Instead, some popularist publications, written outside or from the margins of the discipline, fed the demand for alternative bodily experiences and knowledge with conflicting conclusions.

'Women readers' (chapter 6) gives a historical and first-hand ethnographic dimension to the earlier failure by postwar anthropology to discuss not only sexuality, but also cross-cultural aspects of women's bodily experience. Aspects of sexuality are also pursued in my critique of de Beauvoir. Her excessive disgust at the female body, its form and processes, tell us more about her individual history and acculturated, catholicised self than the body of others or everywoman.

Sexuality was long marginalised within anthropology. After legitimation by Foucault (1979), its historical and cultural construction has become more central within social science. Again, however, Foucault pays precious little attention to gender difference. Thanks also to the impetus from feminist anthropology (Caplan 1987; Martin 1987), anthropology is developing a new sophistication in the cross-cultural ethnography of sexuality and the sexed body.

THEORY THROUGH ETHNOGRAPHY

To conclude, occasionally anthropological analysis has been misread as neutral and unproblematic description, especially by a sociological tradition which makes an intellectual division of labour between theoretical and 'substantive' issues. There should always be a place for ethnographically theoretical anthropology or *graphic* theory. Many of the chapters in this book illuminate theories through ethnographic detail; they are not 'mere' description. Graphic and evocative illustration resounds and ripples. The poetics of anthropology entails more than generalised theory, but also the imaginative attention to detail. These chapters are redolent with examples, individual statements and events. Many of these are from my fieldnotes or are condensed summaries and paraphrases of my fieldwork experience recorded or recalled in that context. They frequently appear in the text as unattributed quotations and narratives. The 1980s' interest in different voices has occasionally been restricted to noting that there are other opinions and standpoints beyond those of the concealed authorial voice. This collection, written both before and after that stage in anthropological discussion, works with many direct quotations or as near as could be recorded at the time. Singular statements and incidents can also act as an epiphany. Interpretation is presented through multiple examples, each with its spatial and temporal specificity, while simultaneously inviting the reader to think and imagine further.

Knowledge of the ambiguities between own or other cultures can become most vivid through heightened sensitivity to the minutiae of cultural and social contexts. If everything is theorised through grand abstraction, then both the anthropologist and the reader may unconsciously supply their own examples in the thinking. They may add their unthought-out experience. They may presume that what seems prosaically familiar at a common-sense level is fully known and understood both by themselves and all others. Alternatively, both classical anthropologist and reader may imagine exotica where it does not exist. So either the commonplace elsewhere is left unnoticed or all strangeness is lost nearby. Any segment of experience, any people, any portion of the globe, should be open to anthropology's poetic sensibility and graphic scrutiny.

NOTES

1 Bloch has stated: 'If the study of Europe or of North America gets a toehold in anthropology departments it tends to rapidly push out studies of other societies because frankly, such studies appear easier to research students . . . . In the LSE we have . . . a fairly traditional anthropology department. If I was replaced by someone studying a French village, for example, I would be replaced by someone studying a culture studied by thousands of people in British universities and there would not be anybody left in any British university in the whole country working on the people of Madagascar, a country of around ten million people. Therefore I am keen on preserving an oddity (the association of anthropology with the exotic)' (in Bloch 1988: 19–20).

2 See Davis (1977) for an overview of southern Europe. Some later texts include Brandes (1980), Ennew (1980), Favret-Saada (1981), Loizos (1981), Strathern (1981), Gullestad (1984), Hastrup (1985), Herzfeld (1985), Martin (1987), Herzfeld (1987), Cohen (1987), Zulaika (1988), McDonald (1989), Cowan (1990), Marcus (1992).

3 In this my colleague the late David Brooks collaborated; bringing Middle Eastern material on gender, femininity and masculinity. This was at a time when postfeminists wrongly claim that our generation concentrated solely on women, and without concern for race and difference.

4 At an interview for a temporary lectureship in the mid-1970s, I was asked by the head of department if I would still be interested in the job if I could not teach anything about women. Presumably, anthropology was unashamedly only about men. I gave this ethnographic example in my 1989 Kaberry lecture, but it was inexplicably deleted from the published article in *Man*.

REFERENCES

Ardener, E. (1987) 'Remote areas: some theoretical considerations', in A. Jackson (ed.) *Anthropology at Home*, London: Tavistock.

Ardener, S. (ed.) (1975) *Perceiving Women*, London: Malaby Press.

Arnold, K. (1977) 'The introduction of poses to a Peruvian brothel and changing images of male and female', in J. Blacking (ed.) *The Anthropology of the Body*, London: Academic Press.

Bell, D. (1983) *Daughters of the Dreaming*, Melbourne: McPhee Gribble.

Bhabhar, H. (1994) *The Location of Culture*, London: Routledge.

Blacking, J. (ed.) (1977) *The Anthropology of the Body*, London: Academic Press.

Bloch, M. (1988) 'Interview with G. Houtman', *Anthropology Today* 4, 1: 18–21.

Bourdieu, P. (1977) *Outline of a Theory of Practice*, trans. R. Nice, Cambridge: Cambridge University Press.

Brandes, S. (1980) *Metaphors of Masculinity: Sex and Status in Andalusian Folklore*, Philadelphia: University of Philadelphia Press.

Bringa, T. (1994) *We Are All Neighbours*, producer D. Christie, Granada television film.

Campbell, A. (1989) *To Square with Genesis*, Edinburgh: Edinburgh University Press.

Caplan, P. (ed.) (1987) *The Cultural Construction of Sexuality*, London: Tavistock.

—— (1992) 'Spirits and sex: a Swahili informant and his diary', in J. Okely and H. Callaway (eds) *Anthropology and Autobiography*, London: Routledge.

—— (1993) 'Learning gender: fieldwork in a Tanzanian coastal village, 1965–85', in D. Bell, P. Caplan and W. Jahan Karim (eds) *Gendered Fields: Women, Men and Ethnography*, London: Routledge.

Clifford, J. (1988) *The Predicament of Culture*, Cambridge, Mass.: Harvard University Press.

Clifford, J. and Marcus, G. (eds) (1986) *Writing Culture*, Berkeley: University of California.

Cohen, A. (1987) *Whalsay*, Manchester: Manchester University Press.

Comaroff, J. and Comaroff, J. (1992) *Ethnography and the Historical Imagination*, Boulder: Westview.

Cornwall, A. and Lindisfarne, N. (eds) (1994) *Dislocating Masculinity*, London: Routledge.

Cowan, J. (1990) *Dance and the Body Politic in Northern Greece*, Princeton: Princeton University Press.

Davis, J. (1977) *People of the Mediterranean*, London: Routledge and Kegan Paul.

del Valle, T. (ed.) (1993) *Gendered Anthropology*, London: Routledge.

Douglas, M. (1966) *Purity and Danger*, London: Routledge and Kegan Paul.

—— (1973) *Natural Symbols*, Harmondsworth: Penguin.

Ennew, J. (1980) *The Western Isles Today*, Cambridge: Cambridge University Press.

Evans-Pritchard, E. (1937) *Witchcraft, Oracles, and Magic among the Azande*, Oxford: Clarendon.

Fardon, R. (ed.) (1990) *Localising Strategies*, Edinburgh: Scottish Academic Press.

Favret-Saada, J. (1981) *Deadly Words*, trans. C. Cullen, Cambridge: Cambridge University Press.

Firth, R. (1988) 'Second Introduction' to B. Malinowski, *A Diary in the Strict Sense of the Term*, London: Athlone Press.

Foucault, M. (1977) *Discipline and Punish*, London: Allen Lane.

—— (1979) *The History of Sexuality, Vol. I*, trans. R. Hurley, Harmondsworth: Allen Lane.

Geertz, C. (1974) 'From the native's point of view', *Bulletin of the American Academy of Arts and Sciences* XXVIII, 1: 26–45.

—— (1988) *Works and Lives: The Anthropologist as Author*, Stanford: Stanford University Press.

Gilsenan, M. (1990) 'Very like a camel: the appearance of an anthropologist's

Middle East', in R. Fardon (ed.) *Localising Strategies*, Edinburgh: Scottish Academic Press.

Goffman, E. (1968) *Asylums*, Harmondsworth: Penguin.

Gullestad, M. (1984) *Kitchen-table Society*, Oslo: Universitetsforlaget; Oxford: Oxford University Press.

Hargreaves, J. (1994) *Sporting Females: Critical Issues in the History and Sociology of Women's Sport*, London: Routledge.

Harris, O. (1980) 'The power of signs: gender, culture and the wild in the Bolivian Andes', in C. MacCormack and M. Strathern (eds) *Nature, Culture and Gender*, Cambridge: Cambridge University Press.

—— (1993) 'Knowing the past: the dilemmas of historical anthropology', paper given to the ASA Conference, Oxford (forthcoming).

Hastrup, K. (1985) *Culture and History in Medieval Iceland: An Anthropological Analysis of Structure and Change*, Oxford: Clarendon Press.

Hastrup, K. and Fog Olwig, K. (eds) (1994) *Finding a Place and Space for Culture*, Copenhagen: forthcoming.

Hertz, R. (1909) (1960 edn) 'The pre-eminence of the Right Hand', trans. R. and C. Needham, in R. Hertz *Death and the Right Hand*, London: Cohen and West.

Herzfeld, M. (1985) *The Poetics of Manhood: Contest and Identity in a Cretan Mountain Village*, Princeton: Princeton University Press.

—— (1987) *Anthropology through the Looking Glass: Critical Ethnography in the Margins of Europe*, Cambridge: Cambridge University Press.

Hugh-Jones, S. (1989) 'Waribi and the white men: history and myth in Northwest Amazonia', in E. Tonkin, M. McDonald and M. Chapman (eds) *Ethnicity and History*, London: Routledge.

Huizer, G. and Mannheim, B. (eds) (1978) *The Politics of Anthropology*, The Hague: Mouton.

Jackson, A. (ed.) (1987) *Anthropology at Home*, London: Tavistock.

Jackson, M. (1983) 'Knowledge of the body', *Man* 18: 327–45.

—— (1989) *Paths toward a Clearing*, Bloomington and Indianapolis: Indiana University Press.

Kaberry, P. (1939) *Aboriginal Woman: Sacred and Profane*, London: Routledge and Kegan Paul.

Kaminski, M. (1980) *The State of Ambiguity: Studies of Gypsy Refugees*, Gothenburg: Anthropological Research.

Kenna, M. (1992) 'Changing places and altered perspectives: research on a Greek island in the 1960s and in the 1980s', in J. Okely and H. Callaway (eds) *Anthropology and Autobiography*, London: Routledge.

Loizos, P. (1981) *The Heart Grown Bitter: A Chronicle of Cypriot War Refugees*, Cambridge: Cambridge University Press.

Luhrmann, T. (1989) *Persuasions of the Witch's Craft: Ritual Magic in Contemporary England*, Oxford: Blackwell.

McDonald, M. (1989) *We are not French! Language, Culture and Identity in Brittany*, London: Routledge.

Macdonald, S. (ed.) (1993) *Inside European Identities*, Oxford: Berg.

Malinowski, B. (1922) *Argonauts of the Western Pacific*, London: Routledge and Kegan Paul.

—— (1929) *The Sexual Life of Savages*, London: Routledge and Kegan Paul.

—— (1967) *A Diary in the Strict Sense of the Term*, London: Routledge and Kegan Paul.

Malos, E. (ed.) (1980) *The Politics of Housework*, London: Allison and Busby.

Marcus, G. and Fischer, M. (1986) *Anthropology as Cultural Critique*, Chicago: University of Chicago Press.

Marcus, J. (1992) *A World of Difference: Islam and Gender Hierarchy in Turkey*, London: Zed Press.

Martin, E. (1987) *The Woman in the Body: A Cultural Analysis of Reproduction*, Boston: Beacon Press.

Mascia-Lees, F., Sharpe, P. and Ballerina-Cohen, C. (1989) 'The postmodern turn in anthropology: cautions from a feminist perspective', *Signs* 15, 1: 7–33.

Mauss, M. (1936) 'Les Techniques du corps', *Journal de la psychologie* 32.

Mitchell, J. (1971) *Woman's Estate*, Harmondsworth: Penguin.

Moore, H. (1988) *Feminism and Anthropology*, Cambridge: Polity Press.

Nader, L. (1969) 'Up the anthropologist – perspectives gained from studying up', in D. Hymes (ed.) *Reinventing Anthropology*, New York: Random House.

Oakley, A. (1972) *Sex, Gender and Society*, London: Temple Smith.

—— (1974) *The Sociology of Housework*, London: Martin Robertson.

Okely, J. (1975) Review of J. Sandford, *Prostitutes*, in *New Society* 34, 20 November, 440–1.

—— (1983) *The Traveller-Gypsies*, Cambridge: Cambridge University Press.

—— (1986) *Simone de Beauvoir: A Re-reading*, London: Virago; New York: Pantheon.

—— (1987) 'Fieldwork up the M1: policy and political aspects', in A. Jackson (ed.) *Anthropology at Home*, London: Tavistock.

—— (1992) 'Anthropology and autobiography: participatory experience and embodied knowledge', in J. Okely and H. Callaway (eds) *Anthropology and Autobiography*, ASA monograph 29, London: Routledge.

—— (1994) 'Thinking through fieldwork', in A. Bryman and R. Burgess (eds) *Analyzing Qualitative Data*, London: Routledge.

—— (1995) 'Gender and diversity', paper given at The Symposium of Chinese Women and Feminist Theory, The Chinese Academy of Social Sciences, Beijing (publication forthcoming).

Okely, J. and Callaway, H. (eds) (1992) *Anthropology and Autobiography*, ASA monograph 29, London: Routledge.

Ortner, S. (1974) 'Is female to male as nature to culture?', in M. Rosaldo and L. Lamphere (eds) *Woman, Culture and Society*, Stanford: Stanford University Press.

Parkin, D. (1990) 'Eastern Africa: the view from the office and the voice from the field', in R. Fardon (ed.) *Localising Strategies*, Edinburgh: Scottish Academic Press.

Pina-Cabral, J. (1992) 'Against translation: the role of the researcher in the production of ethnographic knowledge', in J. Pina-Cabral and J. Campbell (eds) *Europe Observed*, Basingstoke: Macmillan Press.

Pina-Cabral, J. and Campbell, J. (eds) (1992) *Europe Observed*, Basingstoke: Macmillan Press.

Polhemus, T. (ed.) (1978) *Social Aspects of the Human Body*, Harmondsworth: Penguin.

Reiter, R. (ed.) (1975) *Toward an Anthropology of Women*, New York: Monthly Review Press.

Riches, D. (1990) 'The force of tradition in Eskimology', in R. Fardon (ed.) *Localising Strategies*, Edinburgh: Scottish Academic Press.

Rosaldo, M. (1974) 'Woman, culture and society: a theoretical overview', in M. Rosaldo and L. Lamphere (eds) *Woman, Culture and Society*, Stanford: Stanford University Press.

Rosaldo, M. and Lamphere, L. (eds) (1974) *Woman, Culture and Society*, Stanford: Stanford University Press.

Rowbotham, S. (1973) *Woman's Consciousness, Man's World*, Harmondsworth: Penguin.

Said, E. (1978) *Orientalism*, New York: Pantheon.

Sanjek, R. (ed.) (1991) *Fieldnotes*, Ithaca: Cornell University Press.

Scott, J. (1985) *Weapons of the Weak: Everyday Forms of Peasant Resistance*, New Haven: Yale University Press.

Stewart, M. (1987) 'Brothers in song: the persistence of Vlach Gypsy identity and community in socialist Hungary', unpublished Ph.D. thesis, London School of Economics.

Stocking, G. (1968) Review of B. Malinowski *A Diary, Journal of the History of the Behavioural Sciences* IV, 2: 189–94.

Strathern, M. (1981) *Kinship at the Core: An Anthropology of Elmdon, a Village in North-west Essex in the 1960s*, Cambridge: Cambridge University Press.

—— (1987) 'The limits of auto-anthropology', in A. Jackson (ed.) *Anthropology at Home*, London: Tavistock.

Street, B. (1990) 'Orientalist discourses in the anthropology of Iran, Afghanistan and Pakistan', in R. Fardon (ed.) *Localising Strategies*, Edinburgh: Scottish Academic Press.

Sutherland, A. (1975) *Gypsies: The Hidden Americans*, London: Tavistock.

Synnott, A. (1993) *The Body Social: Symbolism, Self and Society*, London: Routledge.

Taussig, M. (1993) *Mimesis and Alterity*, London: Routledge.

Ulin, R. (1991) 'The current tide in American Europeanist anthropology. From margin to centre?', *Anthropology Today* 7, 6: 8–12.

Watson, C. W. (1992) 'Autobiography, anthropology and the experience of Indonesia', in J. Okely and H. Callaway (eds) *Anthropology and Autobiography*, ASA monograph 29, London: Routledge.

Zulaika, J. (1988) *Basque Violence: Metaphor and Sacrament*, Nevada: Nevada University Press.

Chapter 1

Fieldwork in the Home Counties
Double vision and dismantled identity

Malinowski's (1922) advice on fieldwork included the famous pleas to learn the indigenous language and to avoid contact with white men. Such advice would have been inappropriate for my fieldwork. Granted, Gypsies in England are respectably exotic as non-literate nomads, not found in the conventional typologies. Yet we shared the same language, apart from the occasional Romany word inserted into English sentences. Fieldwork did not require progress through grammar books, interpreters and mental translations. This apparent concordance with one's own culture masked other differences.

We are always reassuring ourselves that anthropology highlights the contrasts between cultures. These contrasts are rarely experienced within the same space and time as they are during fieldwork at home. Long-term fieldwork in my own country made explicit the contrast with my customary life. The anthropologist abroad has a different relationship with the society within which the group studied is embedded. He or she is usually a stranger to all contexts. By contrast, in my case, I was moving from a specific experience defined by class, gender, race and education into a stigmatised minority about whom I knew almost nothing, beyond the non-Gypsy ('gorgio', the word used by Gypsies to describe the Other) stereotypes and representations. Until a community worker drove me to a cluster of modern caravans and lorries just off the M1 motorway, I should not have recognised them as members of the exotic category vaguely associated with horses and waggons. Previously, I should have thought I was looking at the caravans of temporary road workers.

You experience the sudden absence of basic amenities like water and a WC on a camping holiday, but usually in a depopulated, rural setting. The Gypsies did not live in the woods of the nursery rhyme. The camps were bordered by major roads and sometimes housing estates. Lorries thundered along the elevated dual carriageway a few yards away. On one camp we nestled beneath a factory floodlit at night. A costly new site was built on a former sewage farm. Cannibalised car bodies, piles of scrap and smoking tyres were my palm trees and coral strand.

To the Travellers I did not appear as an eccentric foreigner but as a member of the dominant persecuting society, albeit a well-meaning student. In this context, Malinowski's (1922) and later, Powdermaker's (1967) suggestions for a preliminary census were inadvisable at any stage. The Trobriand Islanders may on the face of it have been complimented by attention to their way of life. Or perhaps a colonised people has learned to submit to censuses, but nomads everywhere have learned how to evade them. I was warned by one Gypsy friend that I could be burned for writing down a genealogy. Evans-Pritchard (1940) and Chagnon (1974) have also known difficulties in getting mere names.

Unlike anthropology abroad, fieldwork at home is not a matter of memorising a new vocabulary; only slowly did I realise that I had to learn another language in the words of my mother tongue. I unlearned my boarding school accent, changed clothing and body movements. Dropping my 'aitches and throwing in swear words, I was doing an Eliza Dolittle in reverse and without Professor Higgins to supervise me. After some months, a Traveller said, 'Judith, your speech has improved'. Washing and eating became different procedures with the same utensils and food from the same shops up the road (see Okely 1983). My past identity was slowly dismantled in the home counties I had inhabited since childhood.

The view of a famous provincial town from the cab of a lorry crammed with Traveller parents and children looked both familiar and alien. As we drove through districts I had known before, the Travellers would show me another landscape stamped by their past: 'That's where I stopped as a kid with our waggon and horses', 'we tarmacked that forecourt', 'years ago we got loads of scrap from that air base', 'Billy rents this field for his horses'.

One summer, I was calling for scrap and rags in a sleepy village with my regular Traveller workmate: 'Lovely houses these', she said as we passed a desirable Georgian residence. The lilac hung heavy over a white garden seat, I dreamed of a Grantchester tea and imagined the view from a top window; it would make a lovely study, I was thinking. My daydream was fractured by my Traveller companion: 'Lovely houses for calling – those rich people'll have a lot to throw out.' She had rightly seen them as a resource, a place for acquiring goods not a place for habitation. If she had pressed her face against the window pane, it would not be with any longing to enter.

Despite my change in clothing, when calling for 'any old iron, scrap, batteries or rags', I still couldn't get the demeanour right. The housewives would invariably ask me, but not my Traveller mates, what it was for. Eventually, I found it simpler to say it was for charity than reveal that I was an anthropologist doing participant observation as a Gypsy on gorgio doorsteps. Some of the gorgio women looked like myself in another life. I was looking in a distorted mirror. In the company of Travellers, I did experience abuse as a Gypsy at garden gates and in shops, and was chased away where previously I would have been welcome.

An anthropologist abroad does not experience the double knowledge I felt, for example in the following case. My mate Reena persuaded one woman on a private estate to part with an old battery. As it was leaking acid, Reena wrapped it in newspaper. After loading up, Reena's mother Aunt Doll stuffed the newspaper in the hedge, thinking she was being 'tidy'. The gorgio woman had been watching us from her gravel drive. Her views on rubbish disposal were as intimately known to me as those of my Head Mistress. I shrank at her scorn: 'What have you done with that newspaper?' she called out. 'It's all right', said Aunt Doll, 'I've put it in the hedge.' 'That's typical of you Gypsies, you like to live among old car bodies in a dust bowl!' Aunt Doll drew herself up to her full height: 'Madam, I'm not a Gypsy and I don't live in no dust bowl. If you want to know I give up my time for this work, I'm working for charity.' This time it was the gorgio woman's turn to shrink away. Whereas Aunt Doll was detached from the criticism about rubbish disposal, she resented the stigma attached to the word Gypsy. I, on the other hand, was inwardly free of such identification, but I felt her pain. At the same time, I felt it 'wrong' to shove newspaper in that hedge.

The one or two unexpected visits to my camp by gorgio friends brought into sharper focus the contrast between my two existences and double vision in the same country. Anthropologists abroad may also risk intrusions from friends back home but at least the visitors have been partially sobered by the extended journey and the obvious strangeness. My friends, however, drove the same roads as the Travellers.

One afternoon, after an especially dramatic confrontation between Travellers and the police on the camp, a small mini-van pulled in. We wondered if this was another 'pig' in disguise. Out stepped my college friend Mike in chic King's Road shirt, tight Levis and dark glasses. I had to emerge from the cluster of confused Travellers and identify myself. I switched to a fellow intellectual tone and became ungainly in my loosely hung attire. Despite his desire to hang around or sit gossiping in my caravan, I told him to drive me to a tea shop in the town. Mike had been given my exact ordnance survey location by a secretary at my London research centre.

The other male visitor, well over 60, caused a sensation by greeting me with a slight peck on the cheek. He also anticipated a free and easy conversation in my caravan. Soon we were joined by six children and three women, two of whom had never deigned to visit me before. Their presence was actually a useful protection against any accusation that I fitted the Gypsy stereotype of a free-wheeling gorgio woman, something I needed to disassociate myself from. My grey-haired 'uncle' (the only acceptable category I could offer) continued his Hampstead-flavoured literary discussion, naively complaining to me later of the 'immaturity' of the Travellers' uncontrollable shrieks and giggles. My gorgio visitors found my prudish demeanour both comical and unnecessary. It was hard to explain that mixed-gender encounters are treated as sexual liaisons.

Anthropologists abroad, both today and in the past, have had to work under the shadow of officials and their policies towards subordinate groups. In my own case, government intervention occurred even before the research began. A senior civil servant wrote to the governor of our independent research centre reminding them of their partial state funding. He then objected to the centre's proposed Gypsy research, all of which he insisted should be conducted within Whitehall. Fortunately a charitable trust had already offered funding. Anthropologists have to negotiate for permits and visas. Similarly, I depended on some official consent to living on a temporary site. In all cases, there is a risk of identification with the officials, whether or not you study them.

Malinowski was also troubled on occasions by a double vision. He could see the white administrator's view of the Trobriand landscape while he was attempting to understand the Islanders' experience of it, or at least while he was attempting to isolate his own view. When accompanied unwillingly by two officials he wrote: 'I saw and felt the utter drabness of the Kiriwana villages; I saw them through their eyes (it's fine to have this ability), but I forgot to look at them with my own' (Malinowski 1967: 163). Malinowski, like many other anthropologists, responded to this dilemma by cutting white men out of his research (see Okely 1975 and chapter 2, this volume). Fieldwork in one's own country may make this separation of suitable research fields even less tenable. Apart from the theoretical and historical necessity of including the wider context, the effects of those same policymakers are lived with daily in the anthropologist's country both before and after fieldwork.

The research project to which I was originally attached included a study of legislation and government reports (Adams *et al.* 1975). Research into officials entering the camps was as problematic as in colonial times. First, because I had had to negotiate with them for my own entry and secondly because they assumed I would identify with their view of the 'Gypsy problem'. The Travellers also tended at first to identify me with the officials. This identification was hard to throw off. An officer giving me a lift from the County Hall suddenly stopped the car to ask a Traveller family on the roadside to move on. Predictably, that family never trusted me and spread a story that I collaborated with the police.

I was given free access to files at County Hall because it was assumed, despite my explanations to the contrary, that my research centre was attached to the Ministry and also that my write-up would be wholly favourable. My boarding school accent was useful again. This called for another change of clothing. As a female, I was also seen as harmless. The files proved to be a Pandora's box and when my guarded queries betrayed a lack of consensus, some of the files were mysteriously withdrawn. My double identity had become apparent. Later, official controls operated in gentlemanly ways, unique to anthropological fieldwork at home. My research centre insisted on sending drafts of our report to the council who sanitised it and inserted a final paragraph which made nonsense of the rest. It was never considered appropriate to send similar drafts to Gypsy representatives (Okely 1987).

When publication is in the same country as fieldwork, the anthropologist cannot escape being read or misread by a wide range of interested parties beyond the usual academic constituency. The text will therefore bear the marks of such future scrutiny. If the study includes a minority group, the publication will be read more easily by some of its members. This development is to be welcomed, for the anthropologist cannot avoid the political consequences of his or her research. These consequences remain on the anthropologist's doorstep. Any latent tendency to treat people as objects or distant curios has to be confronted, not left repressed in a secret diary. The double vision has to be focused correctly. The fieldworker at home cannot split identities between countries.

REFERENCES

Adams, B., Okely, J., Morgan, D. and Smith, D. (1975) *Gypsies and Government Policy in England*, London: Heinemann.

Chagnon, N. (1974) *Studying the Yanomamo*, New York: Holt, Rinehart and Winston.

Evans-Pritchard, E. (1940) *The Nuer*, Oxford: Clarendon Press.

Malinowski, B. (1922) *Argonauts of the Western Pacific*, London: Routledge and Kegan Paul.

—— (1967) *A Diary in the Strict Sense of the Term*, London: Routledge and Kegan Paul.

Okely, J. (1975) 'The self and scientism', *Journal of the Anthropology Society Oxford*, Oxford, Trinity Term.

—— (1983) *The Traveller-Gypsies*, Cambridge: Cambridge University Press.

—— (1987) 'Fieldwork up the M1: policy and political aspects', in A. Jackson (ed.) *Anthropology at Home*, London: Tavistock.

Powdermaker, H. (1967) *Stranger and Friend*, New York: W. W. Norton.

Chapter 2

The self and scientism

In this chapter I examine some of the background to the debate about subjectivity in participant observation; the primary methodological technique in empirical anthropological research. Earlier versions given at seminars included more detail of my own fieldwork experience. This I have had to leave out for more elaborate analysis in future writing. Meanwhile, I have presented some of my fieldwork as examples in the approaches explored and suggested for participant observation. There is a need for more explicit recognition of fieldwork as personal experience instead of sacrificing it to a false notion of scientific objectivity.

The problem of subjectivity in research is recognised by most con-temporary social scientists mainly to forestall criticism and further argument. The traditional response is to refine the 'objective' methodology by formally eradicating the direct link between observer and observed. For example, the questionnaire method in much empirical sociological research predetermines the subject matter, and questions arising and information transmitted are selective and curtailed. This premeditation and control over interaction is presented as proof of objectivity. The questionnaires are administered by assistants (nameless and usually female) and the 'hard data' written up by (named and usually male) research lecturers. The larger the sample and the more random the selection, the more 'scientific' the findings. The people interviewed are usually willing to volunteer fundamental and unpredictable insights which are merely jotted down under supplementary 'remarks'. Even in more informal unstructured interviews, the inquisitor never abandons his or her dominant role. Other information acquired in less formal contexts is referred to as 'impressions', and 'soft' data to be tested by the hard data (see Young and Willmott 1962: Appendix). The method is inherently authoritarian.

In anthropological participant observation there is greater reciprocity in the exchange of information. Here the problem of subjectivity becomes explicit. The fieldworker, as opposed to those who analyse other people's material, has a peculiarly individualistic and personal confrontation with 'living' data. This close contact has made anthropologists feel vulnerable to criticism from those who employ formal techniques of distancing between subject and object. Hence the peculiar coyness which anthropologists have shown in discussing their relationship with the various people they have studied.

The participant observer does not deliberately impose preconceived notions of relevancy and ready-worked hypotheses on the data to which he or she has access. Despite criticisms from the formalists, this absence of filtering is the source of strength. The individual is open to a complete range of information and not merely what people say they do.[1] This material is of course analysed in the light of existing anthropological theory but not prejudicially at the fieldwork stage. In distinguishing the methods of sociology and anthropology, Maquet (1964) has justified the use of participant observation on purely technical grounds. In non-literate societies, written sources, written questions and answers were not feasible and the totality of customs largely unknown to the observer, thus requiring long stays and 'indirect' observation. Such methods were unnecessary in the study of 'one's own' literate society . . . 'where the whole culture is taken for granted'. The broad difference in techniques which Maquet describes might indeed have this historical foundation, but their merits cannot be judged solely in terms of their subject matter. Participant observation is equally valid in 'one's own society'. To take the whole culture 'for granted' is also to be guilty of subjectivity, more insidious because it goes unrecognised. Both the study of the observer's and another society involve subjectivity, but of a different order. I wonder if the belief in objectivity attained by studying another society is unconsciously explained by geographical not theoretical distance.

As in any research methodology, the participant observer does have a problem of subjectivity. This cannot be resolved by distancing, repression and short-cuts to abstractions. Objectivity is an ideal model to work with, not a fact. In the study of a human being by another human being (and what better medium is there?), the specificity and individuality of the observer are ever present and must therefore be acknowledged, explored and put to creative use. It is fashionable now for authors from a variety of disciplines to give an apologia or acknowledgement of his or her ideological stance as Marxist, liberal, structuralist etc. in a preface. This kind of confession is no substitute for the continuing and conscious working through of these implications. Similarly in psychoanalysis, it is not enough for the patient to be labelled; his/her situation has to be examined and understood through hundreds of hours of analysis. Political interests are also now made more explicit or better understood. This applies especially to anthropologists looking back on the colonial era (Maquet 1964). Less attention is devoted to the individual characteristics of the observer as important subjective factors conditioning knowledge. In any case, in anthropological research, few analytic tools or categories have been developed to explore the various forms of subjectivity.

So far, the remedies suggested by anthropologists have mainly involved greater external control rather than any creative use of the observer's individual resources. To deal with what he called 'the personal equation', Nadel (1951: 50) considered the selection of anthropologists on the basis of 'psychological testing'. I wonder by what culturally loaded criteria would candidates be deemed suitable, and for which culture? As another means of 'overcoming the limitations of the personality' Nadel suggested teamwork. While considering Fortes' and Evans-Pritchard's awareness that the 'passing through a single mind' of the data is peculiarly valuable, Nadel asserts: 'once more we must face the issue that science cannot in any respect, be private' (Nadel 1951). Again, as is the case with many others, impersonal verification is confused with objectivity (Maquet 1964).

Given this distaste for privacy in science, it seems all the more extraordinary that the anthropologist's private and personal experience of fieldwork is *not* exposed to view. Since almost nothing about the people studied is dismissed as private, taboo or improper for investigation, the same should apply to the investigator. I am not suggesting that everything be then put into print or in theses for public scrutiny. Already many things in field notes must remain confidential, and are later dismissed as trivia or disguised. The problem is that the fieldworker's personal reactions and experience are suppressed or dismissed from the outset. A certain personal exposure may in time be seen not as professional disaster but intellectual growth. Revelation of the 'humanistic and experiential' elements of fieldwork has been advocated on moral grounds; as an exploration of moral relativism (Swallow 1974: 58). My reasons for advocating this aspect of fieldwork are not rooted in morality, but relate to the epistemological problem of subjectivity which is perhaps implicit in Swallow's discussion. Too often the personal is represented in opposition to the objective, when the latter merely conceals the personal in pretentiousness. This dichotomy of knowledge is reflected in the sexist division of labour and knowledge in our society. Women are often less inhibited about exploring and expressing the personal element, although they may apologise for this in academic debate. In some cases, women are more likely to comprehend a theory through an example or image whereas men will grasp a theory through generalisation. Given the different upbringings of males and females and the exclusion of women from direct economic and political power, only indirectly obtainable through personal relations with individual men, it is not surprising that the consequences are expressed in mode of thought. Anaïs Nin describes the polarity in her diary:

Now analysis is revealing how little objectivity there is in man's thinking. . . . Man generalizes from experience and denies the source of his generalizations. Woman individualizes and personalizes, but ultimately analysis will reveal that the rationalizations of man are a disguise to his personal bias, and that woman's intuition was nothing more than a recognition of the influence of the personal in all thought.

(1974: II, 23–4)

In this quotation I interpret the concept 'intuition' as culturally loaded and constructed, not as something inherent in all females. If as anthropologists we accept and explore different modes of thought in different societies, we should not be averse to finding them within one society and in neither case does it follow that these variations are genetically determined.[2] Actually women lose out on several counts. In a context where the specific is described as 'hard', scientific and objective fact, its opposite is airy-fairy speculation, emotional and soft – women's domain.[3] In another context where fact is equated with 'vulgar empiricism' and its opposite is theory, women are seen to be the fact gatherers and men the theoreticians.[4]

Rodney Needham, in his discussion of lateral symbolism, suggests that the dualism in this debate 'is a central issue in any humane discipline and as an essentially philosophical problem it may not admit any definite resolution. It has to do with the variable meanings attached to such abstractions as "fact" and "theory"' (Needham 1973: xxxi). In the case of our own society the 'fact'/'theory' dualism is transposed to the female/male division which corresponds to a political and economic actuality and is reinforced by self-fulfilling ideologies. Whatever 'female thought' may be, it is the one which is undervalued. The same goes for so-called 'primitive thought'. There are parallels between the kind of thought which Anaïs Nin associates with women and 'the science of the concrete' discussed by Lévi-Strauss (1966: 15–22). The participant observer is not at one remove from his or her material. The method involves working through images and anecdote.

Nevertheless, whether through scientistic or sexist bias, the personal is often denigrated in anthropological monographs. The 'I' of the observer sometimes disappears altogether as though the material was acquired by impersonal procedures. The classical handbook *Notes and Queries* (1967: 27) tells the fieldworker that really only amateurs suffer from 'bias'. 'Scientific' training successfully obliterates cultural and personal history and presumably the self.[5]

EXAMPLES

Evans-Pritchard's considerable insight into both his methods and personal form of 'Nuerosis' (1940: 9–15), and, indeed, Malinowski's first public account of fieldwork (1922: 2–25) have not always stimulated anthropologists to give more or even as much information about their research.[6] From the 1960s a few anthropologists have presented more autobiographical accounts (Turnbull 1961, 1974; Maybury-Lewis 1965; Read 1965; Mead 1972; Chagnon 1974). Earlier, in the most explorative and sensitive account of the relationship between the outsider and people encountered in fieldwork, Smith-Bowen (1954) felt obliged to fictionalise events and persons and publish under a pseudonym, so reaffirming the tradition of separating the 'subjective' from the public body of academic work.

In some of the publications, the anthropologist emerges as narrator (Conrad-style) and actor alongside other characters in the exotic setting. Detailed descriptions, normally reduced to the opening pages of monographs, are given of scenery and personalities. The stream of events is action-packed. Often the only structural unity of the narrative appears to be the chronology of the stranger's visit. This is a new kind of ethnography based on 'true story', subject to limitations of which literature is free. Such techniques may be a welcome rebellion from the depersonalised monographs of the past, but they have not yet resolved the problems of subjectivity in participant observation research.

Take Colin Turnbull's (1974) study of the Ik which, on the basis of long-term observation, is an informed rival to the genre of travelogues so despised by Lévi-Strauss in his own autobiographical account (1963: 17–18). Turnbull considers it right that 'any description of another people . . . is bound to be subjective'. Since he had no access to previous accounts of the Ik, he believes that he started with 'a clean slate', without 'a preconceived notion', just 'clinical observation' (Turnbull 1974: 13). He omits to mention his pre-conceived notions about all human societies which he brought in his own head and Land-Rover. His personal asides are presented as universals which we readers are supposed to support. They are no more than his own commonplaces; our intellectual journalist reporting. His subjective exposure lacks any self-analysis and he certainly can't analyse his companions. For instance, he interprets laughter as merriment, never as hysterical distancing or catharsis. Smith-Bowen never made that mistake, perhaps because she let herself experience the same.

Napoleon Chagnon (1974: x) has attempted to preserve 'an intimate relationship between ethnography, methodology and theory' and in two chapters (1 and 5) gives a personal account of his fieldwork. There is virtually no relationship between these chapters and his main work, which consists largely of data gleaned by the latest technological gadgets. Details of his fieldwork are justified more in terms of technical/procedural problems of data collection; i.e. which villages he could stay longest in and why he had to leave others, rather than any theoretical link between the self and others. Discussion of the observer's experience is described as 'the non quantifiable aspects of fieldwork' (ibid. 162), thereby conveying the feeling that if something can't be counted, it demands no alternative analysis or description. If, as the preface claims, Chagnon is trying to show how the exotic becomes commonplace (ibid. viii), he fails. His form of personal revelations exploits on every page the exotic or bizarre as would be understood by the North American or European general reader. The chapters make exciting and sensational reading. We are rarely presented with the range of Chagnon's inner feelings, instead his escapades and heroism in the pursuit of science. One night the natives were going to crush his skull, another time he caught a 'raging' fungal infection of the genitals, after borrowing a man's loin cloth.

The opening paragraph titillates the reader's fantasies about Shamen and savages. Familiarity in the exotic is conveyed not by his description of the people around him, but by the 'commercial breaks' for his IBM printout and the Tri-x for his Pentax. Our Napoleon from Pennsylvania is better than Biggles or the *Boy's Own Annual*.

AUTOBIOGRAPHICAL EXAMPLE

Having been so unkind about others, at this point I should show myself amenable to self-examination, especially in relation to the kind of part an anthropologist imagined he or she is playing in the field. Among the Pygmies, Turnbull was romantic and among the Ik a cynic, with the Yanomamo Chagnon appeared a hero; what was I, a lone woman living with the Gypsies in southern England? I could tell some stories; exotic precisely because they are set not in rain forests or deserts, but on the edge of Greater London just up the M1. My supervisor, Godfrey Lienhardt, on reading my notes ex-claimed, 'They're more violent than the Dinka!' I plan to describe the strangeness; but not telescoped and wrested from the commonplace and imponderabilia of the everyday. For the moment let's dissect what I thought I was at, in fantasy not ethnography.

Early in my anthropological studies I was impressed by a common assertion among both men and women anthropologists that the female anthropologist in the field is not 'hampered' by her sex because she is treated as an 'honorary male'. I didn't realise at the time how deeply this appealed to deep contradictions in my own history. This belief is confirmed in *Notes and Queries* (1967: 70): 'Among very unsophisticated natives . . . a woman may find that she is regarded primarily as a stranger and is given the status of male.' To my surprise and perhaps disappointment, when I entered the field I did not find this so. I had to be extremely cautious in talking to men, usually making sure that a woman was present, since non-Gypsy women are regarded disapprovingly as licentious and immoral, just like the non-Gypsy (gorgio) stereotype of Gypsy women. Women, not men, had to be my main informants and allies. The rigid male–female segregation meant that any woman seen talking alone to a Gypsy man who was neither kin nor husband, was accused of sexual infidelity. I had to be careful and more conscious of myself as female and began to wonder if this was so different in some other fieldwork situations.

Increasingly, I suspect that women anthropologists are given ambiguous status in the field, not as 'honorary males', but as members of an alien 'race'. So where did this 'honorary male' come from? The idea has its roots instead in the anthropologist's own society where the ideals of male and female behaviour are as marked. It requires some nerve among women of my society to travel alone without plans and timetables.

Adventure is pulling me out. When a man feels this, it is no crime, but let a woman feel this and there is an outcry.

(Anaïs Nin 1974: II, 51)

Now for self-investigation. In the single-sex boarding school where I was educated from the age of nine to eighteen, the 'world' was divided into four 'houses'. These cosmological institutions were not represented by any buildings; they were groups of girls competing for cups in field sports, conduct, deportment and drama. Most significant to this discussion, the four houses were named Rhodes, Livingstone, Shackleton and Scott. I belonged to the last. So our models were all white colonisers or explorers. The trouble was they were all males. These heroes, not heroines, set an example to which we, as Penelope was to Ulysses, could never, nor indeed, should ever aspire (chapter 8, this volume).

Brought up only to marry or beget a Scott or Livingstone, perhaps I found my journey into Gypsydom especially exhilarating, although I rejected entirely the idea of being a coloniser. I hurtled down motorways in my fifteen hundredweight van, I loaded heavy scrap iron and dwelt with strangers and nomads, so escaping the strictures of the domestic role allotted the females of my own kind. In addition, this *rite de passage* made me an honorary male among those back home. By this experience, the female anthropologist not only achieves equality in her own society, she might unconsciously feel a confident separation from the domestically burdened wives and mothers in the society she is studying.

Whereas the female anthropologist not accompanying a husband is rejecting her conventional destiny by the act of fieldwork, the white male anthropologist is completing his (see also Lévi-Strauss 1963: 42 for a discussion of the function of travel among young French men). That is why a little more self-awareness in motives might be helpful to both male and female anthropologists in the presentation of the self in their fieldwork confessions.

MALINOWSKI'S DIARY

It is ironic that the man who first developed and gave scientific status to participant observation in anthropology also kept a personal diary, which has caused only embarrassment or been overlooked as an invaluable adjunct to fieldwork by his colleagues and academic descendants. Raymond Firth (1967) considers that the diary 'in its purely ethnographic sense cannot be ranked as more than a footnote to anthropological history'. For Geertz (1974), the diary exposes any previous claim that anthropologists had some 'unique form of psychological closeness, a sort of transcultural identification with our subjects'. He neglects both self-analysis and biography as techniques for understanding the interaction.

Malinowski's diary (1967) is a remarkable case study of the concealed subjectivity in fieldwork method and general ideology distorting both evidence and theory. Still today (Swallow 1974), personal and cultural conflicts in the field are relegated to the anecdotal and oral traditions of faculty gossip. Thanks to the consent of Malinowski's widow, we have a record of his on-the-spot reactions. Among other anthropologists their reactions are usually only recalled after fieldwork and therefore changed in their retrospective auto-biographies.

Unfortunately Malinowski did not use his diary in the way which I shall advocate – as a means of exposing and exploring subjectivity. Instead he used it as a privatised escape from the fieldwork situation to maintain a 'sane' and familiar internal order in an alien land, and as a punitive stimulant to his rigid work ethic. His dependence on the norms and values of his own culture were at risk; for example, he was worried he might forget about academic commitments and the obligations of sexual fidelity. The diary became an internal dialogue with a culture-bound conscience where the private and subjective were artificially separated from the professional and objective. On the one hand, he was publicising and eliciting appreciation for the Trobrianders' institutions in his official writing; on the other, he was contending with his hostility to an 'alien race' in terms similar to those of his colonial contemporaries.

There are four aspects which it would be useful to isolate in Malinowski's diary:

1 Attitudes to women and sex (the two for him were rarely separated).
2 Personal feelings about the Trobrianders.
3 Interaction with local white men.
4 Ideas about keeping a diary.

ATTITUDES TO WOMEN AND SEX

He expresses a longing for a white woman, in particular his future wife whom he considers has 'the miraculous power to absolve sins'. Raymond Firth cites this as proof of the depth and sincerity of his love (1967: xviii). This woman is identified with white civilisation (Malinowski 1967: 148). But he also has lustful feelings for another white woman with whom he cannot break contact. His conflict seems to be the classical one in Western civilisation between the pure woman (wife) and the sexual fiend (whore). On a day-to-day level, Malinowski is confronted with his feelings towards the black women who became the victims of his projections and concepts of the whore. Sexual relations with them are seen as 'whoring' and 'sloshing in the mud' (ibid. 181). Sometimes he confesses to his sense of their beauty (ibid. 255) but bitterly regrets having 'pawed' one (ibid. 256). His diary serves to goad his conscience, and control any deviation from his self-imposed sexual code and that of his own civilisation. This can sometimes only be achieved by negating sexuality in women: 'Moral tenets: I must never let myself become aware of the fact that other women have bodies, that they copulate' (ibid. 249). The tendency for women to be seen mainly as sexual objects may well have encouraged anthropologists to avoid or underestimate them as persons and informants (see Ardener 1975: 137–8 and chapter 10, this volume).

For a long time I was guilty of a kind of sexism in my own fieldwork. At first I considered my segregation among Gypsy women only as a disadvantage. I was always trying to get *through* them to the men where I presumed all the action was. It was only gradually that I actually became aware of the important political and economic role of the Gypsy women in their own right and precisely because they were women. My initial prejudice I have tried to rectify (Okely 1975b and chapter 4, this volume). My fieldwork mistakes arose partly because of a belief in the separation of my 'personal' political views on feminism and my 'objective' role as researcher in another culture. After the London Women's Anthropology Workshop in 1973, I suddenly saw that the two were interconnected.

MALINOWSKI'S FEELINGS ABOUT THE TROBRIANDERS

In its strongest aspects, Malinowski might now be accused of racism because of his use of the word 'nigger', just as he could be accused of sexism in his indiscriminate use of the word 'whore'. The first time 'nigger' appears in the published text (1967: 154) there is an evasive footnote giving Webster's definition, and designed rather naively to take away the full impact. If, as the editors claim, the word was non-pejorative for Malinowski, one wonders why he should have so assiduously excluded it from his public texts.

Malinowski's use of the word in a private context is interesting to the reader because it indicates that he was a carrier of the stereotypes and underlying values of his own culture, even though he wanted to take the Trobriand culture seriously. Obviously the strain and stress of fieldwork, for example, the personal isolation and 'alien' lifestyle are bound to bring out the 'worst' in anyone, but that does not explain away the cultural form which the 'worst' takes. Irritation with members of one's own 'race' and one's own sex would be expressed differently; the peculiar faults of the individual rather than his or her social category would be exaggerated and deplored. In examining the dilemmas faced by fieldworkers, a psychologist, Wintrob (1969), tends to examine problems of ambivalence, racism and questioning of motives more as symptoms of stress rather than as valid problems in themselves. Malinowski's 'racism' cannot be described simply as stress, it must also be explained in terms of white man's culture.

The contrast between Malinowski's professional or intellectual aims and his private feelings, which reflect his own culture, appears in a single page. He considers composing a memoir on 'the value of Ethnographic Studies for

the Administration . . . above all the knowledge of a people's customs allows
one to be in sympathy with them, and to guide them according to their ideas'
(note there is the presumption of 'guidance'). Then after being misinformed
about a kula expedition, Malinowski expresses 'hatred for the niggers' (1967:
238). He is not sufficiently self-conscious to set his annoyance at the
Trobrianders' independence in the context of white/black relations.

As a Pole, whose country suffered Austrian rule, Malinowski was, as Lucy
Mair suggests (1957: 232), able to identify with oppressed minorities.
However, this may have blinded him to his status in Melanesia. Déraciné,
he became a cosmopolitan communicating with Europeans, Americans and
Australians and speaking their language. His identification was limited
mainly to white men of the industrial world, so his 'racial' status and origin
became more important than his nationality. In the field therefore, he was
identified by the Trobrianders as a colonial and they obviously concealed
information from him which might prejudice their position. Elsewhere, I have
examined how the Trobrianders' apparent ignorance of paternity, as told to
Malinowski, might be explained by his status as a white man unwittingly
associated with the missionary decrees on sexual behaviour (Okely 1975c).

In one passage,[7] Malinowski makes an explicit connection between his
personal reactions to a Trobriand individual and the policies of a colonial
oppressor. This is followed – in a manner comparable to free association –
by a reference to sex between the races, more importantly his dismay at a
white woman's relations with a black man. Racism is thus interwoven with
sex and sexism, and all are symptoms of white male chauvinism:

> The natives still irritate me, particularly Ginger, whom I could willingly
> beat to death. I understand all the *German and Belgian colonial atrocities*.
> I am also dismayed by Mrs Bill's relations with a handsome *nigger* from
> Tukwa'ukwa.
>
> (1967: 279)

Whereas white male/black female sexual relations may be 'sloshing in the
mud' and a regrettable pastime, black male/white female sexual relations, in
any analysis of white man's racism, is the ultimate taboo, since it undermines
the presumption of white male 'supremacy' and white female 'purity'. In this
racist and sexist system, where the male is considered superior to the female,
the relationship which troubled Malinowski seemingly gives alarming superiority to the black man over the white woman. This passage in the diary of an
individual indicates the links explicit or unconscious between the particular
or subjective and the general.

INTERACTION WITH LOCAL WHITE MEN

In his diary Malinowski reveals a similar ambivalence or hostility to white
men in the Trobriands as he does towards women of any race and the native

Figure 2.1 Bronislaw Malinowski in the field with Trobrianders.
Source: Royal Anthropological Institute Photographic Collection.

Trobrianders. To the lieutenant governor he is obliged to be deferential for the sake of his visa, but regrets that 'paying attention to this crew simply banalises my work' (1967: 128). Firth (1967) praises Malinowski's thumbnail sketch of this 'legendary figure', but I am left dissatisfied. This man at the 'apex of the official pyramid' could have been considered as worthy as the Trobrianders as a subject of study. Malinowski accepts the white adminis-trators' 'power over the natives' (1967: 167). Yet he is always trying to eradicate them; 'What is terrible is that I am unable to free myself from the atmosphere created by foreign bodies: their presence takes away the scientific value and personal value of my work' (ibid. 163). On the contrary, his amnesia towards the white administrators had considerable repercussions on the 'scientific' value of his analysis. The Trobriand society was over-represented as a functional whole, with economic and political self-sufficiency.

The Trobriand Islands were inhabited not only by white administrators but also missionaries and traders. Instead of pursuing the consequences of these immigrant invasions for Trobriand society, Malinowski sees his relationships with the white men as personal intrusions on his objective research. He continually tries to avoid intensive conversations with whites, especially with the trader Raffael whom he finds so intelligent and sympathetic that he fears the man might become his 'main subject of study' (ibid. 264). The ideal model of the isolated, simple society didn't exist, even at the outset of intensive anthropological fieldwork.

Like Malinowski, I found myself, at the beginning of fieldwork, trying to blot non-Gypsies or gorgio administrators from the landscape. I saw them as useful sources of background information, a way in to the Gypsies, rather than as important constraints within Gypsy society. If I had more self-consciously analysed my personal desire to disassociate myself from these petty gorgios, I might have recorded everything about them and treated their words and actions as equally if not more 'exotic' than those of the Gypsies. Again I have tried to rectify this in later analysis (Okely 1975a).

MALINOWSKI'S IDEAS ABOUT KEEPING A DIARY

As I have elaborated above, Malinowski used his diary more as an escape from the field than as an intellectual tool in research, yet in one astonishing passage he recognises its potential:

> A diary is a 'history' of events which are entirely accessible to the observer, and yet writing a diary requires profound knowledge and thorough training; change from theoretical point of view; experience in writing leads to entirely different results even if the observer remains the same – let alone if there are different observers. Consequently we cannot speak of object-ively existing facts: theory creates facts. Consequently there is no such thing as 'history' as an independent science.
>
> (1967: 114)

It is regrettable that he did not extend the diary's function as the link between subjectivity and 'scientific' participant observation.

As in social anthropology, the discipline of psychoanalysis is exploring the problem of the analyst's subjectivity, 'notably because the treatment has come more and more to be understood and described as a *relationship*' (Laplanche and Pontalis 1973: 92). The technical term 'counter transference' refers to the analyst's unconscious reactions to the individual patient. Freud stresses that 'no psycho-analyst goes further than his own complexes and internal resistances permit' (written in 1910 and cited in Laplanche and Pontalis). Hence every analyst has first to undergo analysis. Techniques of dealing with countertransference take several forms: either to reduce it as far as possible by personal analysis, or to exploit it in controlled fashion as a guide to interpretation. The analyst's unconscious is seen as the ideal means to understanding the patient's unconscious (Laplanche and Pontalis 1973: 92–3).

Social anthropology might explore analogous methods. Subjectivity as influenced by individual personality, cultural history and gender should be analysed not repressed, and exploited for finer observation and interpretation. It would be of additional value if the anthropologist had undergone personal psychoanalysis, but this is not the core of my suggestion. Whereas the patient is battling largely with his or her personal history, the anthropologist is also battling with his or her cultural and social history. And here psychoanalysis has something to learn from anthropology. The anthropologist as participant observer is, like the psychoanalyst, involved in a relationship; this time between the self and many others; between different cultures. There is a problem of cultural counter transference.

The methods which I tentatively advocate for confronting and making creative and theoretical use of this relationship are as follows:

1 Self-analysis
2 The diary
3 Autobiography

SELF-ANALYSIS

Whereas a diary is usually a record of conscious thoughts and experiences known to the author but concealed from others, the kind of self-analysis recommended by Karen Horney (1962) demands the discovery of unconscious links in thought and experience. 'This fundamental disinterest in the self is one of the great difficulties in self-analysis' (1962: 144) and 'the real difficulty is not that of intellectual understanding but that of dealing with resistances' (1962: 146). In this context I would describe both Malinowski's and my own disinterest in administrators, white men or gorgios as a cultural resistance.

Since thought moves faster than the pen it would be useful to jot down

key words, concepts and images, as well as apparently disjunctive free
associations. All these may bring insight at the time or at a later date; a
structural analysis of the self.

THE DIARY

As a means of self-exploration, the diary should be regarded as an essential
part of fieldwork methodology. It could be the place for the key words and
jottings of self-analysis, but in addition, the place for more conscious
thoughts and experience. No anthropologist would consider writing a retrospective monograph about the people studied if he or she had taken no notes
at the time of participant observation. Details of conversations and events are
lost with each day of delay in recording, so that the fieldwork risks falling
back on pre-fieldwork presumptions. The same goes for any description of
the self in the field. Moreover the very act of recording stimulates and
develops ideas at the time.

In *Notes and Queries* (1967) the use of a journal is suggested merely as a
supplement to note taking, its function being mainly to record the chronology
of events and seasons. There is a single mention of 'self' (no other concession
to subjectivity), but no indication that its description be in anything other
than medico-spatial terms; it is lost in the 'weather' and 'special events'.
Audrey Richards (1971) recommended the use of a diary along similar lines,
but her additional comments hinted at its potential for self-examination.

In my own fieldwork I recorded all my material in diary form, thereby
avoiding the problem of preconceived categories. Several copies were made
of each typed page and my material categorised in ways which often appeared
relevant long afterwards. I bitterly regret that I rarely thought it 'professionally relevant' to record or analyse at length my personal reactions and
dilemmas as they occurred. In my postgraduate training, examination performance was assessed mainly in the Malinowski paper. I was encouraged to
read virtually all his articles and books *except* the diary.

There was another reason for my dedication to a science which excluded
the self: my notes were to be examined by my employers, a research
organisation, some of whose members had expressed grave doubts about the
'reliability' and 'objectivity' of anthropological methods. At the first stage
of fieldwork, I had to conceal the fact that I was taking notes at all. Instead,
everything was supposed to be recorded in massive questionnaires. These I
hid in a suitcase under my bunk and later sabotaged by giving them to social
workers to administer. The Gypsies gave brilliant and ambiguous answers
which I was told despairingly couldn't possibly be coded.

During some three months' follow-up fieldwork, I kept a diary which of
course could never recapture the details of earlier responses. A proper
development of simultaneous self-analysis awaits my next project. However,
I can explore to some extent the third and final method.

AUTOBIOGRAPHY

Here the writer attempts to describe and recreate the stages of past experience (Abbs 1974: 6–7). The presentation of the past will vary in accordance with the present time chosen to examine it. Retrospective analysis of fieldwork will give another dimension to contemporary analysis and the diary. Perhaps the final product should consist of an analytic combination of all three, the aim being that self-analysis should have influenced and enriched the research at all stages. It is debatable how far the autobiographical exploration should be a self-contained section; at the very least it should be recognised as an integral part of published research. Pocock's valuable 'Idea of a personal anthropology' (1973) recognises and explores a person's assumptions about his own society, embedded in written texts and recorded interaction with another people. In this chapter, I have chosen to concentrate more on the refinement of self-consciousness in the field situation, the actual process of interaction.

In the creative use of autobiography, anthropologists can learn from literature. The greatest writers have often had to work through most explicitly their youthful autobiographical experience: Tolstoy in *Childhood, Boyhood, Youth*; George Eliot in *The Mill on the Floss*; James Joyce in *Portrait of the Artist*; D. H. Lawrence in *Sons and Lovers*. Philosophers have felt compelled to write autobiographies in addition to, and separate from, their main work: Rousseau, J. S. Mill, Sartre and de Beauvoir. For others the autobiography has stood as their single product, for example O'Sullivan (1953).

So far I have emphasised the methodological advantages of self-analysis and autobiography in anthropology. The experience and a full and creative record of it are valuable in themselves. The anthropologist, entering another society, crosses also a boundary of self-definition. Some novelists have dealt with this experience most successfully in recording the passage between youth and adulthood (Balzac, Stendhal, Flaubert and Hesse).[8] Unfortunately the anthropologist's *rite de passage* between cultures has largely been defined only in the context of the anthropologist's natal culture. That is, s/he is said to undergo a painful and isolating experience in a liminal area before he or she returns as a full member of the academic club. This witticism thus disposes of the experience. The anthropologist is then said to enter the field in order to return, he or she is not said to be in anthropology in order to enter the field. Both Malinowski (1967: 161) and Lévi-Strauss (1963: 17, 43) tried to play down fieldwork as a life experience, although their own evidence contradicts this pose. Perhaps Castaneda (1970) has aroused such interest precisely because he is prepared to abandon a formal objective purpose for new and personal knowledge on the other side.

Fieldwork is a dramatic contrast to the private, sedentary and academic demands of university existence. Practical and manual skills may be greatly valued, also the ability to interact with a wide range of people. In participant observation in a non-literate society, my usual manner of dress, accent, past education were sources of stigma. Details of my past, important to me, were irrelevant to the Gypsies, other details to which I felt indifferent were to them most meaningful. All this can be both shattering and exhilarating.

My main fieldwork has been within the geography of my own society. I was travelling through or camping in towns I'd known before, but in this different context the landscape was transformed. When I knocked on doors asking for 'any old iron, batteries or rags', I often came face to face with people of my own 'background' and social class, but they were aliens and they treated me as one. Often I suffered a profound alienation. After crossing an ethnic boundary it seemed I belonged nowhere (see also Lawrence 1935: end of chapter 1). This cannot be eradicated by self-analysis although better understood and used imaginatively. If you let go you see aspects of yourself as mere props. You are made aware of your 'personal anthropology', its flaws and its virtues, not just through retrospective nor even verbal analysis, but through action. Dedication to objectivity is exposed as the ego of your own history.

NOTES

1 Young and Willmott (1962: 14) in their 'classic' conceded: 'For the most part we can only report what people say they do, which is not necessarily the same as what they actually do.'
2 In one's own society at least no one is obliged to accept and encourage this dichotomy as politically permanent. I would agree with Lévi-Strauss (1963: 394) that 'the anthropologist who is critic at home and conformist elsewhere is therefore in a contradictory position'. But I disagree with his suggestion that the anthropologist should take no action in his or her own society for fear of 'adopting a partisan position' elsewhere (ibid. 385). Lévi-Strauss' ideal objectivity is falsified, since acceptance of the status quo is as much a subjective stance as intervention.
3 It is not coincidental that Swallow's paper appears in the special issue on 'Women in Anthropology' (*Cambridge Anthropology* 1974), and that the earliest draft of my paper was first given to the Women's Seminar at Oxford.
4 Even in the discipline I get a sneaking feeling that obscure abstractions are considered among some contemporaries as the sole proof of intellectual power, as opposed to the infinite mental intricacies of fieldwork problems. Is fieldwork destined to be another female occupation like social work? (I asked this question in the early 1970s when there was a temporary crisis of confidence in fieldwork among my contemporary postgraduates. Fortunately, fieldwork continued to be valued for the ensuing period.)
5 As it turns out, the ensuing pages of *Notes and Queries* occasionally reveal some amusing examples of colonial paternalism and wholesale generalisations about 'other' peoples, which social anthropology was itself trying to discredit: 'The unsophisticated native is often suspicious of all strangers' (p. 29); 'patriotic flattery may be useful' (p. 33); 'women can be just as offended by the offer of (to them) unsuitable beads as are European girls, if given presents suitable for elderly women' (ibid.).
6 Raymond Firth (1936 republished 1963: 10) in his very discreet description of

himself and his methods yet feels obliged to apologise for 'this somewhat egoistic recital'.

7 In my original version of this article I excluded the quotation from page 279. This was because of the conditions in which I was writing the final copy for the *JASO* typist. I was sitting in the library of the Oxford Institute of Social Anthropology, about to copy out the offensive passage, when a Nigerian acquaintance lent over me to ask a question about something. I could not write 'nigger' under his gaze, nor could I talk about the text in the silenced library. There is now some controversy as to whether the word was mistranslated in the 1967 publication.

8 Here I refer specifically to Balzac's *Les Illusions perdues*; Stendhal's *Le Rouge et le noir*; Flaubert's *L'Education sentimentale*; and Hesse's *Demian*.

REFERENCES

Abbs, P. (1974) *Autobiography in Education*, London: Heinemann Educational.

Adams, B., Okely, J. *et al.* (1975) *Gypsies and Government Policy in England*, London: Heinemann.

Ardener, E. (1975) 'Belief and the problem of women', in J. La Fontaine (ed.) (1972) *The Interpretation of Ritual*, London: Tavistock, and S. Ardener (ed.) (1975) *Perceiving Women*, London: Malaby Press.

Ardener, S. (ed.) (1975) *Perceiving Women*, London: Malaby Press.

Castaneda, C. (1970) *The Teachings of Don Juan*, London: Penguin.

Chagnon, N. (1974) *Studying the Yanomamo*, New York: Holt, Rinehart and Winston.

Evans-Pritchard, E. (1940) *The Nuer*, Oxford: Clarendon Press.

Firth, R. (ed.) (1957) *Man and Culture*, London: Routledge and Kegan Paul.

—— (1963) [1936] *We the Tikopia*, Boston: Beacon Press.

—— (1967) 'Introduction', in B. Malinowski *A Diary in the Strict Sense of the Term*, London: Routledge and Kegan Paul.

Geertz, C. (1974) '"From the native's point of view": on the nature of anthropological understanding', *Bulletin of the American Academy of Arts and Sciences* XXVIII, 1: 26–45.

Henry, F. and Saberwal, S. (1969) *Stress and Response in Fieldwork*, New York: Holt, Rinehart and Winston.

Horney, K. (1942/1962 edn) *Self-Analysis*, London: Routledge and Kegan Paul.

La Fontaine, J. (ed.) (1972) *The Interpretation of Ritual*, London: Tavistock.

Laplanche, J. and Pontalis, J.-B. (1973) *The Language of Psycho-Analysis*, London: Hogarth.

Lawrence, T. E. (1935) *Seven Pillars of Wisdom*, London: Jonathan Cape.

Lévi-Strauss, C. (1963) *Tristes Tropiques* (trans.), New York: Atheneum.

—— (1966) *The Savage Mind* (trans.), London: Weidenfeld and Nicolson.

Mair, L. (1957) 'Malinowski and the study of social change', in R. Firth (ed.) (1957) *Man and Culture*, London: Routledge and Kegan Paul.

Malinowski, B. (1922) *Argonauts of the Western Pacific*, London: Routledge and Kegan Paul.

—— (1967) *A Diary in the Strict Sense of the Term*, London: Routledge and Kegan Paul.

Maquet, J. (1964) 'Objectivity in anthropology', *Current Anthropology* 5: 47–55.

Maybury-Lewis, D. (1965) *The Savage and the Innocent*, Cleveland: World Publishing.

Mead, M. (1972) *Blackberry Winter*, New York: Touchstone.

Nadel, S. R. (1951) *The Foundations of Social Anthropology*, London: Cohen and West.

Needham, R. (ed.) (1973) *Right and Left*, London: Chicago Press.

Nin, A. (1974) *The Journals of Anaïs Nin 1934–1939*, London: Quartet.

Notes and Queries on Anthropology (1967), London: Routledge and Kegan Paul.

Okely, J. (1975a) 'Gypsy identity', in B. Adams, J. Okely *et al.* (1975) *Gypsies and Government Policy in England*, London: Heinemann.

—— (1975b) 'Gypsy women: models in conflict', in S. Ardener, (ed.) *Perceiving Women*, London: Malaby Press.

—— (1975c) 'Malinowski's interpretation of sex and reproduction: a reappraisal'. Paper given to the Oxford Women's Anthropology Symposium.

O'Sullivan, M. (1953) *Twenty Years A-Growing*, Oxford: Oxford University Press.

Pocock, D. (1973) 'The idea of a personal anthropology'. Unpublished paper given at the Dicennial Conference of the ASA, Oxford.

Read, K. E. (1965) *The High Valley*, New York: Scribners.

Richards, A. (1971) 'The Use of a Diary'. Paper given at the Institute of Social Anthropology, Oxford.

Smith-Bowen, E. (1954) *Return to Laughter*, London: Gollancz.

Swallow, D. A. (1974) 'The anthropologist as subject', in Women in Anthropology. Special edition *Cambridge Anthropology* I, 3.

Turnbull, C. (1961) *The Forest People*, London: Reprint Society.

—— (1974) *The Mountain People*, London: Picador.

Wintrob, R. (1969) 'An inward focus: a consideration of psychological stress in fieldwork', in F. Henry and S. Saberwal *Stress and Response in Fieldwork*, New York: Holt, Rinehart and Winston.

Young, M. and Willmott, P. (1962) *Family and Kinship in East London*, London: Penguin.

Chapter 3

Trading stereotypes

The main concern of this chapter is Gypsy ethnicity and economic exchange. It describes the Gypsies' special economic niche, showing also why it is more appropriate to refer to economic exchange than to 'work', which in an industrial capitalist system is closely associated with wage-labour.

DEVELOPMENT PREJUDICES

A recurrent theme in the literature is that Gypsies' 'traditional' livelihood has gone, and that they will disappear with development. This underestimates their continuing ability to adapt to changes in the larger economy. It assumes that Gypsies have been isolated and cannot survive unless they remain so (Sutherland 1975: 1–3). It has been said of British Gypsies that

> isolation, caused partly by the need for protection and partly out of desire to preserve cultural integrity, has kept the gypsy ignorant of the outside world.
>
> (Trigg 1967: 43)

> Mass communications have removed the barriers. . . . Education, economic pressures and, in due course, miscegenation will do the rest. The long, long history of the gypsies of Britain is coming to an end.
>
> (Vesey-Fitzgerald 1973: 245)

Equally misleading observations have been made of Gypsies elsewhere. Some American development sociologists have classified Spanish Gypsies as 'underdeveloped marginals' whose contact with 'modern sectors' is largely through formal institutions like the police, militia and school (Goulet and Walshok 1971: 456). Certainly, political contact is imposed by gorgios (the Gypsies' word for non-Gypsies), but Gypsies everywhere also initiate economic contact with gorgios. Every day Gypsies seek out gorgios on their doorsteps, at their factories and offices, on their farms and at their scrap-metal yards. One Gypsy put it neatly: 'Work doesn't come to you, but the *muskras* [police] do.'

Gypsies must and do know exactly what is going on around them. They are continually adjusting to and participating in technological and industrial development, although often in ways unrecognised in orthodox economic terms. Thus the study of Spanish Gypsies confidently asserts that if Andalusia were to 'develop successfully, Gypsies would be left with no marketable skills' (Goulet and Walshok 1971: 464). Confining themselves to occasional visits and questionnaires and imbued with nostalgic notions of the 'real' Gypsy, gorgio observers have described only some of the Gypsy occupations. Other occupations are belittled or left undiscovered, and the underlying principles behind all their occupations are ignored.

CONTINUITY

The Gypsies, or Travellers as they often prefer to be described by outsiders, are directly dependent on a sedentary or host community within which they circulate, supplying goods, services and occasional labour. A considerable number of Gypsies in the British Isles are nomadic, at least for part of the year, living in caravans or 'trailers' towed by lorries or vans. Even those who move into houses are not necessarily permanently sedentary: they could take to the roads again. The Gypsies' shift from horse-drawn waggons to motorised transport is one example of their economic adaptation. Modern technology has actually enhanced their nomadism. Larger homes with bottled-gas cooking and heating facilities can now be transported.

Unlike migrant workers who move from place A to place X for 'settled' and wage-labour jobs, Gypsies operate largely independently of wage-labour. The greatest opportunities for Gypsies lie in those occupations which others are less able or less willing to undertake. This is also true of migrant workers moving to the industrialised areas, but they either take up wage-labour employment or operate small fixed businesses. By contrast, the caravan-dwelling Gypsy family is both self-employed and actually or potentially mobile with lorry, trailer and minimum overheads. With these advantages, the Gypsies can cater for occasional needs where there are gaps in demand and supply and market forces are uneven; and where any large-scale or permanent, specialised business would be uneconomic or insecure. The character of Gypsy occupations can be summarised as 'the occasional supply of goods, services and labour to a host economy where demand is irregular in time and place' (Okely 1975b: 114).

The descriptive details and history of a particular occupation (for which see Okely 1975b) become less important than the consideration of aspects common to all. A list of the occupations of British Gypsies is indicative. It would include:

1 The hawking of manufactured gorgio goods – either small items like brushes and key rings, or larger items like carpets and linen.

2 Antique dealing – the Gypsy collects antiques from individual households over a wide area and then trades them to a dealer, sometimes straight to an exporter to the United States.

3 The sale of Christmas trees and holly.

4 Clearance of discarded goods and waste – old cars, cookers, fridges, boilers, machinery from houses, factories or demolition sites; old clothes and rags. The metal and rags are then sorted and delivered for recycling.

5 External building and gardening – tarmac- or asphalt-laying of small driveways, paving, tree-lopping and external house repairs.

6 Seasonal farm work on a contract basis – fruit-picking, potato-picking, beet-hoeing and hop-tying.

7 The hawking of Gypsy-made wares – like wooden pegs and wax flowers, the sale of white heather, fortune-telling and knife-grinding. These last are the occupations which gorgios most frequently associate with Gypsies.

The study on which this chapter is based involved direct personal experience of scrap-metal and rag collection from houses, farms and public rubbish dumps; helping to break up and sort the materials and to weigh them in at scrapyards. It involved selling holly to florists and joining a gang of potato-pickers. It also allowed the author the dubious honour of being insulted as a Gypsy by shopkeepers and householders (see Okely 1983: chapter 3).

The number and variety of occupations reveal the Gypsies' remarkable adaptation to changes in the larger economy. This is most notable in their recycling of scrap-metal. The Civic Trust has suggested that 'Gypsies and Didikois contribute 20 per cent of scrap-metal over the weighbridge supplies to scrap yards' (1968: 8). Because farmwork and rural-based occupations have declined, those who would fix 'real' Gypsies in this setting will assume there are no alternative economic openings. But the Gypsies, like the dominant sedentary population, have become concentrated in urban indus-trialised areas. The 1965 Government Census of Gypsies recorded 43 per cent in the South-East Region and 17 per cent in the West Midlands – compared to 2 per cent in the Northern Region (MHLG 1967: 7). Over a decade later this shift is probably more marked. With it have come problems in finding camping places free of gorgio interference. This is not because of land shortage as often it is alleged – there are plenty of temporarily vacated plots – but because of stricter controls on land usage, especially for caravans. On the other hand, motorisation has enlarged the Gypsies' daily work radius from the camp base.

SELF-EMPLOYMENT AS IDENTITY

Throughout these changes the Gypsies have retained the preference for self-employment which has always been a crucial defining boundary between themselves and gorgios. Economic exchanges with gorgios are, as far as possible, on the Gypsies' own terms. Wage-labour by contrast would entail working to the orders of a gorgio and would put restrictions on the location, times and type of work. One Gypsy said: 'If we took reg'lar jobs it would spoil us.'

Like Gypsies in California (Sutherland 1975), English Gypsies regard welfare as merely a modern equivalent to begging and so not degrading. But wage-labour is contemptible: Gypsies are proud to announce: 'I've always worked for myself.' The gorgio's stupidity is confirmed by his inability to do so.

> There's not much to a gorgio's life – working Monday to Friday the same time in the morning to the same time in the evening. Then the man gets drunk on Saturday. He has sex once a week that night and a lie-in on Sunday. At the end of it all, the man's given a gold watch!

Even short-term contract work on farms is resented:

> I like calling for scrap. It's much better than picking 'tatoes all day. I'd rather work for myself than a farmer or someone else.

But this is as close as Gypsies come to wage-labour. The men of wealthier families dismiss farmwork as 'women's work' and relegate it to their wives (see Okely 1975b: footnotes).

The Gypsies even avoid wage-labour economic relationships amongst themselves. A Gypsy may work with, but not for, another Gypsy. Economic co-operation occurs in work partnerships: two men might enter a temporary partnership to do some tarmacking jobs together. This often occurs between affines. Always: 'We split the money down the middle.'

In contrast to this egalitarian relationship, Gypsies will willingly exploit gorgio labour. There are numerous gorgio tramps or 'dossers' prepared to do the odd day's work for a flat rate. Travellers may call in at doss-houses seeking casual labourers. These dossers, or 'slaves' as they are sometimes contemptuously called, are given the heaviest and most monotonous work in exchange for a fiver and some cigarettes at the end of the day. They may be offered a meal and even a night's sleep in the lorry cab, but always separate from the family, to confirm their permanent exclusion as gorgios from Gypsy society.

Clearly, the Gypsies' economic activities both express and reinforce their separateness from gorgios. Given also the gorgios' hostility and persecution of them as nomadic caravan dwellers, the Gypsies feel they are entitled to make a living from gorgios in any way which suits them.

The Gypsies' rejection of wage-labour in their economic niche demands (1) diversification in occupations and (2) less specific, wide-ranging skills. The non-recognition of these factors in gorgios' analyses partly explains their historical pessimism.

(1) Occupations noticed and recorded by gorgios tend to be those such as

fortune-telling and rural crafts which confirm the host society's stereotype. With industrialisation, the Gypsies' rural occupations have become exotic in the eyes of gorgio town-dwellers. They have tended also to exaggerate the extent of Gypsy craftsmanship. It comes, therefore, as a surprise that Gypsies lay tarmac and deal in antiques, and those who break up cars on the highway verges are dismissed as counterfeit. But nor were Gypsies exclusively rural in the past. When Gypsies were first recorded in the British Isles in earlier centuries, it is likely that they did have more occupations than fortune-telling and horse-dealing but that these were not recognised as 'Gypsy'. Ideally, the Gypsies have a multiplicity of occupations both over time and at any one time. Wealthier families have the greatest spread of occupations and over-specialisation is invariably least remunerative. Gypsies are ready to switch occupation from one week to the next and in a single encounter as I witnessed:

> When I went out 'calling' at gorgio houses with a Gypsy woman asking for scrap-metal and rags, among other things, we were given a carpet and some dresses. At the next village my companion encountered a housewife whom she quickly sized up and we were transformed into travelling saleswomen. We sold the housewife the carpet and some dresses from the rag bag.

(2) Given this absence of specialisation, the Gypsies' wide-ranging skills are appropriate and necessary. Various criteria must be applied to defining a skill. The vast majority of caravan-dwelling Gypsies can neither read nor write. Few have ever attended school. This lack is normally seen only in negative terms. It is said of Spanish Gypsies that:

> Judicious vocational training and the provision of broader job incentives are indicated as a 'must' policy if Gypsies are to be successfully incorporated into development.
>
> (Goulet and Walshok 1971: 466)

In England, the Plowden Report and the 1967 Government Report on Gypsies described Gypsy children as 'severely deprived' and inhibited in intellectual growth (MHLG 1967: 30). While gorgio sympathisers are beginning to recognise the ethnocentrism of this stance, the drive for state schooling for Gypsies still pays only lip service to the Gypsies' alternative skills acquired from early childhood. Travellers or Gypsies themselves say:

> You could put me down anywhere in the world and I could make a living. If there's a nuclear war only the Gypsies'd be able to look after their selves.

The Gypsies' skills include knowing the local economy and the local people; manual dexterity; mechanical ingenuity; highly developed memory; sales-manship and bargaining skills (Okely 1975b: 133–5). More relevant to this chapter are their opportunism and ingenuity in choice of occupation, and their flexibility in role-playing.

Figure 3.1 A Gypsy girl, with painting materials brought by a gorgio, is watched by her grandmother in 'traditional' scarf. Her brother manoeuvres a horse-drawn trolley for scrap work.

Source: *Echo and Post*

ETHNIC IDENTITY

Linguistic evidence reveals some early Indian content in the Gypsies' Romany language. Over several centuries it has also incorporated vocabulary from many European languages. English Gypsies use Romany words and phrases. For gorgios, the Indian origin of Gypsies centuries back has become a mythical charter for acceptance of the Gypsies as a 'genuine' exotic group (see Okely 1983). For Gypsies this is not relevant. Gorgio proponents of the 'real Romany' may pick out individual Gypsies with dark hair and brown eyes to support their exotic prejudices; they will not 'see' the many others; with lighter hair and blue eyes. Gypsies too may note those among them with dark hair and skin, but such features are more distinct among recent Gypsy immigrants from Eastern Europe and may actually be a source of stigma. They are certainly not criteria for membership. Like gorgios, Gypsies entertain ideas of 'pure-blooded' Gypsies, although without the Indian overtones. For both Gypsy and gorgio, 'real Romanies', perceived as a distinct genetic group, is a convenient metaphor for favoured individuals or groups, depending on context and the specific interests of the classifier. The empirical realities are beside the point. X as a 'real Romany' for one observer may be dismissed as a 'half-caste' or 'drop-out' by someone else.

The Gypsies' dogma of 'pure blood' overlays the continuing threat of marriages across the ethnic boundary. In every generation and in every sub-group, numbers of gorgios marry in and numbers of Gypsies marry out, but the perceived boundary remains intact. Membership rests on a principle of descent. Anyone claiming to be a Gypsy and recognised by others as such must have at least one Gypsy parent (Okely 1975a). Membership ascribed at birth must be affirmed by a way of life and commitment to certain Gypsy values. These include self-employment and pollution taboos which express, at a ritual level, the separation from gorgios (Okely 1983).

Whatever their alleged 'racial' status, more significant for the Gypsies in their economic and political relations with gorgios is that, unlike ethnic minorities who are recognisably different from the mass of the resident population, Gypsies are not physically distinct. They can choose to conceal their ethnic identity or to elaborate it.

The gorgios' categories of 'Gypsy' have a long history and are fundamental constraints on the Gypsies' actions. The Gypsies must become acquainted with these categories in order to manipulate them. They may even have a hand in creating them. The confusion in the literature, and the arbitrariness of gorgio criteria as to who or what is a 'real' Gypsy, reflect the Gypsies' success in presenting so many separate appearances. The ability is explicitly recognised. One Gypsy woman explained it succinctly: 'I have a thousand faces.'

The image of the Gypsy as presented to outsiders is variable and adjusted to the needs of a particular context. This use of ethnicity is quite apart from the Gypsies' sense of identity and ethnic consciousness which is usually concealed from gorgios. Whereas economic relations between Gypsies are ideally based on equality and pursued within the framework of certain rules, there are no such rules accepted by both parties in exchanges between Gypsy and gorgio. Even practices which affront gorgio codes are therefore considered acceptable. But caution itself becomes a moral principle. There is the story of a Gypsy who made a deal with the Devil:

> In those days Gypsies traded in salt – it used to be dear. The Devil gave this Gypsy a barrel of salt which never emptied. One day it spilled over and filled the world. It's like that man who touched everything and it turned to gold. The moral of the story, I suppose, is, you must watch what you're getting. Follow through the deal. Think it out.

The Devil is in essence the gorgio. Deals with the devil gorgio must be made with infinite caution. The Gypsy thought the salt barrel would permanently solve the problem of earning a living. The single deal created over-dependence and brought disaster. Whereas a deal with a Gypsy affirms ethnic independence, a deal with a gorgio risks dependence.

In economic interaction with gorgios, ethnicity or ethnic image may be handled in a number of ways, each having a different value. It may be:

1 exoticised +
2 concealed o
3 degraded −
4 neutralised + −

These modes rarely coincide with the Gypsies' own image of ethnic identity.

1 Ethnic image exoticised (+)

The so-called 'traditional' occupations of Gypsies are often those in which it has suited them to present and identify themselves as Gypsies in accordance with an exotic or romantic stereotype. The word 'Gypsy' derives originally from 'Egyptian', a label often given to persons from the East. As fortune-tellers, the Gypsies exploited the myth of their origins in Egypt, a land once associated with magical arts. Today, Gypsies as fortune-tellers do not claim foreign origins; they need only step into the part bequeathed by their ancestors in England:

> You have to put on a scarf, show off your gold jewellery and say 'Cross my palm with silver'. Some of 'em says 'Cross my palm with paper money' now!

The fortune-tellers met in the course of this study rarely believed in any powers to predict the future (see chapter 5, this volume). None the less, the ability to act the fortune-teller and to read character was recognised as a special skill learnt from childhood. Some of the skill lies in correct sub-classification of the gorgio client – in matching preoccupations and anxieties with occupation, social class, age, race and gender: 'You can always say to a middle-aged housewife that she's got worries.' Individual personality is also assessed. Information may be acquired from another Gypsy who, days or weeks earlier, appeared to the client as tarmacker or salesman. The fortune-teller can create confidence by the announcement of this information. If it is followed by ambiguous statements which will be subjectively interpreted by the client, the latter may unwittingly volunteer new facts which add up to a convincing character reading. Several Gypsies interviewed described how they became very frightened when their predictions came true and they gave up fortune-telling altogether. In one case, a Gypsy woman, not being a psychotherapist, did not realise that her predictions had been self-fulfilling. She had imbued her client with the confidence he needed to extricate himself from his difficulties.

Although fortune-telling between Gypsy and gorgio is seen largely as a con, some Gypsy individuals are believed by Gypsies themselves to have super-natural power, including the power of prediction. These are often older women, classified as *chovihanni* (witch). The Gypsies also associate good or bad luck with some particular items, but those hawked to gorgios as 'lucky' and 'gold' (really brass) charms are seen amongst themselves as inauthentic trinkets.

Women pose as fortune-tellers more successfully than men (Okely 1975c and chapter 4, this volume), but some older men combine it with the exotic or romanticised occupation of knife-grinding. Old men and women of any age can be exotic without being menacing. Younger men in the same guise may be considered threatening unless disarmed by a violin or guitar. As a consequence, in some parts of Europe it is lucrative for a young Gypsy to present himself to gorgios as an exotic musician.

Other occupations with romantic if not exotic potential include the production and sale of rural handiwork such as clothes pegs, wax or wooden flowers and 'handmade' lace – the latter bought by the yard from Nottingham factories. Although manufactured by men, the clothes pegs and wooden flowers are distributed by the women.

2   Ethnic image concealed (O)

Gypsies can 'pass' more easily than some other ethnic groups. This may be a permanent or long-term choice when an individual Gypsy becomes sedentar-ised and abandons his or her ethnic group (Barth 1955). More significant for those who continue to identify themselves as Gypsies is the day-to-day practice of passing. Whereas Gypsy women find exoticism remunerative, Gypsy men profit from concealment of ethnic difference. They must disguise themselves as 'ordinary' and 'normal' in terms of the host society. Daily contact gives the Gypsies insight into the gorgio. Here there is an asymmet-

Figure 3.2 A Gypsy woman, on an official visit to London from Finland, discusses her embroidered apron. Exotic identity may also have political power. *Source*: James Hopkins.

rical exchange of information: the gorgio is permitted very few insights into the Gypsy way of life. The majority of gorgios who seek out Gypsies are those intending to impose their own laws – police, public health inspectors, teachers and missionaries. The Gypsies have devised responses appropriate to satisfying the gorgio invader but leaving him ignorant of the Gypsies' view of the encounter.

As tarmackers, landscape gardeners, travelling salesmen or antique dealers, Gypsy men put on 'respectable' clothing – clean trousers, shirts and expensive cardigans:

> When we goes tarmacking, we don't say we're Gypsies. No. We call ourselves businessmen and say we've got a company.

Touches of normality and semblance of literacy are communicated by headed notepaper, acquired from employees of building firms or local councils:

> We don't tell them the price the first time. We say we'll make an estimate and come back later.

These 'estimates' are typed on the headed notepaper by a gorgio associate or literate Gypsy. Advertisements are placed in the local newspaper giving the phone number of an obliging house-based relative or, in one case, of a pub pay-phone with set times during opening hours, arranged without the knowledge of the landlord. Antique dealers may lay hands on cards from a local antique shop and use them as passports of goodwill. Both men and women can successfully operate as sellers of linen and carpets. No addresses are necessary, only immediately visible authenticity and trustworthiness. Here the men wear good quality suits:

> Two Traveller women described how they used to call on the local vicar and ask to hire the church hall. They would arrange for specially printed cards announcing the date and place of the sale.

The selling of second-hand goods also demands a respectable appearance. Preparing to go out selling second-hand clothes, a Traveller woman first removed her ubiquitous apron, then put on a smart dress and imitation pearls (*not* gold jewellery), declaring: 'We mustn't look Gypsified.' The very word 'Gypsify' reveals an awareness that a person can make him or herself more or less a Gypsy in the eyes of a gorgio.

3 Ethnic image degraded (−)

Gypsies may choose to degrade their image for the gorgio, as scavenger, beggar, pauper or fool. Tom, who regularly called for scrap-metal and rags, said he always put on shabby clothing for the purpose. 'You 'ave to look poor, else they don't give you anything. If I 'ad on a smart suit they'd think "'e's doin' all right, I'm not gonna give anything away."'

A woman posing as a destitute wife makes a better beggar. Irish Traveller women often carry a bundle made to look like a babe-in-arms. If men made such persistent demands as do women beggars they might be accused of assault. Gypsy women outside a fashionable London store may grab men and push sprigs of 'lucky white heather' (white ling) at them. This is the exotic stereotype gone sour. The men pay up to rid themselves of embarrassment. Social security may in future become the modern and more lucrative alternative to begging.[1] It is not, as we have said, considered degrading by the Gypsies, although it does require a degraded image − especially on the local-authority living sites which are ill-suited to the Gypsies' needs for mobility and non-wage employment. Salaried gorgio wardens on the new official sites assist in getting state benefits as it is in their interest to recuperate the high local government council rents. Non-literacy may be turned to advantage in so far as it precludes some Gypsies accepting certain jobs available at the unemployment centre. The Travellers appear suitably mortified:

WANTED - MIXED RAGS, ETC.

CALLING BACK IN 1 to 2 HOURS

If no waste please return card

I deal in **rags,** dirty or clean, **Bristle carpet & Velveteen hemp**
wool or **cotton** whether **good** or **rotten**

Please look up your useless lumber, which you may have left to slumber. If only a handful just give a glance, you may never have a better chance

MY PRICE IS RIGHT   **I NEVER ASK FOR TRUST**

I also buy BRASS, COPPER, LEAD and ZINC, OLD IRON
Best Prices Paid for Old Car Batteries

OLD RAGS, GAS COPPERS, FEATHER BEDDING
Air Raid Shelters   Copper Cylinders & Geysers

Any person other than the owner collecting this card will
be prosecuted

Figure 3.3 A Gypsy Calling card.

If only I could read and write, I'd be able to do lots of things. I'm not a scholard like you, I've 'ad no egication.

The degraded image of the helpless illiterate is accompanied by earnest wishes to conform, to 'settle down' and send the children to school 'so they can 'ave a better life', thus reassuring the gorgio of the superiority of his system. The few literate Gypsies often conceal their ability, preferring to seem deprived. Non-literates can casually screw up or burn official forms, free from the intimidation of their texts.

When there are no further returns to a degraded image and the Gypsies have had enough of gorgio contempt, they will retaliate by reverting to the gorgio idiom of respectability.

When I was out calling for scrap with Reena and Aunt Doll, the latter was accused by a house-dweller of being a 'dirty Gypsy, living on a dust bowl'. Aunt Doll denied both that she was a Gypsy and that she lived on a camp. She said that she was giving up her time to work for a well known charity. The gorgio retreated. (See chapter 1.)

4 Ethnic image neutralised (+−)

In other interactions, the ethnic identity of the Gypsy is known by the gorgio but is largely irrelevant to their business transaction.

In such cases exoticism, concealment or degradation are inappropriate. Relations of this kind occur between the Gypsy as client to some regular patron: the tarmac manufacturer; the antique dealer higher up the distribution ladder; the scrapyard owner or employee at the weighbridge; the builder giving sub-contracts; the linen wholesaler; the gorgio horse-dealer; the farmer. The Gypsy will make efforts to individualise or personalise the relationship, so winning special favours. The man at the tarmac yard will reserve small quantities at a lower price; the man at the weighbridge will fiddle the amount and the farmer will give priority to particular families each season. The Gypsies may not be above pulling a fast one and are certainly ready to exploit their bargaining skills, but the gorgio will be on the alert:

> A gorgio horse-dealer said that in contrast to other customers who would ask the price of a horse and take it or leave it, the Gypsies invariably tried to beat him down. They 'made a thing' of the occasion, he said. They would walk away at least three times feigning uninterest before anything was finally clinched. Whereas a non-Gypsy would come back and complain about a second-rate horse, the dealer found: 'I can always count on Gypsies to get rid of a bad horse. They never complain, they just pass it on to someone else.'

Some economic relationships between Gypsy and gorgio are based on equality and more mutual trust than between patron and client:

> Albert sells old cars to Tony, a gorgio who specialises in repairs of specific parts. Tony has contacts who specialise in other parts. Albert is always on the alert for a buyer of the renovated vehicle as he will get a percentage from Tony. Albert said: 'I've known him for years. He's like my own brother.'

These few examples in which the gorgio is given the category 'brother' in no way undermine the ethnic boundary. Liberal gorgios seeking 'friendships' with Gypsies believe that their specific relationships with Gypsy individuals will 'break down the barriers of prejudice'. They assume that such friendships can be multiplied, but to the Gypsies they remain exceptions:

> A Gypsy discussed a gorgio woman who believed that her 'Christian love' could destroy suspicion and hostility between Gypsies and gorgios. 'It's no good,' he said, 'there'll always be Gypsies and there'll always be gorgios. We'll never mix.'

In some long-term relationships with gorgio philanthropists, the Gypsies do not need to play up the exotic image: the gorgios are permitted some amount of insight and their craving for the exotic is satisfied. It is enough that Gypsies are known and perceived by others as 'secret strangers'. The gorgios see the relationship as political: they are working towards the schooling and integration of Gypsies. The Gypsies find their own political advantages: they may ask the gorgio to appear on their behalf in court or to delay an eviction. But unlike the gorgio, they also see the relationship as economic. Charitable loans have been obtained on a scale far exceeding the returns from a one-off customer and 'friendship' may inhibit the demand for repayment.

ETHNIC IDENTITY AFFIRMED

Another ethnic image operates in economic exchanges within the Gypsy society. Internal exchange takes the form of bartering for lorries, trailers, horses, dogs, gold jewellery and antique china, both between kin and between groups distant to each other. Men rather than women exchange all but the last two items. An exchange is publicly clinched when the two parties slap their right hands together. The gesture is called 'chopping hands' and the exchange is referred to as a 'chop'. Prestige is attached to a Gypsy's ability to make a good 'chop'. The procedure is ritualised. At the annual national gathering at Appleby and, to a lesser extent, at Epsom and at regional fairs like Barnet and Stow, Gypsy men engage in horse-dealing. This is not only a commercial activity but a form of communication and affirmation of Gypsy identity. Gypsies who may be strangers to each other, without a history of competition for land, work or allies, can establish a relationship, albeit ambiguous, over a 'chop'. The exchange is usually in front of witnesses but, in any case, a common code is observed. In contrast to economic exchanges between Gypsy and gorgio, those between Gypsy and Gypsy are symmetrical: each should be aware of the other's tricks and ruses. If a Gypsy makes a poor deal with another, he cannot cry shame. It is shame on him (compare the gorgio who returns to complain to the dealer in the example above). At a large fair with hundreds of Gypsy participants, each transaction will affirm or diminish an individual's prestige. In establishing contact with someone from a distant region, a Gypsy is also protecting his status in his own region.

The horse is given special status among Gypsies. It is considered ritually clean, not *mochadi* (ritually polluted) as are cats, dogs and some other animals (Okely 1983). The horse is an important intermediary between Gypsy and gorgio as an item of exchange, and between Gypsies it has special significance. Since both parties should be experts in the judgement of horses, its exchange affirms their identity and skills as Gypsies. The ability to make a 'chop', and especially a 'chop' of horses, is an art to be learnt from childhood:

> Billy and Sylvie took me with them to a regional fair. Billy, recently housed, had taken his six-year-old son out of school that day. 'My son's

Figure 3.4 Gypsy men consent to being photographed at Epsom races in a generalised location where ethnic identity is affirmed.
Source: Homer Sykes.

got to learn. Gypsies don't need to be educated like the gorgios are. A Gypsy has to learn to chop; know what to say. Did you notice that old man with the waistcoat and gold watch chain? He said: "Look at this horse, if you take her you can have my wife for the night." Now you couldn't learn that in school! Can you see a gorgio doing that? He wouldn't know what to say!'

Readiness to have a 'chop' is linked with manliness. It is a humiliation to refuse, an admission of incompetence before the first round. Having a 'chop' is often the first overture between families meeting on the road. A Gypsy man might say, 'What do you have about you?', 'If I'm half a man for this', or 'I'm a man for exchanging this'. It is no answer for a man to say he will not part with something:

> Albert told me he had been approached by Ned, a man of great fighting ability and political stature, to do a chop over Albert's black and white horse. Albert wanted neither to risk dealing with Ned nor to exchange the horse. He said it wasn't his horse but belonged to his five-year-old son. Ned accepted this, and Albert's dignity was preserved.

The Gypsy woman's ethnic and sexual identity is not affirmed by internal economic exchange as much as by the observance of female pollution taboos (Okely 1975c and chapter 4, this volume). Ideally, like the Gypsy man, she is self-employed in earning a living from gorgios. Traditionally, it is the woman's responsibility to acquire food for the family. Gypsy women often remark that gorgio men do not make their wives go out to work.

CONCLUSION

Ethnicity should be distinguished from ethnic identity. The first refers to the sense of difference and the image presented to the outsider and may be either repressed or elaborated. Ethnic identity rests on group self-ascription (Barth 1969: 14) in theory and in practice. The Gypsies maintain an ideology of racial purity which is made to work by a biased selection of ancestors. The Gypsies' self-image contrasts with the image offered to others, but the two are interconnected. The Gypsies are and, indeed, must be alert to gorgio expectations of Gypsy ethnicity and normality and must supply them, while maintaining intact their own view.

Many Gypsy economic activities have been overlooked because gorgios have needed to define Gypsies only as exotic and/or degraded in their terms. For the Gypsies these are only two out of several available alternatives. Even the host society's concepts of exotic or degraded will change. In the early nineteenth century the Gypsy was considered 'depraved' (Hoyland 1816: 158) as a heathen, rather than 'deprived' (Plowden 1967: Appendix 12) as an illiterate. But whereas charitable financial resources once centred in the churches, they tend now to be concentrated in bureaucratic departments of the state. The Gypsies may have access to these resources in the name of development and education if they are willing to adapt their degraded image to the idiom of bureaucratic allocation. In the United States (Sutherland 1975) and in Sweden the Gypsies have successfully accommodated to welcome welfare provisions and have exploited suggestions for training programmes – although not necessarily in the manner or with the effect that gorgios intended. An American newspaper item is indicative:

> While many of the nation's women seek to break away from housework roles, 10 young gypsy women here are learning to use sewing machines and dress patterns. And some are learning to read as they sew. Many of the women can't read or write.
>
> 'For 2000 years gypsies have avoided education because of traditional mistrust of outsiders,' said N, a gypsy leader who counsels and arbitrates disputes among his people. There are about 500 gypsies in the area. 'Their society is closed and the women have a role of wife and mother and that's it,' said Sue, a sewing instructor. 'To let the young girls out to go to class is a real breakthrough.'
>
> The $17,000 program, financed by the federal Comprehensive Employment Training Act, is administered by a federal–city agency called Work Experience of Adults. Most of the women are teenagers or young adults. They attend classes 30 hours a week and are paid $2.30 an hour to participate in the sewing classes. 'Those girls aren't doing it for the money,' N said, 'it's for the education.'
>
> *(Kansas City Times,* 20 October 1976)

Paradoxically, Gypsies have thrived both on paternalist liberal efforts to absorb them and on the host society's craving for exotic differentiation. Non-Gypsy observers have failed to understand that Gypsies have an alternative and sometimes contradictory model of their own actions. And they cannot, by definition, see Gypsies at all in situations where Gypsy ethnicity is either neutralised or invisible. Gorgio confusion has been Gypsy survival.

NOTE

1 Since this was written, mass unemployment and social security cuts have meant an increase in begging among gorgios.

REFERENCES

Adams, B., Okely, J. *et al.* (1975) *Gypsies and Government Policy in England,* London: Heinemann.

Ardener, S. (ed.) (1975) *Perceiving Women,* London: Malaby Press.

Barth, F. (1955) 'The social organisation of a pariah group in Norway', *Norveg,* reprinted in F. Rehfisch (ed.) (1975) *Gypsies, Tinkers and Other Travellers*, London: Academic Press.

—— (ed.) (1969) *Ethnic Groups and Boundaries*, Boston, Mass.: Little, Brown and Company.

Civic Trust (1968) *Disposal of Unwanted Vehicles and Bulky Refuse*, London: Graphic Press.

Geertz, C. (1963) *Peddlers and Princes*, Chicago: Chicago University Press.

Goulet, D. and Walshok, M. (1971) 'Values among underdeveloped marginals: the case of Spanish Gypsies', *Comparative Studies in Society and History* 13, 4.

Hoyland, J. (1816) *An Historical Survey of the Customs, Habits and Present State of the Gypsies*, London.

Ministry of Housing and Local Government (1967) *Gypsies and Other Travellers*, London: HMSO.

Okely, J. (1975a) 'Gypsy identity', ch. 2 in B. Adams, J. Okely *et al.* (1975) *Gypsies and Government Policy in England*, London: Heinemann.

—— (1975b) 'Work and travel', ch. 5, in B. Adams, J. Okely *et al.* (1975) *Gypsies and Government Policy in England*, London: Heinemann.

—— (1975c) 'Gypsy women: models in conflict', in S. Ardener (ed.) (1975) *Perceiving Women*, London: Malaby Press.

—— (1983) *The Traveller-Gypsies*, Cambridge: Cambridge University Press.

Plowden Report (1967) *Children in their Primary Schools*, London: HMSO.

Rehfisch, F. (ed.) (1975) *Gypsies, Tinkers and Other Travellers*, London: Academic Press.

Sutherland, A. (1975) *Gypsies: The Hidden Americans*, London: Tavistock.

Trigg, E. (1967) 'Magic and religion among English Gypsies'. Unpublished D.Phil. thesis, Oxford University.

Vesey-Fitzgerald, B. (1973) *Gypsies of Britain* (enlarged edn), Newton Abbot: David and Charles.

Chapter 4

Gypsy women
Models in conflict

There is an extraordinary contrast between the outsider's stereotype of the Gypsy woman, and the ideal behaviour expected of her by the Gypsies themselves; the two are more closely connected than the conventional opposition between fact and fantasy, the real and the ideal. The relationship is reflected in the Gypsies' beliefs in female pollution. This cannot be satisfactorily explained through the Gypsies' internal organisation alone, but can be properly understood only when set in the context of the Gypsies' external relations and of the more general pollution taboos between themselves and outsiders or gorgios (to use the name given by Gypsies to all non-Gypsies).[1] I also examine how the Gypsy women use their special relationship with outsiders to resolve problems of formal subordination to men. The disjunction between the outsider's stereotype and the insider's ideal, expressed in pollution taboos, is to some extent bridged by an exchange of fantasies between the women and men of opposing groups.

GORGIO VIEW OF GYPSY WOMEN

Throughout Europe the Gypsy woman is presented as sensual, sexually provocative and enticing. In England a stereotype of the Spanish Gypsy is often thought to be typical and is so depicted in popular paintings: a black-haired girl in low *décolletage*, with flounced skirts and swaggering walk, hand on hip – every operatic Carmen walks this way. One of the *Concise Oxford English Dictionary* definitions of Gypsy is '(playful) mischievous or dark-complexioned woman'. She is thought to be sexually available and promiscuous in her affections, although sexual consummation and prostitution are elusive in the image. Sometimes the suggestion is explicit: in the eighteenth century, a farmer in the area where I did my fieldwork referred to the local Gypsies as follows:

> These miscreants and their loose women, for no doubt all of them are so, as they lie and herd together in a promiscuous manner . . . a parcel of Rogues and Trollops.
>
> (Ellis 1956: 78)

Usually the image is more romantic. Borrow wrote:

> The Gypsy women are by far more remarkable beings than the men. It is the Chi and not the Chal who has caused the name of Gypsy to be a sound awaking wonder, awe, and curiosity in every part of the civilized world . . . upon the whole the poetry, the sorcery, the devilry, if you please to call it so, are vastly on the side of the women.
>
> (Sampson 1930: 123)

Arthur Symons' poem 'To a gitana dancing', published at the turn of the century, carries in essence the gorgio male view of the Gypsy female:

> You dance, and I know the desire of all flesh, and the pain
> Of all longing of body for body; you beckon, repel,
> Entreat, and entice, and bewilder, and build up the spell.
>
> (ibid.: 135)

Ultimately, possession of this 'witch of desire', as Symons called the gitana, can never be achieved. Frequently we find analogies made between Gypsy women and animals or the wild;[2] Mérimée compares Carmen to a filly from a stud farm (Sampson 1930: 133) and Francis Hindes Groome wrote of a Gypsy girl that:

> Of a sudden her eyes blazed again and you were solely conscious of a beautiful wild creature.
>
> (ibid.: 128)

The Gypsy woman, from an alien culture, but not in a foreign land, is in dangerous and ambiguous proximity. She is placed in nature and in contradistinction to the sedentary culture. Non-Gypsies transfer to her their own suppressed desires and unvoiced fears. As Goffman has suggested in *Stigma*: 'Social deviants . . . provide models of being for restless normals' (Goffman 1968: 172). Nothing about her is ordinary; if pretty she is made outstandingly beautiful, if old she is considered a crone. The implication is that Gypsy women are beautiful, despite or in contrast to the projected inferiority of their Gypsy males, who are victims of more derogatory stereotypes and negative projections. Borrow revealed the same bias:

> How blank and inanimate is the countenance of the Gypsy man . . . in comparison with that of the female Romany.
>
> (Borrow 1874: English Gypsies)

Gypsy males are dubbed parasites, thieves, and unclean – menacing but belittled. One reason for the denigration is that the Gypsy male, rather than the Gypsy female, is seen as a potential 'home-breaker'. He may liberate a house-dweller virgin à la D. H. Lawrence (1970), or abduct a woman to be his own in Gypsy society. This male fear is expressed in the popular ditty about a rich lady who goes 'off with the Raggle Taggle Gypsies O'. The

Gypsy woman does not offer the same threat to house-dwelling society, partly because the house-dweller male is credited with an independent mind in his choice of partner, while the female is not.[3] Unmarriageable but endowed with sexual attraction, the Gypsy woman's marginality also gives credence to strange, supernatural powers: for instance, her presumed ability to foresee the future and tell of the past by the 'black' art of fortune-telling. Also, depending on the outsiders' response, she can bring either bad luck by her curse, or good luck by her blessing.

GYPSY VIEW OF GYPSY WOMEN

The gorgios' stereotype clashes with the Gypsies' own ideal for women. The Gypsies are aware that Gypsy women are attributed a special eroticism, and a tendency towards prostitution; they have in turn a derogatory view of gorgio women, whom they contrast with their own. A male Gypsy said to Jeremy Sandford:

> We're not like gorgios: gorgios just take their women as they are. But our people have always been called whores and Christ knows what. Our women, when they get married, they're scrutinized, they're examined to make sure they've stayed a virgin.
>
> (Sandford 1973: 81)

A Gypsy woman must remain a virgin until lawful marriage. Traditionally girls were inspected by married women. More recently, another procedure has been adopted, as I discovered in my fieldwork:

> It's wrong to do it before you've married. When I was going out with a boy, my mother, as soon as she heard, sent me straight down to the doctor's for an examination . . . then I took a certificate back to my mother. She did that with all my sisters.[4]

After marriage, a wife must remain sexually faithful to her husband. To maintain her reputation she must even avoid being alone with another man or being seen in conversation with him on the camp, lest she risk the accusation of infidelity. I was present when a gorgio man called at a Gypsy trailer for the husband, who was out. The unsuspecting visitor remained, so he was instructed to stay near the open door, as far away as possible from the wife and myself. Another Gypsy woman soon appeared: 'What's going on here?' The wife replied, 'It's all right, *she's* here,' indicating my presence – another woman to safeguard her reputation. The presence of a child old enough to relate events was also considered a protection. A woman should ideally remain with one husband for life and, although divorce or separation were not rare among those groups I knew, a woman was condemned if she initiated a separation. One such woman said: 'If a travelling woman has two men [husbands] in her life, they call her a whore.' Within marriage, a wife is supposed to be subordinate to her husband's orders. In addition, her deportment and dress are dictated by certain restrictions which go further than the tenets of 'modesty' associated with house-dwellers. Far from being a flighty *séductrice*, the Gypsy woman is burdened with many domestic duties. A wife is expected to give birth to numerous children and has the main responsibility of childcare. Food purchase, cooking and cleaning are also the woman's domain.

The Gypsy woman (perhaps more in the past than now, although the tradition is still the ideal among most families) is expected to work outside the camp earning a living from house-dwellers. Such activities as hawking, fortune-telling, scrap and rag collection, and begging, come under the activity which the Gypsies refer to as 'Calling'. In some circumstances a woman may also do casual farmwork. She is greatly valued for her ability to obtain goods and cash from the gorgio, a process which may involve conning and trickery:

> My aunt had loads of gold rings she'd got from gorgios. When I was with her, she'd say, 'Do you like that suit the lady's wearing? Well you'll have it.' The lady'd be talked into giving it. Some'd take their earrings off. They didn't dare tell their husbands. Auntie'd say, 'See the ring she's wearing? Well, I'll have that.' And next week I'd see her wearing it.

It seems that in the past the woman was almost wholly responsible for obtaining food and other domestic requirements:

> In the old days the women earned the money. The men sat in the camp all day and the women went out.

An old woman recalled life thirty years ago:

> I'll say this for my husband, he kept a good roof over our head, but I had to get everything else.

The man was responsible for providing shelter and transport, e.g. the wagons and horses.

> Gorgio men give money to their wives. They don't make them work. Maybe it's not like it used to be, but in the old days a Traveller's wife *had* to work. Otherwise they'd beat them.

Today, with greater industrialisation and the switch to motorised transport, in many cases, the man's contribution has increased relative to that of the woman. Some of his earnings are handed over for food and domestic expenses, yet it is still considered important that a woman should be able to earn a good living, if only in crises.

> I'd take my last pegs from the line, clean 'em, and sell 'em 'fore I let my kids starve.

CONTRADICTIONS

There is a paradox embedded in the Gypsy woman's role. Within her own society she is hedged in by restrictions, expected to be subservient to her husband and cautious with other men. Yet nearly every day she is expected to go out to 'enemy' territory, knock on doors of unknown people and establish contact with new customers, some of whom will be men. Success in obtaining money or goods will depend on her ability to be outgoing and persistent, and her readiness to take the initiative. She must be aggressive – quite the opposite to some of the behaviour required of her in the camp.

There do exist formal restrictions on the woman's activities outside the camp. Fred Wood, a Gypsy writer, has claimed that in the past, at least, when a woman knocked at a door and a man answered, she was to ask for the mistress of the house, and if she did not appear the Gypsy was expected to leave forthwith (Wood 1973: 29). Such restrictions explain the apparent inconsistency in the husband's boasting of his wife's mechanical knowledge, 'She knows all about motors', while at the same time discouraging her from learning to drive a vehicle. The latter would give her considerable independence: 'I'm not having you running about; I want to know where you are.' Mechanical knowledge is acceptable so long as it is not used by the women for independent transportation. When out Calling, the woman is expected to travel on foot, or on the more constricting public transport.[5] None the less such controls over the woman's activities outside the camp are either trivial or unenforceable. When Calling with the women, I discovered that they frequently conducted business with men alone and actually stressed the advantage of such a procedure:

> If you get the men by themselves and keep them talking, you can sell quite a few flowers. Tell them to get a present for their wives. They don't know what their wives want.

POLLUTION[6]

Clearly, external control over the women's sexual activities can only be effected by supernatural beliefs, and ones fully internalised by the women. It is here that fears of ritual pollution have power. In addition to the pollution beliefs which the Gypsies use to erect and maintain boundaries between themselves and gorgios, there are certain polluting powers attached to women which can be fully understood only in the context of Gypsy–gorgio pollution. The general pollution beliefs are illuminated by an awareness of the special ecological niche which the Gypsies hold in the larger society.

Unlike most nomads, Gypsies are directly dependent on the economy of another society which is usually sedentary, around which they circulate supplying goods and services. By exploiting their mobility and by not restricting themselves to one occupation, they fill occasional and intermittent gaps in the system of supply and demand (Okely 1975c). To ensure their economic survival and independence, they must initiate regular friendly contact with gorgios and develop a multiplicity of roles and disguises: those who sell carpets will conceal their Gypsy origins, while fortune-tellers will exploit them. The scrap and rag collector, picking through material which the gorgio classifies as 'dirt', is prepared to adopt the posture expected of a despised scavenger. The same society that offers a wealth of economic opportunity for nomads simultaneously makes it hard for them to survive in other ways, because they have different patterns of land-usage and they resist bureaucratic control. This is temporarily resolved by a policy of persecution by gorgios and of evasion by Gypsies. However, when confronted by gorgio authorities, a subservient and humble posture may be necessary. All roles, whether trickster or victim, carry the risk of self-degradation and a dangerous sense of unreality unless the inner self is protected intact, or group integrity is maintained and expressed in an independent society.[7]

The problems arising from this relationship with the gorgios are resolved and symbolised in the Gypsies' attitude to the body. My suggestion, which I shall try to document, is that they make a fundamental distinction between the inside of the body and the outside.[8] The outer skin with its discarded scales, accumulated dirt, by-products such as hair, and waste such as faeces, are all potentially polluting. The outer body symbolises the public self or role as presented to the gorgio. It is a protective covering for the inside, which must be kept pure and inviolate. The inner body symbolises the secret, ethnic self (Okely 1983). Anything taken into the body for its sustenance must be ritually clean. Attention is directed not only towards food but also towards the vessels and cutlery that are placed between the lips. The outer body must be kept separate from the inner: even a person's shadow can pollute food. Washing habits are a crucial arena: food, eating utensils and the tea-towel for drying them, must never be washed in a bowl used for washing the hands, body or clothing.

> He's a real Gypsy. You wouldn't find him washing his hands in the same bowl as he washes his cup.

A washing-up bowl used for other activities is permanently contaminated and can never be made clean. The personal washing and laundry bowls are potentially polluting and are usually placed outside the trailer. A woman explained to me that both her washing-up and personal washing bowls were stainless steel. She sensed that others might accuse her of confusing them. So she threw away the personal washing bowl and replaced it with an old plastic bucket.

Gypsies clearly distinguish between something being dirty and something ritually unclean. The word *Chikli* (from *Chik* for dust or soil) means 'dirty' in a harmless way. But the word *mochadi* means 'ritually polluted'. Another meaning offered only by Borrow (1874) is 'unclean to eat'. The gorgio is condemned as *mochadi* for his eating and cleaning habits and because he does not distinguish between the inner and outer body; for example, gorgios possess and use kitchen sinks for multiple purposes. Gypsies either board up their sinks or commission caravans without them and instead use a variety of bowls.

If you look at a Gypsy's trailer, you won't find a sink, that's what gorgios use.

People say we're dirty . . . they don't see that we think they're dirty . . . . Sometimes you go to houses and maybe the outside and the garden look all right but you should see what's inside.

In trying to relate pollution beliefs to other factors, Mary Douglas (1973: 132–3) explains the Pygmies' absence of rules of purity and sacramental religion in terms of their social organisation, which is decentralised and fluid. The Gypsies' social organisation is very similar, with one major difference: their need for regular interaction with an encompassing, hostile society. The Gypsies' rules of purity fit with an obsession with an external ethnic boundary. The internal fluidity of their society vanishes when juxtaposed with the external gorgio society. The Hadza, studied by Woodburn and cited by Douglas, have a similar organisation to the Pygmies, but are notable for a strong male/female segregation with a menstrual taboo and menstrual couvade. In a divorce-ridden society with frequent husband/wife disputes, Douglas writes, 'this formal taboo' expresses 'the pressure of social relations' (ibid.). I suggest that, unlike the Hadza, the male/female pollution beliefs among Gypsies cannot be explained only in terms of the internal organisation, but specifically by the organisational relationship and pollution taboo between Gypsy and gorgio. Here the woman's dual external and domestic role is important.

In addition to the paradox in the behaviour required of Gypsy women in the encampment, compared to that outside, there is another with which they are connected. Unlike pastoral nomads or hunters and gatherers, Gypsies must obtain the bulk of their food from a wider society. Gypsies may have been able to obtain more wild game in the past, but even then a large amount of food had to be purchased or obtained from the gorgio cultivator. With greater urbanisation, this dependence has increased. Thus food, which must be clean for the inner body, is acquired from the potentially dirty gorgio. The Gypsy woman is the crucial intermediary in this transaction since she has the main responsibility for acquiring or purchasing food, as well as its preparation or cooking. She goes between the unclean, alien, and, by implication, unsocialised or 'wild' gorgio and the clean Gypsy group: she is the link between uncontrolled 'nature' outside the Gypsy system and controlled 'culture' inside it.[9]

Women must be careful as to their method of obtaining food, the type of food acquired, as well as its preparation, which may involve cooking. One danger is that they might obtain unclean food: a fear often voiced is that gorgios could either deliberately or inadvertently poison food.

But another danger is that the women might trade their sex for food and thereby threaten the ethnic inheritance of the group.[10] The pollution taboos associated with Gypsy women largely reflect these problems: the woman's need to control her sexuality in certain contexts; the separation between her external, unclean Calling role and her internal, clean culinary role; and the necessity for discrimination between gorgio and Gypsy males as sexual partners.

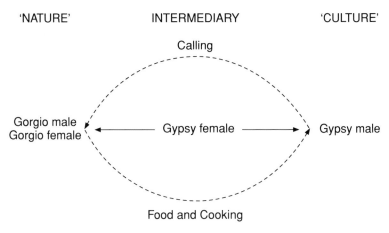

Figure 4.1 Calling and cooking for Gypsy culture.

In the 1920s, T. W. Thompson, a Gypsiologist, recorded aspects of female pollution current among English and Welsh Gypsies of the time (Thompson 1922, 1929). My own fieldwork revealed the continuation of some pollution taboos,[11] although it was often difficult to obtain distinctly positive or negative information on many occasions. The Gypsies are notoriously circumspect with outsiders: direct questioning, even with trusted friends, was usually greeted with silence, avoidance or deception. If, indeed, female pollution taboos have become less important, this coincides with the relative decline in the women's external economic role, and thus my case that the two are interconnected is strengthened. The Gypsy woman's external contribution was still vital in the 1920s and the preceding years for which Thompson recorded his information. A meticulous ethnographer, he has noted the facts but he can offer no explanation. The power of the Gypsy female to pollute a Gypsy male I would summarise in these three alternative ways, using both Thompson's and my own material:

1 Female sexuality is inherently polluting if mismanaged.

2 Menstruation is associated with pollution.
3 Childbirth is polluting.

Thompson finds greater emphasis on (1) and (3), a stress which was confirmed in my own fieldwork.

1 Sexuality as inherently polluting if mismanaged

The woman must be careful not to expose certain parts of her body or to bring it into contact with a man (private sexual intercourse within marriage being the only permissible context in which this may occur). Both in the past and today this is exemplified in restrictions in the woman's dress. Today, shorter skirts are permitted than formerly, but not mini-skirts. I found that blouses must cover the body up to the base of the neck. Tight sweaters and hot-pants are banned. If trousers are worn by women, the hips and upper thighs have to be covered by a dress or smock. The woman has to be careful in her movements. According to Thompson, her legs must be held close together and she must not bend forward from a standing position, especially with her back turned to men. This was confirmed in my fieldwork:

> When that gorgio woman first came on this site she didn't understand. She kept bending – in a skirt right up here . . . the men had to cover their eyes . . . and she had a low neck, that was terrible.

> Travellers don't like girls to sit with their legs apart . . . even a girl of that age [6] would be told. It wouldn't be allowed.

Thompson recorded that a woman had to take special precautions in her toilet habits. A woman's underwear had to be washed separately from the men's clothing otherwise this could be polluted. It had to be dried out of sight. I never saw women's underwear on the crowded lines, except sometimes when hidden inside other clothing. Thompson also recorded how men could be polluted by touching women's clean linen or by walking under such a clothes-line. A woman's dress could also pollute men's underwear, according to Thompson. A woman had to wash her body in complete privacy and ideally from a special bowl reserved also for washing her underwear. Any man inadvertently seeing a woman relieving herself, i.e. exposing herself, was also liable to pollution. In my fieldwork one of the major reasons given by Gypsies against unsegregated toilet blocks was that a man might catch a woman by surprise. Breast-feeding, according to Thompson, was also to be done in private. I found that the vast majority of women avoided breast-feeding altogether and opted for bottle-feeding, despite the contrary advice of midwives and health visitors.

> I breast-fed only one of mine. But I locked myself in the trailer first and drew the curtain. We wouldn't let a man see. That's filthy.[12]

Thompson records that sometimes husband and wife, if not every member of the family, had to have separate crockery. I found cases where each member, whether adult or child, retained his or her own cup. Thompson's material indicates that food preparation and Calling require distinctly separate ritual procedures, thus, I suggest, reinforcing symbolically the separation between the woman's external and internal roles. The woman risks polluting a man via his food. Thompson records that food or water was polluted if a woman stepped over it, held it too close to her, or touched it inadvertently with her skirt. Frequently it was said that a woman could pollute red meat if she touched it before cooking, and did not use an implement. Further fieldwork may reveal whether this is still the case. Traditionally, for cooking or food preparation, the woman had to wear a large white apron encompassing her lower body, front and back. Today these are smaller and patterned, but still considered the mark of a 'true Gypsy'. The apron for a gorgio housewife has a diametrically opposed function which is to protect the dress from the 'dirt' of food and cooking. For the Gypsy, the apron is to protect the food and cooking from the 'dirt' of the dress, which is ritually contaminated by the outer body and specifically the sexual parts. (See Figure 3.2, p. 54)

Thompson described the elaborate preparation required traditionally of a Gypsy woman going Calling:

> After removing the ample white apron she wears in camp, she fastens the money-bags in position round her waist; puts on her hawking apron, which is of black with an embroidered hem; fixes the monging-sheet [i.e. begging sheet] – a square damask cloth – behind her so that it is accessible from either side; re-ties the kerchief she is wearing on her head, and puts on over it her long-poked, lace-trimmed bonnet.
>
> (Thompson 1922: 19)

Then she ties her shawl into a sling to hold her baby, puts on a red cloak and takes up her basket. Notice how the money is placed beneath the hawking apron which acts as the shield between the potentially polluting dress (and sexual parts) and the potentially pure monging-sheet which often contained food, and had thus to be protected from contamination. The hawking apron (black) was never to be worn while cooking as it would in this other context be considered by some as *mochadi*. Some women still wear black embroidered pinafores for Calling or for funerals.[13] I found that black is also associated with mourning and death, which seems to be considered extremely polluting (Okely 1983).

Although Thompson has recorded the polluting power of the female body, her clothing, her contact with food and Calling activities, he has not emphasised the more specific mismanagement of her sexuality (that is: illicit sexual intercourse, not simply the suggestion of sex): 'If a man marries an "unmarried mother", they say he's a fool because she isn't *pure*,' I was told (see Okely 1983: chapter 12).

Uncleanliness comes from illicit sex both before and after marriage. It is said that a husband once had the right to throw his wife on the fire for a transgression. Of one woman believed to be associating with gorgio men, it was said: 'She's been picking up men. She should be burned, that's what she wants.' To which the speaker's husband replied: 'Time was a *moosh* [man] would put his wife in the canal or push her in the fire if she did that.'[14]

More recently it was reported that a Gypsy branded his wife 'with a red hot cleaver when she refused to answer questions about her sex life' (*The Times*, 27 February 1974). Fire is considered to be the suitable purifier for *mochadi* articles (e.g. the possessions of the dead), and so presumably also for impure women. The possibility that illicit sex is more polluting for the female may be where the symbolic and biological potential of the body is used: for a man, sexual intercourse involves temporary absorption into the other, while for the female it may entail permanent absorption, by conception, of the 'other' into the inner body. Since the gorgio is generally considered *mochadi,* there is the implication that sexual relations between a Gypsy female and a male gorgio are especially polluting. Moreover, the offspring from a casual sexual encounter between Gypsy and gorgio is more likely to be born into the Gypsy group, if the mother rather than the father is Gypsy. Thus sexual infidelity with gorgios by Gypsy women is more threatening to the group than that by Gypsy men. Possibly, pollution via illicit sex may not occur between a Gypsy woman and man.

Defloration, however, even within the context of marriage, can be seen as an unclean act, a loss of purity. Both Thompson's (1927) and my own material indicate that it is usual for a young couple wishing to marry, to 'elope' or run off together, ostensibly without the knowledge of the parents. They return after a few days for formal acceptance and, in a minority of cases, for a Registry Office ceremony and feast. The act of defloration has occurred in a *liminal* place away from the camp and the Gypsy group.[15] I suggest that defloration is probably seen as polluting, and comparable with polluting events such as birth and death, *rites de passage* which should also occur outside the camp. While Thompson has discussed at length the pollution associated with birth and death, he has not examined such possibilities in marriage, although his material elsewhere hints at this (1927: 123).

2 Menstruation as polluting

Thompson's records and my fieldwork indicate a milder emphasis on this as a source of pollution. Only among some groups was the woman not supposed to cook during menses. Then, either her husband or other women took over this task. I was able to confirm this from only two such cases, but the occasional trips I noticed to fish-and-chip shops by husbands may have been to protect themselves from pollution. Sexual intercourse seems to be prohibited at this time.[16] Specific mention of menstruation is not supposed to be made in front of men, because they might risk pollution (see also Thompson 1922), so information is limited, especially for male fieldworkers. T. Acton (1971) has suggested that the taboo has declined because of the invention of the sanitary towel. He inadvertently reveals ethnocentric bias by his assumption that a 'neater' or seemingly more 'hygienic' containment would solve the whole symbolic problem. Moreover, even the technical problem is not solved by a modern invention: one married woman who, together with her family, showed no inhibition about dispersing all manner of rubbish and uncovered faeces a short distance from their camping spot, told me: 'I never throw them [sanitary towels] out. I don't believe in that. I always burn them.' The implication was, perhaps, that these articles were especially ritually polluting.

3 Childbirth as polluting

Thompson considers that the Gypsy woman is the greatest potential source of danger to men during and following childbirth. Traditionally the woman retreated to a special tent during labour and for a time after the birth. She had her own crockery and was not allowed to prepare food for men for some weeks. Later the tent, bedding and utensils were burnt. The new-born baby was also considered *mochadi* for a time and had to be washed in a special bowl, and so also its clothes. Today the woman and baby are still regarded as temporarily *mochadi,* and cooking must be done by other women or older children. Moreover the woman is forbidden to discuss her experience with any man or even to tell any man other than her husband (which she will do only reluctantly) the fact that she has entered labour and requires aid. A young woman was warned by the hospital to report immediately she had pains as serious complications were expected. One evening, when she was in the company of an uncle as well as her husband and aunt, labour pains began:

> I was doubled up. My uncle asked what was the matter. I couldn't tell him, he was a man. You don't tell men those things . . . . They went out for a drink and I had to wait till my husband came back. I walked up and down thinking, 'If only there was a woman I could talk to.'

As in the past, men must not assist women in labour. The almost universal preference for childbirth in hospital has been misinterpreted as a conversion to gorgio medicine and the Welfare State. Yet women I encountered in fieldwork were reluctant to attend prenatal clinics and often jettisoned any prescriptions such as iron supplements. Any attendance at clinics indicated more a desire to ensure a hospital bed. It is significant that the Romany word recorded by Smart and Crofton (1875) for doctor is *drabengro*, the same word as used for 'poisoner'. Hospital food is avoided because it has been cooked by gorgios and in a polluted place. The women usually discharged themselves early, to the consternation of the medical authorities.

The nurses at the hospital said, 'We're sick of the Gypsies. They never come to the appointments at the clinics.' Mary wouldn't eat the food. She wouldn't let them wash her. She cried a lot.

Many Gypsies even complained of rough treatment and poor attention during the birth. Rather than being a safety measure for the women, hospitalisation is a convenient way of dealing with a polluting act. The gorgios are given the task of supervising the process and disposing of polluted articles.

From the last two sections we can see that at menstruation and childbirth the woman's ability to pollute is temporarily intensified because they are occasions for the outlet of bodily waste. The female sexual orifice is a 'natural' point of exit for polluting bodily waste, in the light of the Gypsies' distinction between the inner and outer body, where rejected matter from the inner body is especially polluting.[17] While, for some families, menstruation may not be considered especially polluting, childbirth seems always so. A certain shame is attached to pregnancy. Women must conceal their shape with coats or other very loose garments (coats are otherwise rarely worn). Pregnancy is proof that the woman has had sexual intercourse. Conception is a dangerous affair and must not be misplaced, i.e. the father must be a Gypsy. The term used by Gypsies is to have 'fallen', or 'when I fell for . . .', the added name being that of the child not the father. The baby is ambiguous matter because it has been covered by the blood and waste of birth: the inside come outside. The baby remains polluting for a while, possibly because it has not been 'made' a Gypsy until some socialisation has taken place.[18]

J. S. La Fontaine, in discussing women's *rites de passage* in relation to the mode of descent in a society, has suggested that the elaboration of ritual connected with the defloration of Gisu females reflects the importance of male control in a patrilineal society, whereas the greater elaboration of ritual at first menstruation among the Bemba is consistent with a matrilineal society. She does not 'know of a cognatic society in which *rites de passage* reach the scale and elaboration' of those she discussed (La Fontaine 1972: 184). For the Gypsies, a cognatic society, those *rites de passage* associated exclusively with one of the sexes are not 'elaborate' in La Fontaine's sense. There is little ritual attached to first menstruation as such, it is merely the point at which girls become capable of polluting men.[19] Defloration is a dangerous and private transition, not so much a demonstration of male possession. Conception and childbirth are again dangerous but made private. The problem is not one of control by a particular descent group or kinship line, with name and property to transmit, but the protection of the ethnic group as a whole from the dominant society.

It is notable that the women's ability to pollute men, while heightened at certain times, is also ever present, and is not merely associated with certain events or *rites de passage*. The elaboration and public aspects of precaution-ary ritual lie in *continuing daily* observances. Gypsy men are innately pure, almost by predestination, whereas the women have to aspire to an elusive purity by good works, whether as virgins or wives.[20] Since, in their external role, Gypsy women are always vulnerable to sexual contamination by the non-Gypsy, they must be taught that their ever-present sexuality and fertility are dangerous. The woman's dress, deportment and behaviour are matters for constant public scrutiny. They must shield their sexual parts and control their movements and misplaced desires. If women were distinctly polluting merely because of their unique bodily waste, then aprons would presumably be required only at childbirth and menstruation. However, women's sexuality is always potentially polluting to Gypsy men. The Gypsy women must protect all Gypsies from pollution by controlling their sexuality: if indiscriminate and casual with Gypsies, they could be so with gorgios.

For the Gypsies, the mouth is a possibly dangerous point of entry into the inner body, and must absorb only ritually clean food. Women have an added vulnerability because of their sexual anatomy, which is somewhat analogous to a mouth. The woman's sexual organ is regularly polluting as a source of waste, but is also always vulnerable to pollution by the absorption of foreign polluting matter, mainly by sexual intercourse with the gorgio. The ambiguity of the woman's sexual orifice, as point of exit and entry, is reflected in the separation made between it and food. In both the woman's Calling and culinary roles, aprons symbolically protect food from contact with the lower body. Ritual control of sex is connected with control of the con-sumption of food.

The separation between food and female sexuality manifests itself further in a way which is distinctly related to the Gypsy woman's external role. In figure 4.1, the Gypsy woman's roles were shown as a circular process: Calling on the gorgio, followed by the importation of food and its cooking for the Gypsy. Calling and cooking are *activities,* the only apparent *object* is food. The missing commodity or 'object' in the first stage of the cycle is sex, which must never be exchanged for food. Hence ritual observances separate objects as well as actions. It is precisely because of their identity as members of the female sex that women are singled out for their roles. Therefore sex in some form, if only as gender, is ever present in the exchange, although sexuality is not released. In the second part I shall demonstrate how gender and latent sexuality are used.

WOMEN'S PERSPECTIVES

Here a standard male-oriented enquiry might end. However, I am interested in the women's perspective: something which has aroused greater interest since Feminism took new confidence in the Women's Liberation Movement. Frequently in anthropological enquiries women have been seen as separated from major political and economic decision-making, and the extent to which they may participate informally or influence indirectly is not often fully explored. Emphasis has been placed on the male interpretation of events. Anthropologists have often been in closer contact with the menfolk of particular societies and they have found them most articulate. The field-workers, whether male or female, have also imported a male bias which has filtered their observation of the alien society at every level (London Women's Anthropology Workshop 1973; E. W. Ardener 1972).

There are some basic problems which women in nearly every society have to resolve. These were present long before the Women's Liberation Movement and therefore have wider, historical significance. But my mode of presentation arises specifically from the position of women recently in industrialised society.

1 Women in the West, if not elsewhere, have been formally assigned a single economic (and usually unwaged) role rather than a choice from the multiple alternatives open to men. While women often have the main responsibility of childcare, food preparation and domestic work, their economic contribution outside the home, however essential, has been either denied and belittled or grossly under-rewarded relative to that of men.
2 Women have rarely been given or achieved formal or actual political power. Their political activity has been largely by influence and usually through a male intermediary.
3 The biological difference between male and female has frequently been used as the basis for a dichotomisation of social quality. The female has been deemed subordinate. The animal, irrational or supernatural charms associated with her are merely another way of describing and reaffirming that inferiority.
4 Women have often been subject to greater controls on their sexual needs and desires than men. Virginity, sexual fidelity and abstinence have in many cases been demanded more of women than of men.

If we assume that these imbalances have to be culturally imposed without much assistance from innate qualities, some conflicts may have to be resolved. Women from birth may be confronted with an alternative, superior model reserved exclusively for males. These conflicts are of a different order from those in a society where some members, both male and female, are subject to restrictions which do not apply to other men and women from a different family, race or class, for whom alternatives exist. Sexual discrimination is built right into the natal family and may therefore be the most provocative or most powerful restriction. Even if carefully socialised, women may not automatically be prepared to accept the major domestic role, minimum external economic and political participation, implied inferiority, and greater restrictions on their libido. They will find ways of avoiding them. Simone de Beauvoir (1949: II, Introduction) has emphasised the evasions made by women: 'Il est donc nécessaire d'étudier avec soin le destin traditionnel de la femme. Comment la femme fait-elle l'apprentissage de sa condition, comment l'éprouve-t-elle, dans quel univers se trouve-t-elle, enfermée, quelles évasions lui sont permises.'[21]

I am not suggesting crudely that men alone have necessarily imposed these restrictions; women have assisted by some complicity, consciously and unconsciously (Okely 1963). Men as well as women may need to find ways of circumventing the same restrictions.

Edwin Ardener has suggested that a closer examination of aspects such as ritual may reveal that women have their own conflicting cosmology which may be observable at the level of belief rather than the verbal. This could be further extended: women's alternative view may be observable in almost all non-verbalised activities or behaviour, not simply ritual, and also within the crevices of verbalised activities. The observer may be able to reveal new connections, alternative statuses implicit in the women's situation, sometimes by logical analysis or by association, especially where there are paradoxes or inconsistencies with the male model. The women's implicit situation may never be made explicit, never voiced (even if a sympathetic female anthropologist were to encourage the women to talk in confidence). The resolution of certain problems may occur only at an unconscious level. (This analysis of social positions, acted out but not articulated by a group of persons within a specific society, may be compared to the method of psychoanalysis where conflicting or dangerous phenomena may be repressed by the individual and only articulated with the assistance of an analyst.)

So far, the material on the Gypsy woman has implied that she is little more than an intermediary between the Gypsy male-dominated society and gorgio society – slightly more active than in the view that women are passive objects exchanged in marriage between two male-dominated groups (Lévi-Strauss 1969: 65). The Gypsy women are overtly subordinate to the men in the internal Gypsy society. However, the Gypsy society cannot be seen in isolation from gorgio society. It is my contention that Gypsy women resolve some of their problem of subordination to Gypsy men in their external relation with gorgio society. They liberate themselves in devious, unspoken ways.

ECONOMIC ROLE

Although Gypsy women within their own society have the major responsibility for childcare, food preparation and domestic work, as we have seen they are expected to go Calling at gorgio houses. At one level they are 'forced to' by their men, and allegedly beaten if they don't earn enough.

> She has to go out with a thin woollie and her pinny, with a basket selling lace in all weathers. Her husband doesn't give her any choice.

However, this duty should also be seen as an escape from a domestic role. The same woman who gave me the statement above was described as follows:

Mum does love to be out. She's happiest then . . . . She's had to earn her living since she was twelve. Her dad made her.

I found that many women gradually being settled on local authority sites complained of boredom. Sedentarisation restricted their external activities and intensified their domestic role. One woman who had ceased to go Calling said:

When you think of a woman's job, all it is, is pots and pans, cleaning and children. It's all right for some women whose husbands let them drive off in the day. My husband won't let me. There's not much to a woman's life.

When Calling, the woman makes contact with people outside her domestic sphere, beyond even her own society. Her identity is not simply as a wife and mother or member of a kin group, but that of an independent worker. In contrast to the lot of most 'working wives' in the larger industrial society, Gypsy women avoid monotonous wage-labour: for example, low-grade factory jobs which are often reserved exclusively for females. One woman who did take a factory job for a few weeks said: 'I hate factories: the same thing every day and you have to come in at the same time, otherwise they knock some money off your wages.'

She also compared Calling with farm labouring: 'I like Calling for scrap. It's much better than picking potatoes all day. I'd rather work for myself than a farmer or someone else.'

Calling involves self-employment as opposed to wage-labour. The work offers an opportunity for decision-making, independent of men. It requires a multiplicity of skills acquired through a long process of participatory education from childhood. Also, in contrast to many female occupations in the wider society, the Gypsy woman's work is not simply an extension of a woman's supportive and domestic role, as is often the case with cleaners, primary school teachers, nurses and secretaries.

Given the dangers of sexual infidelity and contamination of the ethnic group, it might seem odd that men expose their women to such risks and do not monopolise the external economic activities themselves. Crude explanations might be that this is due to laziness or exploitation. A more satisfactory explanation is that they do so because women are more successful at Calling than men would be. Here the Gypsies can exploit the house-dwellers' ideal or stereotyped woman, whether Gypsy or gorgio. In the dominant society, economic support is usually considered primarily the male's duty, so the Gypsy woman out Calling conceals her role as major breadwinner and often poses as an abandoned, near-destitute wife and mother. By eliciting the pity of the gorgio, she can extract a greater economic return.

PHYSICAL COMBAT

Gypsy women are considered by gorgios to be physically less threatening than their men, since they are not credited with abilities to attack or defend, and they are thus able to make closer contact with gorgios than their men can. The Gypsies are aware that women are expected by many house-dwellers to be non-violent. When a gorgio woman, who was married to a Gypsy, was involved in a fight with a Gypsy woman, she was complimented: 'You're not a gorgio. You hit back.' While exploiting their presumed vulnerability, the Gypsy women actually cultivate fighting abilities. I heard a mother repeatedly chant the following maxim to her seven-year-old daughter, after the girl had been hurt by another:

> Don't throw stones, stripe 'em up then they won't come back no more. If you can't hit 'em, kick 'em; if you can't kick 'em, pull their hair; if you can't pull their hair, pinch 'em; if you can't pinch 'em, bite 'em; if you can't do that, you're bloody useless. You'd better lay down and take your punishment.

She said her own mother used to tell her that. The woman's reputation as a fighter is important for her self-esteem. One woman who lost a fight which I witnessed, tried to convince her neighbours that her misfortune was merely an accident:

> You know this morning, I went to hit her like that [she crooks her elbow]. But she leant that way. She moved a different way than I was expecting. And you know how I fell down? That was 'cos I had my arm up. With all her weight on me. She's a big woman, well I couldn't stay up . . . I'm not *trashed* [scared]. That woman could come up here. I can look after myself.

Fighting prowess is useful in external relations and with other Gypsies. It follows that unlike the ideal in bourgeois society, the Gypsy woman is not especially valued for 'femininity'. Physical frailty and the use of cosmetics leading to obsessive narcissism and mirror self-consciousness are not generally encouraged, although smart fashionable clothing and elaborate hair-styles may be worn on special occasions, such as fairs or weddings. Jewellery (such as gold earrings for pierced ears and sovereign brooches), however, is more important. Large rings are highly valued as weapons in a fight.

POLITICAL ROLE

In the decentralised, non-literate Gypsy-Traveller community, which has neither chiefs nor fixed leadership even within the competing flexible groups linked by kin ties, in so far as it is possible to talk of a political–jural sphere, women's rights and roles are usually subordinate to those of men. Within marriage the husband has formal power over his wife in decision-making. It

is frequently said that in a domestic quarrel the husband has the right to beat
the wife. Her kin rarely intervene, and the woman has little defence:

> If I come up against my husband, I don't fight with him 'cos I know it's
> no use. I can't win and if I go on at him too much, he starts smashing up
> the things in the trailer [which she has to replace]. So you know what I do?
> I scratch myself, dig my nails into my hands and my skin and I pull my
> hair. That's the only thing I can do.

Apart from this inverted aggression, the wife has a formal right of retaliation:

> The woman's one right is to leave her husband. But he must come and fetch
> her. She mustn't eat humble pie and return by herself. Otherwise she loses
> face with the other Travellers . . . . The husband does a lot, maybe he beats
> her, but it's her one way out to leave him for a while.

It is still said that the husband even has the power of life or death over his
wife for major transgressions.[22]

In inter-family and inter-group relations the women sometimes act as
important negotiators or representatives. I am uncertain, however, how far
they can initiate strategies; perhaps they merely communicate and discuss
issues decided by the men. Older women are certainly sought specifically for
advice in crises. In some disputes, the women are expected to fight. This does
not occur simply in a situation of hysterical loss of control and not for purely
'subjective' reasons as in the male-oriented description of women fighting.
Frequently 'sexual jealousy', a psychological explanation, is given for female
combat, while 'social status', a sociological explanation, is given for male
combat. Neither explanation should exclude the other. It does happen that
women, in defending their social status acquired via a spouse, may have to
fight a sexual rival. But Gypsy women also assume more blatantly political
roles. One woman may take on the equivalent representative from another
family in order to defend the interests of her husband and family, for example
in a dispute over camping land. In one such case the husband, whose wife
had challenged another woman, said: 'We're gonna beat up Annie before she
goes on that site. I tell you she's not going on that site.' While not
participating, her husband identified himself with his wife's action. In another
case, a wife threatened to fight the man of a rival family:

> It's gonna be a case for hospital. I don't mind if I go to Holloway [a London
> women's prison]. I'll beat him. I'll take his neck and screw it . . . . I'll
> make him drink his blood. There's gonna be blood running down that site
> . . . I weren't interested in the place 'til he came shit-stirring. He wants to
> be over everyone.

On other occasions the men may assume the fighting role.

As in her external economic role, so in her political relations with the
gorgio society, as already suggested, the Gypsy woman is able to exploit the

gorgio ideal of women being the weaker sex. Regarded by gorgios as non-violent and incapable of independent decision-making, the women are left by their men to cope with visiting gorgio authorities. The women can be suitably evasive and indecisive. When Gypsies are threatened with eviction the men usually disappear from early morning to night. The women have to offer excuses and plead with the police, public health inspectors, security agents and social workers. Safety for the family from prosecution or permission for a prolonged stay on the camping site will depend partly on the women's success. The women deal with unwanted journalists and cameramen:

> Once they came with those things that go round [ciné-cameras] and Elsie and I went for them, threw them up in the air . . . smashed them. They didn't come back.

Men more than women are vulnerable to the superior force of gorgio authority: husbands not wives are arrested, prosecuted, fined, imprisoned and taken for military service. At least one Gypsy man spent the whole of the war in women's clothing, thus eluding gorgio control. His simple transformation assured him the near-magical safety with which females are endowed. The female's seemingly greater vulnerability is her very protection. As already indicated, the Gypsy woman is well prepared for possible attack. 'I always keep some hot water boiling. All I need do is sling it at any man that tries anything.'

Sometimes the women will act to defend their husbands:

> One day the *gavvers* [police] turned up. John had just come back from work and I was making his tea, he was tired. They said they'd have to take him to the station. I asked if he could have his tea first and they said no. This *gavver* was standing in the doorway and I said, 'You can have your tea', and I picked up the kettle and threw the water in his face . . . . At the station the same *gavver* said, 'Oh no, not her'. He thought I was mad.

Few Gypsy women are charged with assault.

RITUAL EQUALITY AND SEXUAL RIGHTS

Edwin Ardener (1972: 6) has suggested that men are usually more aware of other cultures than women through greater contact, and so are more 'likely to develop metalevels of categorization' which distinguish themselves plus their women from other men plus their women. Here I disagree. Gypsy women, and doubtless women in many other cultures, are not lacking contact with the outsider. Although 'culture contact' by itself may not necessarily bring articulated independence of the dominant model, it is important to remember that the women may make different use of this experience to their *covert* advantage, and manipulate the dominant models of *both* groups or societies.

Whether or not Gypsy men see gorgios and Gypsy women alike in certain contexts, as part of non-mankind, they do classify their women as ritually unclean. Whereas both Gypsy men and women are equal in their need to protect themselves from pollution from the outer body in their eating and washing habits, women are additionally and inherently impure by reason of their sex, and Gypsy men are vulnerable to such pollution. The opposite is not the case. The Gypsy male is superior and inherently pure, in opposition to his inherently impure and inferior female. However, the Gypsy female, when placed in opposition to the dirty gorgio, acquires some compensatory superiority. (Both Gypsy men and Gypsy women are belittled and may be regarded as polluting by the wider society; Okely 1973.) This sense of superiority is observable, but not consciously articulated, in two encounters between Gypsy women and gorgio men: one where the woman acts out a sodomite role; the other with an implicit fantasy of castration:

A gorgio man, visiting a Gypsy on business, stood with his back to the wife who sat on her trailer step, in the company of women and children. She grabbed a hand brush and kept pushing it towards the man's buttocks: 'Stick it up his arse . . . right up!' The women shrieked with laughter.

When out Calling in a van, we drove towards a workman to ask directions. Rose thought I was going to hit the pink conical road markers: 'Mind the tinkerbells!' Her mother retorted contemptuously: 'I thought you meant the tinkerbells between 'is legs. We wouldn't want to damage those!'

The various ritual restrictions demanded of the Gypsy woman will appear somewhat humiliating in the context of her own society. But when seen in terms of her relation with gorgios they may be voluntarily acceptable reminders of her own limited power: her decision whether or not to enter sexual relations with a gorgio determines the ethnic purity of her people. On the other hand, the Gypsy women have no alternative if they wish to remain as respected members of their ethnic group.[23]

We have seen that the Gypsy woman is subject to greater restrictions on her libido than are Gypsy men. Loss of male virginity and extramarital relations with gorgio women were not greatly disapproved of among Gypsy men, and might even be a matter for boasting. Women seemed to resign themselves to this. One wife ignored what her husband did outside the camp. Another said:

Men are born hunters. They'll always be looking out for a woman . . . . My husband's father is still good-looking. His wife's been beaten up. She looks old. He's had loads of women and he talks about them in front of her. Sometimes she talks about the women as well. She's got to put up with it.

Joking behaviour of a sexual nature was the accepted form between Gypsy men and any gorgio women visiting the camp. It was positively encouraged by their wives, perhaps as a defence measure. 'My husband would like to take you out in his motor. He'll take you to the pictures.' However, no such joking was permissible between a Gypsy woman and a gorgio male on the camp. Extramarital sex brought ostracism if not punishment for a Gypsy woman. Extramarital relations between two Gypsies within the society were more restricted than between a Gypsy male and a female gorgio, although when adultery happened between Gypsies, it usually preceded or accompanied a permanent realignment in marriage, often without great upheaval.

Given these restrictions on their sexual behaviour, how do the women evade them? First, when women talk among themselves, they are able to express their sexuality without inhibition in what they refer to as 'a sex talk':

> It's all right us having a laugh and joke together – just us women having a sex talk, but not when the men are there.
>
> You know X, she was standing above me on the step and she had no drawers on. I definitely had my photo took! [Here the woman's vagina is wittily compared to a camera.]
>
> A (to visiting gorgio girl): 'We'll ask you proper.'
> B 'Have you ever had intercourse? A penis, have you ever had it up you?'
> A 'Nuts! That's what we mean, nuts!'
> C (brandishes large horn-shaped, cut-glass vase): 'Have you ever had that? What do you think of that?' (Roars of laughter.)

I have omitted other examples for reasons of discretion.

Confronted with greater tolerance towards male infidelity, among themselves the women indulge in fantasies of revenge, even if rarely implemented:

> If my husband went with another woman, I wouldn't have him back, but I'd beat him. I'd beat that thing up till his legs were broke, till there was no life in him. [Notice that in contrast to the case of adulterous wives, no symbol of purification, e.g. burning with fire, appears in the fantasy.]

Perhaps more satisfactorily than in mere fantasies, the women also resolve the problem of restriction by manipulating their actual relations with the external society. Here we return to the gorgios' stereotype of Gypsy women, which cannot be explained solely as a transference of repression. It reflects also the paradoxical behaviour required of Gypsy women among gorgios. Gypsy women are aware of their ambiguous role whereby aggressive salesmanship can be mistaken for sexual aggression. So, I suggest, despite the effectiveness of ritual safeguards, they exploit the stereotype, not only for economic ends, but for another purpose, concealed from their men. By acting a provocative and erotic part, they are vicariously escaping the constraints of the sexual role in their own society, while ensuring that no union is consummated. Subtly, the Gypsy woman is flouting a role imposed by her fellow Gypsies. Aggressive and alluring behaviour is tolerated by the Gypsy male because the woman pretends that nothing is really going on inside her, beyond the desire to titillate for money. It is seen by the men as a performance which is done only for economic gain and is not regarded as a real expression of Gypsy women's sexuality.

Borrow, in *The Romany Rye* (1969: 65), is assured by Ursula that if, when in a pub with her menfolk, a handsome young officer were to wink and invite her outside, her men would be 'under no apprehension'. She would go out and merely 'make a fool' of the gorgio. Borrow is understandably sceptical but considers only the obvious possibilities, not the woman's hidden mental experience. Then as in modern times, the women reject consummation because of their belief that the gorgio is unclean. Their reputation is intact and they are pollution-free. But meanwhile they have enjoyed their power. Clébert (1967: 218), writing of French Gypsy women, describes how they have no taboo about exposing the breasts and wash at public fountains with 'no consciousness of the slightest lasciviousness'. However normal this may seem to Gypsy men, it seems unlikely that the women are unaware of the outsiders, for whom the breast is forbidden fruit. Even Clébert admits to admiring the sight. He also writes that gorgio observers have misinterpreted Spanish Gypsy women's dances: 'They are not erotic. At least they are not so intentionally.' Again I doubt whether the dancers are oblivious to their observers' response.

I give two cases from my fieldwork: on one occasion, when we were alone, a young wife described to me her acquaintance with the farmer for whom she and her family were fruit-picking. He asked her to 'come away' with him. 'He showed me all the week's wages. He said he'd give me that and more, and a nice house.' She made use of his home and telephone, but only when his wife was present. She recalled his remarks with obvious pleasure: 'He said, "I can't go to sleep at night, you know why? – you women are much more lively than our kind. Our women are dead".' She revealed only part of the story to her husband when the farmer became too demanding. On another occasion I went out one evening with three women whose husbands believed we were going for a quiet chat at the local. We drove some distance to a more exotic pub. We got talking to several men, one of whom secretly offered one woman whom I will call 'X' some 'hot' (stolen) copper. The women were friendly, flirtatious, but avoided any intimacy. As we drove back:

Y 'That man was trying to ask me out. He asked why we'd all come here. I said, "We're only here for the beer!"' (Laughter)
Z 'We can't tell them [husbands] about it.'
Y 'No, my husband mustn't know. If he knew we'd been talking to those men there'd be murders!'
X 'We'll say we just went down the road.'
Z 'Yes, you mustn't tell them, understand.'

Ursula admits to Borrow that she will steal and lie to obtain things from gorgios, but is extremely insulted when he suggests she might also play the *lubbeny* ('prostitute'). The very word *lubbeny* is unutterable by her. 'A person may be a liar and thief, and yet a very honest woman' (Borrow 1969: 63). I also found the words 'prostitute' or 'whore' virtually unspeakable; they were communicated to me in a whisper, in contrast to 'cunt' which was used frequently and indiscriminately even to young babies. The idea of prostitution crops up in strange ways. There is a repeated mythical tale of a grandmother:

> Grandmother used to drink like a man. She ran a brothel. Wicked woman. At the end she owned two houses . . . . When grandmother was in the pub one night, a man with a long beard came in. He goes up to her and says, 'Have you got a light, my pretty?' meaning to ask her if she was willing. My grandmother gets some paper, rolls it up, pushes it in the fire, and says, 'Here's a light, my pretty', and she puts the paper to his beard and it goes up in flames!

Here again is an example of a Gypsy woman expressing ritual superiority over a gorgio male. The beard, a common psychoanalytic symbol of genitals, is purified by a burning phallus. One young woman with whom I went Calling jokingly suggested we should manage a brothel. Neither the grandmother nor my friend were prostitutes themselves. Instead they favoured exploiting prostitutes, or rather *exploiting prostitution*, without tainting themselves. The possibility of selling sex for food is formally suppressed but thus pushes its way into stories and jokes.

Prostitution appears more blatantly by projection in the Gypsies' stereo-type of the gorgio woman, which is comparable to the stereotype held by gorgios of Gypsy women. Gypsies attribute to gorgio women the inverse of behaviour expected of Gypsy women. Gorgio women do not control their sexuality: they 'show their arse', wear no knickers, strip-wash in front of men, and put on provocative make-up and revealing dress. For Gypsy men gorgio women are fair game, if not actual prostitutes. During the early part of my fieldwork three men joked with me. My naive response was repeated amidst uproarious laughter around the camp:

> *Male Gypsy* 'If I gave you two hot pennies out of the fire, what would you do then?'
> *Female gorgio* (the anthropologist) 'I'd drop them.'

The joke partly said that the gorgio woman, i.e. the anthropologist, would drop her knickers for the price of two pennies: a cheap prostitute indeed. (The pennies could also be seen as purifying sexual organs.) I doubt whether this joke would ever be played on a Gypsy woman.

The boundary erected by both Gypsy and gorgio between the two societies becomes a useful device for resolving powerful areas of conflict by compart-mentalisation. Different role potentialities in a single individual are split between two societies. Lévi-Strauss (1969: 38) expresses these potentialities in marital terms: 'This deep polygamous tendency, which exists among all men'; Freud would state the problem more explicitly as a sexual drive. Lévi-Strauss reserves such tendencies exclusively for men. It is more credible that just as men may be dissatisfied by the ideal woman and ideal role they have created for themselves, so may women be troubled by alternative images and tendencies within themselves. Both men and women protect themselves by giving these tendencies, oversimplified, to an alien people. Thus (as in figure 4.2) virginity, monogamy and sexual abstinence, the ideals, are placed on ego's side of the ethnic boundary, while prostitution, promiscuity and passive availability are placed on the other. A woman who does not conform to any of the first set will be automatically classified under the other pejorative set. Although possibly originally articulated by men, these divisions are usually accepted by women. Within the larger gorgio society, an ethnic boundary may not always be used.

There appears to be no ready Gypsy category in which to place Gypsy women resorting to prostitution and remaining in their own society. Also, empirically, prostitution is extremely rare. I encountered only one example. Deserted by her husband, the young mother wished to keep her children with

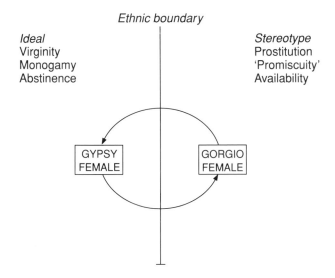

Figure 4.2 Sexual projection and ethnic boundary.

her. Until her eventual re-marriage she temporarily offered sexual favours for money. Her sense of duty made her behaviour excusable to the Gypsies. But she was likened to a gorgio. She was told: 'You shouldn't do that. You're like the land girls.' For Gypsy women the separation between the ideal and the fallen woman is reinforced by pollution beliefs, on a par with the separation they must make between sex and food. The few gorgio women drifting into Gypsy society as real or honorary prostitutes and conforming to the stereotype, were treated as polluting. Their apparent ability to pollute other *women* was derived from their uncontrolled sexuality, not simply from their eating and washing habits.

> She was eating a meat pie and picking some of it out; 'I don't like that jelly', she said. I told her: 'I reckon you like the jelly . . . you're dirty. I wouldn't have you drink tea with me, not let you touch my cups.'

Even the few gorgio women who enter the society with the respectable status of wife are at first held in contempt and ostracised, until they have demonstrated meticulously their desire to conform to a Gypsy identity.

As a counterpart to their sense of ritual superiority towards gorgio men, which I have already indicated, Gypsy women assumed an aggressive and dominating attitude towards gorgio women. Gorgio women, thought to show uncontrolled and polluting sexuality, were described in the following ways: 'Just a big hole with lots of hairs in it'; 'red' or 'cranky cunt'. The Gypsy women's response to this image was frequently: 'I'll put my boot up her cunt.' Gorgio women, ever open and available, were thought to want the crudest of sexual satisfaction, if not rape.

When prostitution is resorted to deliberately as a way of life, by either the Gypsy or the gorgio, then the ethnic stereotypes assume new significance. The few 'regular' prostitutes of Gypsy origin had moved into gorgio society and become house-dwellers. They concealed their origins and dressed and behaved not as Gypsies, but as they pictured gorgio prostitutes to be. For them, being a prostitute may initially be the enactment of a fantasy. As the traditional control of their sexuality breaks down, they act out the opposite stereotype. In order to consummate an illicit relationship, they cross the ethnic line. An eighteen-year-old girl who had left her family and moved into lodgings visited her cousin on an encampment (while, it was said in the camp, recovering from an abortion). She wore hot-pants, a tight sweater and lots of make-up:

> I might move to London, you could earn £15 a day at striptease, or you could stay in a flat and have a photographer visit you and take pictures. No one else would see you. If I got money, I'd buy a motor bike and all leather gear.

Her attempts at prostitution were still fairly amateur.

Like Gypsy women acting in real or make-believe fashion in gorgio society, some gorgio women also appear to use man-made stereotypes to meet their needs. Escaping certain roles within their own society, they go off with the 'raggle-taggle' Gypsies. I am referring specifically to women in transit, not those who assume the role of permanent wife with all its restrictions. I encountered two such drifters who, in breaking all the rules of dress and behaviour, invited anger and scorn from the Gypsy women. It is only retrospectively that I understand their deliberate tactlessness and apparent irrationality. They were fully aware of the correct code for Gypsy women and occasionally conformed to it. Generally they were not aiming for honourable acceptance but were instead enacting their own fantasies. They seemed to like the idea of the Gypsy male as exotic seducer and images of themselves as peculiarly seductive, either as outsiders or as stereotyped Gypsy women. Although in their case not fictitious, their form of prostitution was freer and more amenable to fantasy than in gorgio society, where prostitution is more routinised and supervised by men.[24]

This use of the Gypsies to soften and romanticise the prostitute's harsh role and image reappears within gorgio society. For example, there is the curious phenomenon of the gorgio stripteaser without any Gypsy connections, who assumed the name of 'Gypsy Rose Lee', later celebrated in the film and musical, *Gypsy*. The stripteaser expressed most blatantly the gorgio stereotype of the Gypsy woman who is sexually arousing but untouchable. This masquerade takes another more satisfactory form: Clébert (1967: 208), in affirming the absence of prostitution by or among Gypsies, notes the existence of gorgio prostitutes in Pigalle dressed up as Gypsies. Here the unobtainable is made obtainable through living fantasy.

The ideal, stereotyped and illicit relations between female and male Gypsies and gorgios are represented in figure 4.3. Each of the two social

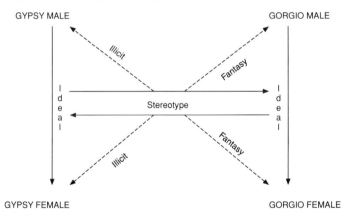

Figure 4.3 Stereotype, ideal and fantasy across gendered ethnicity.

Key

The vertical line from male to female represents the public Ideal woman within the group.

The horizontal double lines of exchange represent the public stereotype of the women, if not the men, of the opposing group. This is the inverse of the Ideal.

The diagonal broken lines represent the illicit fantasies exchanged between individual women and men of opposing groups.

The Ideal man for either group is 'missing' because, from the male point of view, at least, and unlike the Ideal woman, it is not the inverse of the stereotype of the men in the opposing group.

groups idealises and marries its own kind. The women, if not the men, of the opposing group are attributed stereotyped qualities which are the inverse of the ideal. Since both sexual and marital relations between the two groups are disapproved of, if not prohibited, no real exchange of sexual or marital partners should take place. On a statistical level such exchange is indeed rare. There is, however, an illicit, unorganised exchange of fantasies between the male and female of opposing groups. These fantasies are the unconscious link between the ideal and the taboo. Men have fantasies about the 'other' women and women have fantasies about the 'other' men. Both have fantasies about themselves in this rapport.[25] At the level of fantasy, Gypsy women, confronted with greater sexual control than men, equalise their situation. Nothing is actually given, but the possibility is admitted. Perhaps the Gypsies may be more aware of the stereotypes which gorgios attach to them than is the case in reverse, and exploit these.

To conclude: I have argued that the ideal of Gypsy women held by Gypsies, and the pollution taboos associated with women, are interdependent with the relationship between Gypsies and gorgios, and also with the stereotype which gorgios have of Gypsy women. Further, while conforming to the ideal, and conscious of the gorgio stereotype, Gypsy women seek expression, on less recognised levels,[26] for their conflicts with men of both groups.

NOTES

1 Gorgio is the Romany word for 'stranger' or 'outsider', and has similar pejorative associations to those that the title 'Gypsy' has for some house-dwellers. Although many English Gypsies may refer to themselves as 'Travellers', especially to outsiders, I have chosen to use the title 'Gypsy'. The definition of a Gypsy or Traveller, where descent is a necessary condition, I have discussed elsewhere (Okely 1975a). The chapter 'Gypsy identity' was published as part of a research project organised by Barbara Adams at the Centre for Environmental Studies, and sponsored by the Rowntree Memorial Trust, to all of whom I am indebted. An earlier version of the present chapter on Gypsy women was first read at the Women's Anthropology Group, Oxford, and I am grateful to Shirley Ardener for her encouragement. My own material was based on fieldwork between late 1970 and early 1972 among Gypsies with whom I lived mainly in Southern England, and more especially near the larger industrial centres.This fieldwork was later supplemented throughout the 1970s after the completion of this article, for a time with an SSRC postgraduate award.

2 For the placing of other women in the wild, see Edwin Ardener (1972). In this case house-dwellers may associate Gypsy women, more than gorgio women, with the wild.

3 This sexual discrimination is comparable to that embedded in the racist's frequent fear that a black man might marry a white man's daughter. There is less preoccupation with the fear of a black woman marrying a white man, because the latter is considered less vulnerable to seduction without reasoned choice.

4 All unacknowledged quotations are from my field notes; they are reconstructions

of conversations which were written up as soon as practicable after the event. Direct recording would have been inhibiting and in most circumstances extremely provocative to this non-literate people who have learnt to associate note-taking with police harassment.

5 Before motorisation, women were permitted to go out Calling with a pony and open trap, which were presumably more inhibiting to sexual activities than is the privacy of a motor vehicle.

6 It will be obvious to the reader that in my discussion on pollution, boundaries and the symbolism of the body, I have been greatly influenced by the work of Mary Douglas, and more specifically her *Purity and Danger* (1966). So implicit are her ideas that I can no longer give page references.

7 This schizoid situation can be compared with that portrayed by Laing in *The Divided Self* (1965), where the public role and the personality projected for outsiders are separated from the private, inner self. Increasing separation may endanger the inner self and its sense of reality. (I am grateful to Martin Thom for drawing my attention to this and for our discussions on aspects of this chapter.) In contrast to the isolated individual, the Gypsy can display and nourish his or her 'inner self' with all members of his ethnic group, who are all in a similar predicament.

8 Anne Sutherland's study of Gypsies in California (1975) places greater emphasis on the upper and lower part of the body. I am grateful to her for the stimulus of her working papers which raised questions I then had to answer in my own fieldwork.

9 I note here Edwin Ardener's (1972) use of 'nature' and his amplification of Lévi-Strauss.

10 The Gypsies have an ideology of 'pure blood' although in fact those with one gorgio and one Gypsy parent can be assimilated.

11 Thomas Acton (1971) claims that the emphasis on the uncleanliness of women has virtually disappeared. However, his own material sometimes contradicts this. Moreover, he does not discuss the pollution associated with childbirth.

12 The restriction on public exposure of the breasts is in marked contrast to the Gypsies in California studied by A. Sutherland (1975) and Gypsies in France (Clébert 1967: 218). However, Sutherland recorded that a woman could pollute a man by lifting her skirt and exposing the lower part of her body (cf. S. Ardener 1973).

13 These pinafores, sometimes specially commissioned from local dressmakers, have no sleeves and cover the upper and lower body, front and back.

14 Personal communication, B. Adams, 1972.

15 Victor Turner (1970: ch. 4) in discussing the liminal period in *rites de passage* emphasises its temporal and ceremonial aspects. Although both Turner (1970: 98) and Douglas (1966: 96) mention the possibility of a liminal person being removed elsewhere, neither fully explores the idea of a liminal place. For the Gypsies, the choice of location, unaccompanied by elaborate ritual and public ceremony, may, in some instances, demonstrate a marginal state.

16 One man jokingly made me repeat some words which sounded like *Rattvalo Kauri*. These he refused to translate. The other witnesses appeared tense. I discovered later, via Smart and Crofton (1875: 128, 92), that the words meant 'bloody penis'. Presumably this had a special horror because it implied tabooed sexual intercourse during menstruation. It had been engineered so that the words were uttered appropriately by a gorgio woman.

17 Presumably semen is clean because of its fertilising qualities. It is not waste by definition, although it may be wasted.

18 Despite the Gypsies' ideology of purity of blood, they sometimes adopt gorgio

babies and, provided these are socialised as Gypsies, their genetic origins become irrelevant. See Okely (1975b).

19 It appears (although further fieldwork is necessary to clarify this) that women past the menopause are still capable of polluting men.

20 This distinction was clarified for me after noticing a similar theme in Julie Du Boulay's (1974) work on Greek women, first read at the Women's Anthropology Group, Oxford.

21 I have restored the full reference and quotation from de Beauvoir because its theoretical implication is central to my argument (see chapter 9, this volume).

22 See also Borrow (1969: 76), recording customs in the nineteenth century: 'A man by Gypsy law, brother, is allowed to kick and beat his wife, and to bury her alive if he thinks proper.'

23 I have restored some of my original text which, before editing, drew attention to the constraining consequences of pollution requirements on Gypsy women. To be outcast from the group is the greatest sanction and one which far outweighs any sense of power. A much abbreviated version appeared in Okely 1983.

24 The ex-prostitute 'J' in Millett (1972: 120) recalls: 'It's very hard to find a prostitute who hasn't got a pimp.' Nevertheless, prostitutes may have the ideal of independence: 'If you have a lot of men . . . then you're not dependent on any one of them' (ibid. 86). See also de Beauvoir on prostitutes (1949 II).

25 This relationship between two ethnic groups can be compared to the asymmetrical relationship between black and white races. In cases where sexual and even marital relations occur, each partner may continue to live out his or her fantasies in the concrete situation. See Bastide, 'Dusky Venus, black Apollo' (1972), for an examination of the continuing inner conflicts in mixed marriages.

26 Men, also at an unarticulated level, may have another view of their situation.

REFERENCES

Acton, T. A. (1971) 'The functions of the avoidance of Mochadi Kovels', *Journal of the Gypsy Lore Society*, third series, I (3–4): 108–36.

Ardener, E. W. (1972) 'Belief and the problem of women', in J. S. La Fontaine (ed.) *The Interpretation of Ritual*, London: Tavistock.

Ardener, S. (1973) 'Sexual insult and female militancy', *Man* 8: 422–40; and in S. Ardener (ed.) (1975) *Perceiving Women*, London: Malaby Press.

Bastide, R. (1972) 'Dusky Venus, black Apollo', in P. Baxter and B. Sansom (eds) *Race and Social Difference*, Harmondsworth: Penguin.

Beauvoir, S. de (1949) *Le Deuxième sexe*, Paris: Gallimard.

Borrow, G. (1874) *Romano-Lavo-Lil*, London: J. Murray.

—— (1969) *The Romany Rye*, Everyman edn, London: Dent.

Clébert, J. P. (1967) *The Gypsies*, trans. C. Duff, Harmondsworth: Penguin.

Douglas, M. (1966) *Purity and Danger*, London: Routledge and Kegan Paul.

—— (1973) *Natural Symbols*, Harmondsworth: Penguin.

Du Boulay, J. (1974) *Portrait of a Greek Mountain Village*, Oxford: Oxford University Press.

Ellis, W. (1956) 'The nuisance and prejudice of the Gypsy vagrant to the farmer', cited in V. Bell *To Meet Mr Ellis*, London: Faber and Faber.

Goffman, E. (1968) *Stigma*, Harmondsworth: Penguin.

Hindes Groome, F. (1930) *Kriesgspiel*, cited in J. Sampson (ed.) *The Wind on the Heath*, London: Chatto and Windus.

La Fontaine, J. S. (1972) 'Ritualization of women's life-crises in Bugisu', in J. S. La Fontaine (ed.) *The Interpretation of Ritual*, London: Tavistock.

Laing, R. D. (1965) *The Divided Self*, Harmondsworth: Penguin.

Lawrence, D. H. (1970) *The Virgin and the Gypsy*, Harmondsworth: Penguin.

Lévi-Strauss, C. (1969) *The Elementary Structures of Kinship*, trans. J. H. Bell, J. R. von Sturmer and R. Needham, London: Eyre and Spottiswoode.

London Women's Anthropology Workshop (1973) Collected papers, unpublished.

Mérimée, P. (1930) *Carmen*, excerpt from ch. III cited in J. Sampson (ed.) *The Wind on the Heath*, London: Chatto and Windus.

Millett, K. (1972) 'Prostitution: a quartet for female voices', in V. Gornick and B. K. Moran (eds) *Woman in Sexist Society*, New York: Signet.

Okely, J. M. (1963) 'The spectre of feminism', *The Messenger* (4): 45.

—— (1973) 'No fixed abode'. Talk given on BBC Radio Three, 9 September.

—— (1975a) 'Gypsy identity', in B. Adams, J. Okely *et al. Gypsies and Government Policy in England*, London: Heinemann.

—— (1975b) 'The family, marriage and kinship groups', in B. Adams, J. Okely *et al. Gypsies and Government Policy in England*, London: Heinemann.

—— (1975c) 'Work and travel', in B. Adams, J. Okely *et al. Gypsies and Government Policy in England*, London: Heinemann.

—— (1983) *The Traveller-Gypsies*, Cambridge: Cambridge University Press.

Sampson, J. (1930) *The Wind on the Heath: A Gypsy Anthology*, London: Chatto and Windus.

Sandford, J. (1973) *Gypsies*, London: Secker and Warburg.

Smart, B. C. and Crofton, H. T. (1875) *The Dialect of the English Gypsies*, London: Asher and Co.

Sutherland, A. (1975) *Gypsies: The Hidden Americans*, London: Tavistock.

Symons, A. (1930) 'To a gitana dancing', in J. Sampson (ed.) *The Wind on the Heath*, London: Chatto and Windus.

Thompson, T. W. (1922) 'The uncleanness of women among English Gypsies', *Journal of the Gypsy Lore Society*, third series 1: 16–43.

—— (1927) 'Gypsy marriage in England', *Journal of the Gypsy Lore Society*, third series 6: 101–29.

—— (1929) 'Additional notes on English Gypsy women taboos', *Journal of the Gypsy Lore Society*, third series 8: 33–9.

The Times 27 February 1974.

Turner, V. W. (1970) *The Forest of Symbols*, Ithaca and London: Cornell University Press.

Wood, M. F. (1973) *In the Life of a Romany Gypsy*, London and Boston: Routledge and Kegan Paul.

Chapter 5

Fortune-tellers

Fakes or therapists

The rationality debate has focused on the alleged non-rationality of the non-Western other or former primitive.[1] Instead, I wish to draw attention to the non-rational beliefs among citizens of the dominant Western context. In this case the mysterious other, the non-literate Gypsy, caters to the needs, desires and troubles of the literate, supposedly rational majority. What is even more unexpected is the fact that whereas the literate, often relatively educated client has faith in the Gypsies' powers to predict the future, the Gypsy specialist does not. It is a puzzle as to why clients entertain such a belief and a puzzle as to how the Gypsies continue successfully to practise this 'art' which they don't believe in. The Gypsies or Travellers are the ones who are faced with the kind of questions which Evans-Pritchard (1937), confronted with Azande practices, had to answer and make intelligible to an incredulous Western readership. For fortune-telling to work among non-Gypsy clients, the latter must believe that Gypsies believe in their own supernatural powers. This chapter aims to unravel these puzzles not only for Western readers but also for non-Westerners who have been led to think that exotica and magical beliefs have been eradicated from Western suburbia and the metropolis.

EXOTIC TRADITIONS AND INVENTIONS

The economic and structural position of Gypsies makes them especially suitable to be seen as marginals and holders of exotic knowledge with supernatural powers, i.e. with access to the unpredictable and as predictors of the future. The historical context shows both the exotic legitimation used by Gypsies and their long-term practice of fortune-telling. The word Gypsy derives from 'Egyptian', an exotic nomenclature. Whether or not the so-called 'Egyptians' first officially recorded in the British Isles in the early sixteenth century came from abroad is a matter of controversy. 'Egyptian' was a loosely used label for anyone from abroad. Elsewhere (Okely 1983), I have suggested that the majority of Gypsies even in the earliest period were largely persons of indigenous origins, thrown into a nomadic way of life during the collapse of feudalism. It suited them to adopt an exotic nomenclature, especially for occupations like fortune-telling. Credibility was more likely to be given to persons from afar. Later commentators, and sometimes it seems the Gypsies themselves, explained their special powers as deriving from Egypt, a land of ancient wisdom.

The earliest records of 'Egyptians' in Scotland describe them as 'pilgrims' (1505), and then as dancers entertaining the King (1530). The first record of an 'Egyptian' in England is indeed of a woman fortune-teller in 1514 in a Dialogue of Sir Thomas More. She 'had been lodging in Lambeth but had gone overseas a month before, and . . . could tell marvellous things by looking into one's hand' (see Vesey-Fitzgerald 1973: 28). I suspect that she did not go abroad, but travelled within the country. It added piquancy to her powers to be 'here today and gone tomorrow'.

The aristocracy were at the same period dressing up in their own images or fantasies of Gypsy women. A chronicler, Edward Hale, refers to ladies at a court mummery and at a state banquet dressing in elaborate, exotic costumes 'like the Egyptians' (Vesey-Fitzgerald 1973: 28). It is plausible that the travelling Gypsies in turn dressed up to entertain the aristocracy whose fortunes they told. In 1530, the first of many repressive acts of parliament against Gypsies refers to their occupation as fortune-tellers and to official scepticism. They were described as 'outlandyeshe People callynge themselfes Egyptians' who had

> gone from Shire to Shire and Place to Place . . . and used great subtyll and crafty means to deceyve the People, berying them in Hande that they by Palmestre could tell Menne and Womens Fortunes and so many tymes by crafte and subtyltie had deceyved the People of theyr Money.
>
> (Vesey-Fitzgerald 1973: 29–30)

It is debatable as to whether the Gypsies' alleged foreign origin encouraged them to exploit exotic occupations, or whether the opportunities in fortune-telling encouraged indigenous nomads to feign a foreign origin.

GORGIO PERCEPTION

Whatever their origins, Gypsies are believed by others to exist on the margins of the dominant society. While attempts have been made to control, disperse or destroy them, an alternative response has been the inclination to exoticise Gypsies. Inarticulate powers are vested in those who are a source of disorder (Douglas 1966). Members of the dominant sedentary society of non-Gypsies, or gorgios, project onto the Gypsy group a range of attributes which are often the inverse of their own ideal. Since Gypsies are believed to exist beyond the bounds of 'normal' society, credence has been given to their healing powers and to esoteric knowledge, including the ability to tell fortunes.

Since Gypsies are associated in a dominant sedentarist ideology with 'anti-structure' (Turner 1969) and threatening forces, it seems that they are believed to understand their non-rational workings and offer predictions about them. These Gypsy–gorgio consultations often occur in places and times of anti-structure – fairs and holiday, seaside towns – in addition to the more mundane but liminal space of the house-dweller's doorstep. Gorgio clients have also visited Gypsy sites, made peripheral in the sedentarist landscape, in search of fortune-tellers.

There is a wealth of representations in the literature and the media of the

Figure 5.1 Romany Belles by Dame Laura Knight, *c.* 1938. Gypsy fortune-tellers at the races.
Source: City of Aberdeen Art Gallery and Museums Collection.

exotic supernatural quality of Gypsies. Non-Gypsies who themselves write about fortune-telling make use of misleading beliefs about Gypsies to add credibility to their own manuals, for example: 'Handwriting analysis has been a favourite of the Gypsies for centuries. The Romany folk were no doubt the first people to popularise this character-reading technique' (Martin 1972: 189). This claim is largely false since Gypsies have a non-literate tradition. The same author claims that Gypsies 'sincerely believe' in palmistry (ibid. 1972: 49). There is in turn a circular flow of information and invention; a few literate Gypsies consult these non-Gypsy manuals for new ideas. Gorgios thus help to construct the Gypsies for them.

FEMININE GENDER, CONTAINMENT AND ABSORPTION

The stereotype of Gypsy women, immortalised in Carmen (cf. chapter 4), has added lustre to their role as fortune-tellers. Carmen combines both un-controlled desires and strange powers. She deals the cards and can foretell both others' and her own fate. In fact, Carmen is a distortion or projection of a gorgio imagination – mixed up with grains of ethnographic truth. Mérimée, the French literary creator of the story of Carmen in 1845, had minimal first-hand contact with Gypsies but drew on others' material, including Grellman (1787) and Borrow (1841). Although the latter consistently rejected any suggestion that Gypsy women were sexually uncontrolled, Mérimée insisted on the creation of the sexually impulsive Carmen. Bizet, who had never visited Spain, then further embellished the fantasy in his celebrated opera. Today, the exotic stereotype of Carmen – a French gorgio creation of a Spanish other – mingles in expectations about Gypsy fortune-tellers in Britain. The archetype can be compared to Flaubert's model of the Oriental woman (Said 1985: 6).

Both in the past and today, Gypsy fortune-tellers have tended to be women. They are seen as less menacing than men when calling at doorsteps (see chapter 4). Confidence is important for establishing an immediate intimate and face-to-face relationship. Women are also more often associated with a caring role. In contrast to doorstep fortune-tellers, gorgio astrologers and fictive Gypsies giving predictions in the mass media are frequently male. They do not work by face-to-face relationships with their readers and believers, so that a caring intimacy is not a requirement. Instead, astrologers rely more on a scientistic stamp of mathematical authenticity.

In some instances, non-Gypsy male astrologers exploit ambiguous 'camp' stereotypes or the image of the Indian Guru. But on the whole, male astrologers exploit the rational, scientific image, so much so that in the 1980s a male astrologer in Britain received a weekly government grant to set himself up in a 'small business' (the Guardian, 27 October 1983). It is unlikely that such grants would be given to Gypsy women fortune-tellers, with an exotic presentation. Fortune-telling has no scientistic 'masculine' pretensions; it is closer, I shall argue, to the more grounded practices in psychoanalysis.

The Gypsy woman's association with the margins provides invaluable anonymity. Stories, desires and anxieties can be revealed by clients without obvious repercussions. The information is safe with her. Moreover, the Gypsy is uniquely suited to syphon off the bad into the margins. A concept from the practice of psychoanalysis, namely that of 'containment', is relevant. For the analysand, there is a problem in getting rid of bad feelings because they have to be contained somewhere, otherwise it is feared that they might hit back. Priests, shamans, scapegoats, prostitutes, hitch-hikers and therapists have all been used as containers for the sufferings and bad feelings projected by individuals and groups. The Gypsy fortune-teller can likewise be seen as an effective container or transporter of bad luck. Unlike the therapist who is seen to process the bad through theorising and interpretation, and unlike the priest who may recycle evil through prayer, the Gypsy simply takes the bad away with her. Since the Gypsy woman is believed to belong to the bizarre, the disorderly or even the unclean, those aspects of a client's life history can be rejected and distanced from the client and placed in the Gypsy who is seen as a psychic refuse collector. She pipes out pessimism and anxiety. She is treated as a waste pipe to another world. There are parallels with the role of the funeral priest at Benares who has to absorb pollution (Parry 1980).

STRUCTURAL AND IDEOLOGICAL RELATIONS

Given this exotic or erotic space which Gypsies, especially women, hold in the dominant imagination, I shall examine more generally the Gypsies' economic and ideological position in relation to non-Gypsies. Differences can be exploited. These include (1) the Gypsies' detachment from non-Gypsies' daily working and financial concerns, (2) the Gypsies' privileged asymmetrical knowledge of the gorgio other, and (3) the Gypsies' contempt for gorgios, expressed through pollution beliefs.

(1) As nomads or Travellers, Gypsies are geographically mobile, unhoused and of no fixed abode. They have persistently rejected wage-labour. Although some move into housing and occasionally resort to wage-labour, the ideal and practice for many Gypsies in Britain and often elsewhere is travel and self-employment. Now with trailer-caravans, Gypsies or Travellers have different priorities from house-dwelling persons in the sedentary economy who must rent or buy housing. Non-Gypsy house-dwellers depend on wage-labour employment and are rendered especially vulnerable when faced with eviction, redundancy, rises in rents, taxes or mortgages. The Gypsies have their own problems of eviction, constant harassment, prosecutions and unpredictable earnings, but their economic and social priorities and strategies are different. They do not dream of promotion, a decline in mortgage interest rates or winning the pools as an escape from the pressure. It would seem therefore at

first sight that Gypsies are unsuited to give solid guidance through fortune-telling on matters of contrasting priority to house-dwellers. But this difference can be advantageous; they are not distracted by identification, they are creatively detached.

(2) Despite the gorgio representation of Gypsies as on the margins, the Gypsies' economy is enmeshed with the dominant economy. The Gypsies earn their living from gorgios by providing a variety of goods and services – including fortune-telling. Their range of occupations entails regular contact with gorgios (Okely 1983). Successful trading rests on close acquaintance with gorgio needs, interests and differentiation by class, gender, region, ethnicity, age and personality. Gypsies or Travellers must learn to read off the characteristics of the individual gorgio in each context (see chapter 3). Gorgio weaknesses can be and must be known. Such detailed knowledge of the 'enemy' is not reciprocated. Skills at observation and quick responses to specific contexts provide an essential foundation for fortune-telling.

(3) Gorgios are equally the victim of Gypsies' stereotypes. The Gypsies' view of gorgios is hardly one of admiration, although they are dependent on them. There is contempt, in addition to mistrust. The gorgio is stupid, cannot earn a living by his or her wits and is attributed the inverse of Gypsy ideals, sometimes rather similar to those accredited to Gypsies – the gorgio murders, sexually molests young children, rapes and persecutes. The gorgio women are also considered to be sexually uncontrolled (see chapter 4). The Gypsies maintain their distance by means of pollution beliefs. The gorgio is seen as dirty and polluted with filthy eating and washing habits (Okely 1983).

The practice of fortune-telling is consistent with these aspects of the Gypsies' position. A nomadic people, 'here today and gone tomorrow', may be attributed strange powers precisely because they seem to live untrammelled by the conventions of house-dwellers. Daily contact and detailed working knowledge of gorgios by Gypsies give scope for sound character reading. The gorgio is known, but held in contempt. Pollution observances and sexual controls ensure that the necessary distance is maintained. Reciprocal intimacy is never accomplished and the fortune-teller retains her mystique.

CONTRADICTION

There is a contradiction with regard to the Gypsies' suitability for the art of fortune-telling. Both from my own fieldwork and from the reliable literature on Gypsies here and elsewhere, it seems that Gypsies consider the ability to predict the future to be a confidence trick; in this respect fortune-telling is a fake. It is just another lucrative way of earning a living off gorgios. The Gypsies sell 'lucky gold charms' along with their fortune-telling, but like their predictions, they know and consider them to be fakes. One Gypsy explained succinctly: 'We sell lucky charms because *you* believe in them.'

Sometimes it seems they are almost pushing their own luck at deception and parody. A Gypsy fortune-teller whom I encountered in the North-east of England was selling to gorgios small plastic 'white elephants'. She was literally and symbolically selling something which she considered to be useless. I observed this when I was no longer living with Gypsies. When I lived as a resident over a period of two years on several Gypsy camps, no one offered to tell my fortune and the Gypsies did not tell each other's. Hence my limited material on fortune-telling from my encampment field notes.

Here is one example of a Gypsy, unusually a man, describing his work:

> There was this woman on holiday at the seaside. She'd had a nervous breakdown. She'd been told to leave her house. I told her she should stop worrying, that when she got back she'd be offered a better house than the one she'd got now. Well, she could enjoy her holiday then couldn't she? It was no good her worrying. She paid me for it.

In several instances where Gypsies found their predictions to come true they became alarmed. One woman, whose case I discuss in detail below, told me of such an experience, so she gave up fortune-telling for good. She did not appear to realise that her prediction had been self-fulfilling.

The Gypsies or Travellers do entertain some specific notions of good or bad luck, for example it is bad luck or even polluting to utter the word 'rat' inside a caravan or trailer (Okely 1983: ch. 6). A few beliefs had an element of prediction. It was said that the sight of a type of person, perhaps an old woman or cripple, on the road at the start of a day's work may be interpreted as a sign that the day will be unproductive. The day's outing might then be cancelled. However, these warnings for the Gypsies are only applicable to immediate and short-term problems. They offer little scope for long-term prediction. Some older Gypsy women may be considered to be witches (*chovihanni*) but they are not credited with powers of fortune-telling. A younger Traveller woman told me of one such 'witch' who had asked her for a valuable china plate hanging on her wall. When she refused, the old Gypsy woman told her that it would fall off and break. This happened a week later and was seen as a warning not to reject the woman's demands.

Amateur opportunist Gypsy fortune-tellers should be differentiated from long-term specialists. Although considered fake, fortune-telling is seen by Gypsies as a real skill. Those who discussed the practice with me insisted that children should start learning it by observing adults at work. They are said to need a considerable apprenticeship. If a Gypsy does not learn from a sufficiently early age, it was said that she or he would never make a good fortune-teller. Unfortunately, I was unable to accompany Gypsies during such work, nor was I able to talk at length with many specialists. They remained wary of exposing their art. But a number of Gypsies were prepared to describe some of their experiences to me. From the other side, I have also accumulated a number of accounts by gorgios of their experiences as clients.

FLEXIBILITY VERSUS PLANNING AND SEDENTARY SECURITY

There are differences between the travelling Gypsies' view of the future and that of the sedentary society. There is a contrast, if not real conflict, in priorities between a nomadic group committed to self-employment and those of a sedentary society marked by a fixed abode, and, at least until the 1990s, the ideal of permanent wage-labour employment. The Gypsy–Travellers invariably move through and camp on territory owned and/or controlled by others. Not only is flexibility required in choice of occupation, but also in choice of camping site. Travellers seek a living and a stopping place wherever and whenever available. They are ever vulnerable to being moved on even when there is work around. They are more vulnerable to short-term changes – immediate eviction from land and unexpected losses or gains in earnings. To counteract this unpredictability, they must live by opportunism, must seize the chance. Instant reactions are required. Often they cannot plan on working and staying in one place even for a few days. Long-term planning is counter-productive. Travellers or Gypsies recognise that they have no control over the long term; only some manoeuvrability of the moment. So they have made a virtue of it.

I watched an older Gypsy woman rebuking a Gypsy man for saying that he'd be back at Christmas on a specific camp site even though the authorities planned to close it. She said, 'Bill don't cross your bridges. . . . Wait till it comes. . . . I never plan. . . . You must never plan, you don't know what'll happen' (cf. Okely 1983).

By contrast, the priorities of a sedentary, literate and bureaucratised society have been towards planning. The ideals are ever greater predictability and control. There may be pressures to make irrevocable decisions concerning employment, residence and investment but where, however detailed the information available, it is impossible to predict the alternative outcomes of decision x or y or z. Fool-proof prediction would be invaluable; hence the potential opportunities for Gypsies in fortune-telling. The paradox is that members of the sedentary society should seek guidance from persons who have neither interest nor experience in long-term planning.

In discussing the healing powers of a shaman who may (like the Gypsy) practise deliberate deception, yet bring change and cure in the client, Lévi-Strauss (1963: 180) suggests a relation between psychosomatic illness and degree of security:

> Disorders of the type currently termed psychosomatic which constitute a large part of the illnesses prevalent in societies with a low degree of security, probably often yield to psychotherapy.

According to this view, it would follow that Gypsies would suffer from a high level of psychosomatic illness since their way of life is marked by a low degree of 'security'. I found little evidence for this. Moreover, there is a hint of sedentarist ethnocentricity in Lévi-Strauss' assessment. A travelling, nomadic group will have different notions of security from those defined by a dominant sedentary society. Too often this is overlooked. For example, a non-Gypsy administrator of Gypsy local authority education asserted that Gypsy children suffered from 'turbulence' due to their travelling way of life. He was judging the children's experience out of its cultural context. Gypsies have developed strategies of flexibility and opportunistic skills in the face of long-term unpredictability. Contrary to Lévi-Strauss, it would seem more appropriate to consider the occurrence of psychosomatic illness and the need for psychotherapy in the society from which Gypsies draw their clients; where long-term planning and the notion of a 'secure future' are idealised and institutionalised, but in practise imperfectly achieved.

There will always be areas elusive to prediction and control for both individuals and groups. When it comes to decision-making, whether in public or personal matters, an individual can be bombarded with rational, factual information about two options, but still be unable to know how to make the perfect, 'correct' decision. There are unknowns both ways. Faced with this dilemma, the individual might as well flip a coin. A society governed by an ideology of certainty and security is ripe for a magical solution through fortune-telling.

CREDIBILITY AND AUTHENTICITY

The advent of science and technology and increasing secularisation have not ensured the disappearance of so-called superstitions and belief in fortune-telling. Despite the numerous revelations in the literature and in newspapers of the Gypsies' faking, and more important, despite the Gypsies' apparent inability to foretell the future, the practice of Gypsy fortune-telling has continued through the twentieth century and in Western 'scientific' societies. Gypsy fortune-telling is a lucrative industry in major cities in the USA and Canada (Cohn 1973; Gropper 1975; Sutherland 1975). Gypsy fortune-tellers regularly visit and find willing clients all over Britain; in both rural enclaves and the metropolis and large cities. Moreover, fortune-tellers may not always depend on a one-off encounter; I have examples of Gypsies with regular clients. One such client was an old lady suffering from a painful illness who welcomed an annual visit from a Gypsy fortune-teller. Not all the clients are so obviously vulnerable. Another, a chief architect in North-east England, depended on a weekly visit from a Gypsy fortune-teller in his smart new office suite in the city centre. He would make no major decisions before consulting her. It was only by chance that I heard of this potentially embarrassing secret normally kept within the man's immediate family. Public knowledge of the man's dependence on a Gypsy fortune-teller would have damaged his professional credibility.

Several academics have been shaken by a Gypsy's observations. A Fellow of Kings College, Cambridge, and philosopher visited a Gypsy fortune-teller's booth. Having not identified his profession to the Gypsy the academic was told: 'I see many books coming from you but you must take your time.' He was both astonished at her recognition of his ambitions and comforted by her advice, since he found the process of writing painfully slow! Some fifteen years after this encounter, her prediction of many books remains unfulfilled. Possibly her insights into his slow productivity proved over-reassuring.

The non-Gypsy literature on Gypsy fortune-telling reveals some consistency with my own later material. The popularist writer Vesey-Fitzgerald has, like others, recorded the Gypsies' acknowledgement of their duplicity, but his reaction to its continuity is as follows:

> It must be remembered that deceit and imposture alone could never have built up and supported a practice that has withstood the passage of centuries and the constant attacks of progress. There must also be truth.
>
> (Vesey-Fitzgerald 1973: 126)

He recognises the practice of character reading. He is familiar with the fourteen basic rules for fortune-telling given by the nineteenth-century Gypsiologist and first President of the Gypsy Lore Society, Charles Leland. For example:

> It is safe in most cases with middle-aged men to declare that they have had a lawsuit, or a great dispute as to property, which has given them a great deal of trouble. This *must* be impressively uttered. Emphasis and sinking the voice are of great assistance in fortune-telling. If the subject betray the least emotion, or admit it, promptly improve the occasion, express sympathy, and 'work it up'.
>
> (Leland 1891: 182)

Despite the deception, Vesey-Fitzgerald (1973: 134) considers that 'there yet remains a considerable residue that is absolutely honest and uncannily accurate, and which can be explained ... only by postulating the gift of "second sight"'. He suggests that it is 'a form of involuntary prophetic vision either direct or symbolical ... nowadays at any rate, it seems to be connected mainly with Celtic peoples ... especially of ... the wild and mountainous regions' (ibid. 135). He, like other non-Gypsies, attributes supernatural powers to those on the perceived geographical margins.

Vesey-Fitzgerald gives examples of accurate predictions, including that given by a Gypsy to him. This expert can only explain the puzzle in terms of the supernatural, *despite* the Gypsies' own confessions of deception. Thus even some of those closely acquainted with Gypsies seem to be committed to the fantasy of the Gypsy fortune-teller's magical powers. By contrast, Leland (1891: 181), in the final analysis, dismisses any supernatural explanation:

> I do *not* insist that there is anything 'miraculous' in Gypsy fortune-telling. It may be merely the result of great practical experience and of a developed intuition, it may be mind or 'thought-reading' – whatever that really is – or it may result from following certain regular rules.

Leland instead explains the Gypsies' abilities in fortune-telling in terms of heightened and well-trained powers of perception.

Like Leland, and in contrast to Vesey-Fitzgerald, my explanation for the Gypsies' continuing credibility and financial good fortune in their profession lies not in any genuflection towards the supernatural. Their power and effectiveness lie elsewhere. Non-Gypsies in the larger, dominant society bestow that power upon Gypsies because they associate them with the non-rational. The Gypsies then rationally exploit gorgio; the other's non-rationality.

THE DYNAMICS OF FORTUNE-TELLING

It is insufficient merely to be a member of the Gypsy group for the effective practice of fortune-telling. There are precise skills involved which include authoritative self-presentation, typological assessment of strangers, perceptive diagnosis and the instigation, perhaps unwittingly, of self-fulfilling prophecies. The Gypsies or Travellers I encountered saw the exotic identity as crucial for fortune-telling. They used the phrase 'to look Gypsified', thus explicitly stating that a specific image had to be adopted in that context: 'You have to put on a scarf and your gold jewellery. You used to say "cross my palm with silver", now it's "cross my palm with paper money"' (see chapter 3). Thus the Gypsies' work is sustained by the gorgio's expectations which Gypsies labour to fulfil.

Practical credibility to this shimmering but insubstantial image is lent by the preliminary revelation of some basic facts about the potential client. These facts may be inspired or obvious guesses. But whenever possible, the Gypsies will exploit or seek out prior information. Workmates who called around the houses previously on different business, e.g. tarmac laying or scrap collection, will make it their business to note any potential clients for fortune-telling. They may find out his or her marital status, number of offspring, occupation, current situation and past history. The subsequent revelation of these facts to the client will assist the fortune-teller's credibility. They are also useful stepping-stones to any additional clues as to personality, class, etc., from the client's general demeanour and home surroundings.

Some of the literature (Leland 1891: 173) and my own material suggest that the activity of reading the palm is of little practical worth compared to the reading of the face. Indeed it may be that the holding of the open palm is merely a diversion. While the client is engrossed in staring at his/her hand, the fortune-teller is able to concentrate on the face unbeknown to the client who will expose him/herself unselfconsciously. With or without firm facts, the fortune-teller may proceed by ambiguous questions. These can be disguised as pronouncements which appear to convey information, while in effect covering up misfired guesses and confirming speculation. The opportunist fortune-teller may complete the session with a number of quick pronouncements, often optimistic. Other more experienced fortune-tellers will use a specific technique for character reading and for predictions which fit with the individual's wishes, fears and possibilities. A century earlier, Leland had his own choice of terms to describe this part of the fortune-teller's procedure and insists that there is no clairvoyance:

> As she looks into their palms, and still more keenly into their eyes, while conversing volubly with perfect self-possession, ere long she observes that she has made a hit – has chanced upon some true passage or relation to the girl's life. This emboldens her. Unconsciously the Dream Spirit, or the Alter Ego, is awakened. It calls forth from the hidden stores of memory strange facts and associations, and with it arises the latent and often unconscious quickness of perception, and the Gypsy actually apprehends and utters things which are 'wonderful'.
>
> (Leland 1891: 173)

Clients have described to me, and I have also witnessed at first hand, how at key junctures the Gypsy fortune-teller stares into the middle distance and no longer appears to be focusing on the minutiae. It is then that some dramatic revelations, some predictions or prophetic utterances are made.

One day in Durham City, a Gypsy woman (who did not know my identity) caught sight of me looking aimless. I was indeed wrestling with a personal dilemma and the need to make an important decision. I responded to her beckoning, although fully versed in the knowledge of the Gypsies' own scepticism. My collusion could be explained both as personal interest and as in the cause of 'science'. Nevertheless, as participant, long acquainted with Gypsies, I found it impossible to behave as the passive client, let alone detached observer. I quickly informed the Gypsy woman of my problem, so by-passing any demands on her to prove any immediate revelatory powers through guess-work. Compelled yet further to get over the shoddy legitimating business of guesses and crude manipulation, I continued to feed her with facts. But she would have none of it and protested: 'You're interrupting me, let me speak on.' She was focusing her gaze away from me and delivered a torrent of utterances and predictions with the dramatic and flowing force of an orator. Interruptions would have broken her concentration. Despite all scepticism as a social scientist, I found the experience therapeutic and useful.[2]

PSYCHOANALYSIS

There are aspects in the fortune-teller's methods akin to the procedure of psychoanalysis, although the fortune-teller and psychotherapist or analyst have entirely different aims and interests. The content of their concerns are also very different in focus. The state of mind adopted in the process of fortune-telling is comparable to that recommended by Freud to the psycho-analyst. It was called a 'state of attention' where the analyst was to let things emerge without concentrating on anything specific. A later disciple, Bion, recommends that the analyst should be just floating or suspended, troubled by neither memory nor desire (1977). The Gypsy fortune-teller has different aims, but she apparently adopts a similar perspective of receptivity and unfocused or middle-distance concentration. Like a psychoanalyst, the fortune-teller must also be alert to what the client may be unconsciously conveying. She, like the analyst, may use her own unconscious to do so. The client may unwittingly convey hidden desires or anxieties. The fortune-teller must be attuned to a range of information within and beyond what the client believes he or she is revealing. And the most successful technique may be by precisely not focusing on what the client is most trying to put across. Thus my clumsy attempts to speed up the fortune-teller in Durham, detailed above, may have interfered with her state of attention. In some cases the Gypsy fortune-teller may brilliantly pick up on the client's secret ambitions (e.g. the case of the academic quoted above).

Additional dimensions to the fortune-teller's skills and methods would require further investigation. Meanwhile, some broad distinctions can be suggested. In his comparison Lévi-Strauss refers to the shaman's prerequisite role as that of orator while the psychoanalyst's is mainly that of listener (1963: 199).By contrast, the fortune-teller is both listener and orator. In terms of speaking time, the psychoanalyst may be mainly a listener, but he or she makes fundamental interventions and interpretations. The analysand is encouraged to work through things past, recognise and resolve unconscious or conscious conflicts. The analysand responds to the analyst's interventions and interpretations and thinks through them in order to recognise the symbolic meanings and repressions in his/her free associations and transference relationship.

The Gypsy fortune-teller's role, by contrast, is not explicitly to expose symbolic meanings to the client and any inappropriate repetitions from the client's childhood. It does happen that the Gypsy, through her apparently magical revelations of facts from the client's circumstances, can stimulate the client to confront and talk about matters habitually repressed. Distressing aspects of the client's past and present can be unburdened onto the Gypsy who is accredited the power to know and to handle them, although not to explain them. Confidential details offloaded by the client are not considered dangerous indiscretions, since the fortune-teller, with unfathomable powers, is believed to know the basics already and, as an elusive nomad, is often anonymous.

In the majority of cases, the Gypsy fortune-teller prophesies an optimistic outcome to the client's troubles. The future scenario is one of hope and certainty in accord with the client's spoken or unspoken wishes. It is here that the Gypsy's 'suspended attention' (Bion 1977) offers scope for intuiting the client's hidden, unconscious wishes. Advice is also given about difficult decisions, but masked as prophecy. This form of masked advice is therefore different from that which can be given by an ordinary friend or relative. For, without the magical overtones of prophecy, mere advice leaves the client with the responsibility of choice and decision. If, on the other hand, the choice lies with a fate already revealed, the client need only submit to its arbitrary outcome. The illusion is that the future scenario has been drawn from outside, from the Gypsy on the margins, whereas in fact it has been drawn from the client, via the Gypsy's sensitised assessment of what the client would most desire. The fortune-teller colludes with and sells wish fulfilment.

By contrast, the psychoanalyst tries to expose the inadequacies behind the analysand's wish fulfilments which are inauthentic resolutions to other less acceptable wishes. The psychoanalyst aims to reveal the unconscious wishes which can then be related to conscious reality. Compared to the psycho-analyst's interests, the Gypsy gives the client wish fulfilment in a wide range of matters, e.g. wealth, property, work, marriage, romance and travel. Of course, selling hope is a deception and the collusion with wish fulfilment could be a diversion from a repetitive problem. However, it can be argued that the offer of certainty and hope may so relieve the client of anxiety that he or she feels free to continue, to act with optimistic strength to control his/ her fate, while simultaneously not knowing that the action has come from within.

The fortune-teller does not always offer optimism. She adds to her mystique by saying sometimes that she will not reveal all, that she thinks it best not to reveal the bad. In other cases, especially when the fortune-teller is confronted by a sceptic or a rejection of her services, bad things are prophesied. Just like the prophecies of good things, the bad prophecies can be self-fulfilling or remembered after the event. The Gypsy's curse is a defensive weapon and, like her offers of good luck, are effective because non-Gypsies believe in them.

Earlier, I drew attention to several paradoxes; why is it that Gypsies with a different *modus vivendi*, with different priorities and attitudes towards future planning, as well as contempt for their gorgio clients, seem so effective in telling non-Gypsies' fortunes? I have suggested that it is precisely the Gypsies' detachment from and disinterest in gorgios' concerns which make them effective. They are unimpeded by 'desire or memory' (Bion 1977).

Although Gypsies or Travellers may have their own ambitions, these do not coincide with those of their clients. The Gypsies are in a permanent rather than temporary liminal state with regard to the dominant society. Gypsies have a vantage point for a detached and inspired gaze. Without personal and emotional involvement, they can advise non-Gypsies effectively. They do not identify with the client's problems, so they are not overwhelmed by them. A therapist or psychoanalyst has to cultivate a certain professional detachment, but would still claim to care. The Gypsy fortune-teller does not have to cultivate this detachment; pollution beliefs and practices already express and reinforce the separation between the ethnic minority and the wider society. The gorgio is the other to the Gypsy.

CASE STUDY

The following case study from my field notes shows both something of the techniques of fortune-telling and the self-fulfilling outcome which the Gypsy woman did not recognise as a result of her own intervention. 'Meg', a Gypsy woman, explained that when invited into a house to tell someone's fortune, 'You have to look around and try and guess . . . you tell all the facts that you know and then it's up to you . . . . Usually middle-aged housewives have problems.' Meg didn't really believe that she had any special powers: 'But once what I said came true and I've never done it since.' She was frightened by the correct outcome of her prediction:

> It happened the previous year. Her mates came to her and said there was a man who wanted his fortune told – 'He ain't half got a lot of money'. She didn't make it clear whether she was told the salient facts before the interview or not. But in any case when he came to her trailer some time later, she didn't make out she knew the facts – he told her most of them.
>
> *Meg*: 'I always send the others away, I couldn't do it, if I knew they were near the trailer.'
> *Question by the anthropologist*: 'Because you might laugh?'
> *Meg* (laughs): 'Yes.'
> (There may have been more reasons which my suggestive question forestalled.)
> *Meg*: 'I put him at his ease, offered him a cup of tea . . . I said, "You've got a lot of troubles". He said, "Yes, yes", and I said, "Don't worry, in the end everything's going to work out right", because it's always best to say that. He seemed very happy and said "go on". I said, "I can't tell you no more . . . not until you've crossed my palm with silver . . . now I'm not going to look . . . I'll turn away and put my hand out and you put what's in your pocket into my hand". But when I turned back, I didn't look at it, just held it, I was very interested to know how much it was . . . . Then you know you have to go on from there.'

He had already poured out his problem, without any overt guessing from Meg. Apparently his wife was 'going with' another man and wanted to get her husband put in an asylum so that she could obtain his share of the property. They appeared to be joint owners. Once the man had tried to commit suicide and had been in a mental home for a short while. The wife played on this and set fire to a room in the house and pretended that it was her husband so she could get him committed to the mental home. The man was in a desperate state.

> *Meg*: 'I said, "There's a woman in your life; another one" (while Meg was telling me this, she indicated that such statements are always safe bets). "She's either going to make you very happy or else she will destroy you". He said, "Yes, yes, you're right, there's a girl in the office".' [Meg:] 'And you haven't really noticed her much.'
>
> *Gorgio client*: 'Yes, you're right, she's been friendly but I haven't been out with her because even tho' my wife's been unfaithful, I don't want to be unfaithful to her.'

Meg described to me how she need only make a few odd comments and the man would supply a mass of helpful information. Later, I wondered whether this was not also my position with Meg. She was supplying me with extensive information after minimum prompts.

> *Meg*: 'He kept saying, "Let's see if it's the same one, what's she look like?" . . . . You have to guess with this but try and imagine what kind of woman it might be . . . I said, "She's between 25 and 30". He said, "Yes, it is the same one"' [i.e. the man was not considering testing the fortune-teller, he was prepared to believe anything about a woman].
>
> *Question*: 'What if you'd guessed wrong?'
>
> *Meg:* 'Well you can make out it's another woman he hasn't met yet . . . . The man wanted to know more about her . . . I said, "She dresses well, she likes nice things" and the man said, "Yes, come to think of it, she does" . . . . . He was all over me. I said, "You're going to go out with her and go to her room and you are not going to do anything that would make you feel you've done wrong. You're going to have a nice time".'

This was exceedingly clever – the man could now go and fulfil her prophecy because it would involve no moral struggle. Meg was virtually telling him to go and do what he might want to do. She was not conscious of the outcome as a self-fulfilling prophecy.

Then Meg told the man she couldn't tell him any more . . . things would be all right but she needed more money in order to tell him. If she didn't have the money, things might not turn out good. She asked the man if he had more money. He said he had some in the bank and would get it. She told him not to tell anyone of what had passed between them, otherwise things might turn out bad. She told him to get the money and wrap it in some cloth, and leave it in a certain bush down the road.

> *Meg:* 'When I was listening to him talking about his troubles, I wasn't thinking of that, I was thinking of Jonnie's [her husband's] troubles – how he needed to get his motor taxed. . . . The man got his money and guess how much was there? £15!' [This would have been worth considerably more at the time.]

Meg had not expected as much as that. She then told him: 'By this time next week something will have happened, something very important, a big change.'

Meg acknowledged that she was deliberately vague, she said she didn't make out whether it was to do with his wife and the house or romantic entanglements. The man went away saying, 'Oh, I feel so relieved – I feel like a great weight has been taken off my chest.'

Meg: 'Yes, I thought to myself, you have lost a load – all that money.'

The man came back before the week was out, really happy. He said that a big change had happened. Meg told me this with amazement, wanting me to react to the extraordinary prediction. She had no awareness that she herself had induced the change by her own action. He thrust more bank notes into her hand: 'For nothing, just for coming and telling me that what I had said was true!' Meg didn't show much interest in telling me what had actually happened, again indicating that she didn't realise the significance. I asked her and she told me casually: 'Oh, he said that he had employed a detective to follow his wife and he got it proved that she was mixed up with another man. So the wife couldn't try and send him to an asylum once that had been shown.'

I suggest that the man, through being told that everything would turn out good, was motivated into positive action. He had been aroused from his helpless passive depression into defending himself. Meg admitted that fortune-telling had to be learnt – i.e. what to say and to whom. This she picked up from other experts. But she believed her major skill was limited to guesswork. She appeared to have no idea that she had had the power to induce change. She believed only in a certain knack at prediction and even that frightened her when it proved accurate.

PRACTICAL KNOWLEDGE

The Gypsy fortune-teller's work does not rely solely on the exotic image. Credibility is gained with the aid of practical knowledge. The Gypsies' apparent nomadic anonymity is linked by non-Gypsies to the assumption that Gypsies are ignorant of the larger society, whereas in fact Gypsies must be thoroughly acquainted with it. The fortune-teller is adept at judging both the general type and specificity of the potential client. Whenever possible, she finds out in advance individual details about the client who rarely considers this as a possible explanation for the fortune-teller's apparent clairvoyance.

The ability in Gypsies to classify non-Gypsies into types is something which clients may find most difficult to acknowledge. I was struck by the resistance by some non-Gypsy informants to accepting that the predictions given them by fortune-tellers could be seen as intelligent guesses consistent with age, gender and class. A client seems to be committed to identifying him/herself as a unique individual with a unique fate. To accept that the Gypsy fortune-teller saw the gorgio client as merely a social type would be to deny individuality.

Fortune-telling works in part because it entails effective specialised knowledge and techniques. The fortune-teller is practised in sensitive guesswork, and in some cases, it seems, a state of 'suspended attention' in order to intuit the unspoken or unconscious desires and wishes specific to the client.

Pronouncements are delivered with convincing and reassuring authority. The gorgio client is relieved of the burden of choice in some difficult decision and, through an apparent glimpse into the future, is offered the illusion of greater control over his/her life. In many instances therefore the prediction of 'good fortune' may be self-fulfilling. Anxiety and immediate uncertainty are relieved and the client may act positively. Whereas a therapist may offer explicit inner-directed control over the patient's future, the Gypsy fortune-teller only implicitly offers inner-directed control over the future. This is disguised as an external prediction which the client is more likely than not to see come true, since the skilled fortune-teller does not make totally wild pronouncements.

There is a selective memory of the Gypsy fortune-teller's predictions. Those which come true are recalled, those that do not are forgotten, redescribed or reserved for a more distant future. Gypsy fortune-tellers even safely claim long after certain famous events that they had predicted them. Many a 'Gypsy Rose Lee' at the Epsom races claims that she had predicted the abdication of Edward VIII. Vesey-Fitzgerald (1973: 135) gives some similar examples without sceptical comment.

Since there is a time lag between the prediction and its alleged fulfilment the Gypsy will be conveniently out of the district and unaccountable if any inaccuracies are exposed. In the short run, optimism will not easily be discredited. In any case, the clients are unlikely to object. They are self-selected, at risk and in a permanent or temporary state of gullibility. Clients seem to have a profound commitment to affirming the authenticity of any encounter with a fortune-teller, if they held it to be true at the time. They do not want to recognise that the experience might have been one based on cynical deception. Moreover, a client such as the 'rational' architect referred to above is as vulnerable as any other person because he would not dare confess his dependency on a fortune-teller, nor his uncertainty in decision-making. Gypsies who have outwitted people in other ways recognise that 'they don't like to show they're fools'.

CONCLUSION AND ANTHROPOLOGICAL COMPARISON

I have outlined the reasons why Gypsy fortune-telling continues to thrive in the larger supposedly rational society. Gypsies are eminently suitable for the task. Their marginal, exotic position gives credence to magical powers and they have developed techniques to ensure credibility, although they themselves may neither fully articulate nor be conscious of the dynamics of the encounters. The effectiveness of fortune-telling cannot be explained simply as skilful deception. It works so long as the dominant society constructs its fantasies about the unknown minority group which is used to find certainty or wish fulfilment. Even when considerable empirical evidence is available as to the Gypsies' disbelief in their own powers of prediction, and that a scientific ideology contradicts such powers, the practice is not discredited. Non-Gypsies have a vested interest in their own not simply the other's fantastic beliefs.

I end with a peculiarly apt but unconventional comparison with Evans-Pritchard's arguments in the celebrated case of the Azande in Africa. A Westerner's interpretation of the (ir)rationality of exotic others can be turned back to interpret the (ir)rationality of Westerners.

Social anthropologists have tended to credit only so-called primitive people or those on the rural fringes with belief in magic. Evans-Pritchard contrasts the European with the Azande when discussing the latter's belief in a poison oracle. The Azande system survived undiscredited. If a diagnosis or prediction by an Azande oracle was incorrect, it was said that either its operation was incorrectly carried out or that mystical forces had intervened. It is a closed system. More importantly, Evans-Pritchard suggests that a scientific experimental method for testing the veracity of the oracle was not available: 'Azande cannot go beyond the limits set by their culture and invent notions' (1937: 351).

In the case of fortune-telling, we find a quasi-magical practice resorted to by members of a society imbued with belief in the scientific method. Educated, urban Westerners are among the Gypsies' clients, not just those in some allegedly rural periphery. Yet, more surprisingly than among the Azande, these clients do not allow this scientific tradition to modify their behaviour. The two areas of experience are kept distinct.

Fortune-telling flourishes so long as non-Gypsies maintain beliefs in the Gypsies' exoticism and Gypsies are prepared to collude with them. So powerful are the image and the performance of the all-knowing fortune-teller in some cases that I also found myself mesmerised in my encounter as client with a Gypsy in Durham (described above). She fielded all my attempts to convey my long-term field experience with Gypsies. My years of research, first-hand knowledge of many families and even my awareness of their scepticism could not break through. She appeared as a living icon of the 'real' Gypsy fortune-teller. This power of our own cultural representations helps to explain the coexistence of scientific knowledge and supernatural or magical beliefs. If in the following quotation we substitute the word 'gorgios' for 'Azande' and 'Gypsy fortune-teller' for 'poison oracle' and 'benge' (poison),[3] then Westerners might be able to use the analysis of another culture to understand their own, and through the eyes of a Gypsy who is just as puzzled by the gorgios' credulity. The 'we' will therefore be taken to refer to Gypsies. Gorgios, or Western non-Gypsies, become the 'other':

To understand why it is that gorgios [Azande] do not draw from their observations the conclusions Gypsies [we] would draw from the same evidence, we must realise that gorgios' [their] attention is fixed on the mystical properties of the Gypsy fortune-teller [poison oracle] and that her [its] natural properties are of so little interest to them that they simply do not bother to consider them . . . . If a gorgio's [Zande's] mind were not fixed on the mystical qualities of the Gypsy [benge] and entirely absorbed by them he would perceive the significance of the knowledge he already possesses. As it is the contradiction between his beliefs and his observations only become a generalised and glaring contradiction when they are recorded side by side in the pages of an ethnographic treatise.

(Evans-Pritchard 1937: 318–19)

The mystical, magical qualities of the Gypsy are created by non-Gypsies despite, or because of, the prevailing scientific and rational ideology. It is only from within the dominant system that the beliefs can be demystified. The Gypsies are not mystified, only puzzled by their clients' gullibility. Bearing in mind the Gypsies' livelihood, I am confident that outlining the 'contradiction' in an article or any 'ethnographic treatise', as defined by Evans-Pritchard above, will not affect the Westerners' recourse to fortune-telling by Gypsies.

NOTES

1 I am grateful to James Hopkins for comments and suggestions. Early versions of this article were given at the 1983 British Medical Anthropology Society Conference, Bristol, and the 1984 ASA Conference, the LSE, London. Illness prevented revision for its inclusion in the resulting volume (Overing 1985).
2 It was this self-confessed involvement which goaded one of the reviewers to recommend rejection of this article for the journal *Social Science and Medicine*. Since I failed to reassure the reader sufficiently early on that I was not a 'believer', my presentation risked bringing social science into disrepute. To avoid future anxiety, I have added 'scientific' comfort to the text.
3 'Benge' (a poison) is administered in varying doses to a chicken after yes/no questions are asked of the oracle. The survival or death of the chicken is interpreted as the answer.

REFERENCES

Bion, W. F. (1977) 'Attention and interpretation', in *Seven Servants*, New York: Jason Aronson.
Borrow, G. (1841) *The Zincali* (Gypsies in Spain), London: Murray.
Cohn, W. (1973) *The Gypsies*, Reading, Mass.: Addison-Wesley Publishing.
Douglas, M. (1966) *Purity and Danger*, London: Routledge and Kegan Paul.
Evans-Pritchard, E. (1937) *Witchcraft, Oracles and Magic among the Azande*, Oxford: Oxford University Press.
Grellman, H. M. G. (1787) *Die Zigeuner* (trans.), London.
Gropper, R. (1975) *Gypsies in the City*, Princeton: Darwin Press.

Leland, C. (1891) *Gypsy Sorcery and Fortune-Telling*, London: Fisher Unwin.
Lévi-Strauss, C. (1963) 'The sorcerer and his magic' and 'The effectiveness of symbols', in *Structural Anthropology*, vol. I (trans.), New York: Basic Books.
Martin, K. (1972) *The Complete Gypsy Fortune-Teller*, Berkeley: Putnam.
Okely, J. (1983) *The Traveller-Gypsies*, Cambridge: Cambridge University Press.
Overing, J. (ed.) (1985) *Reason and Morality*, London: Tavistock.
Parry, J. (1980) 'Ghosts, greed and sin: the occupational identity of the Benares funeral priest', *Man* 15, 1: 88–111.
Said, E. (1985) *Orientalism*, Harmondsworth: Penguin.
Sutherland, A. (1975) *Gypsies: The Hidden Americans*, London: Tavistock.
Turner, V. (1969) *The Ritual Process*, London: Routledge and Kegan Paul.
Vesey-Fitzgerald, B. (1973) *Gypsies of Britain* (new edn), Newton Abbot: David and Charles.

Chapter 6

Women readers

Other utopias and own bodily knowledge

WOMEN'S LIBERATION, THE SEXED BODY AND POPULIST ISSUES

The search for alternative modes of being in the exotic other is often propelled by an internal critique. This is what inspired women after the Liberation Movement to look outside their own society in the early 1970s for resolutions and utopian answers to their questions. Women's subordination, gender divisions, the sexed body and women's bodily experiences became the subject of intense popular interest to the general woman reader. Examples from other cultures could possibly indicate the provisional nature of Western gendered culture. Given the undergraduate demand for courses which addressed these issues, they were also of interest to women and some men anthropology students. At the time, these concerns remained or had become largely peripheral to academic social anthropology. The vacuum was filled by a few popularist books addressed to a non-specialist readership and which made use of cross-cultural examples. They were written from the margins or outside the anthropological academy.

The peripherality of these gendered issues may be explained by the gender of the practitioners and by the ambivalence towards scholarly research on gendered sexuality and the body. Although it is now a commonplace that the categories 'woman' or 'man' are not unitary, broad externally imposed categorisations have continuing implications for people's experience, access to and construction of knowledge. Knowledge and persons have been subject to gender demarcations and asymmetrical power relations.

Since the higher proportion of women to men students of anthropology has not been matched and indeed has been reversed at research and professorial level, the agenda of anthropological research has rarely if ever been set by women. Whatever the variation in their masculinist interests, men have formed the large majority in the power base where anthropological knowledge is generated and published.

Until the 1980s and after, concern with gendered bodily issues had a life of its own largely outside the anthropological academy. Here I draw on material largely from Britain, but there are significant echoes in the United States. Although there were parallel movements worldwide, the Women's Liberation Movement emerged in the West in the late 1960s, following a critique of Western capitalism. Prospects of relative full employment and a new youth consumerism empowered Paris students in 1968 to unite with industrial workers to challenge the status quo. Demands were made for greater political participation and the democratisation of institutions. US students, and men faced with the draft, were backed by large sections of the Western intelligentsia in resistance to US involvement in the Vietnam War. The Black Power movement emerged to question racist majorities. Women were entering higher education and the labour force in greater numbers. New technologies of birth control helped change sexual mores. At the same time, women began to resist being treated as sexual objects rather than as persons. They objected to masculinist rhetoric and to being assigned mere servicing roles by the great white revolutionaries. At the Miss World Contest at the Albert Hall, London, flour was thrown at Bob Hope, the compère. A Black Power spokesman, in asserting that the only position for women in the movement was 'prone', continued to represent women in terms of their sexed body. With a renewed consciousness, both black and white women embarked on a gendered critique.

Questions were again raised about the naturalness and fixity of gender divisions, sexuality, bodily experience and personal relations. Earlier, within anthropology, Margaret Mead had broached such topics, and written with popular appeal, but the profession largely ignored her, especially in Britain. For example, my postgraduate anthropology degree in 1969–70 contained not a single reference to Mead among the multiple course reading lists. Her *Male and Female* (1949) had become an important extra-curricular text for feminists in the 1960s. In the 1970s, de Beauvoir's *The Second Sex* (1949) witnessed renewed popularity among women readers especially in the States. De Beauvoir's assertion that 'woman is made not born' was rediscovered, to challenge the biological basis to difference. Although social anthropology had at an early stage in descent and kinship studies distinguished the social from the biological, these distinctions were scarcely developed in relation to gender.

With the Women's Liberation Movement, there was an interest in exploring the specificity of women's lived experience and their consciousness as women. Although in this multi-faceted movement, some might have suggested that women naturally shared things in common, there was a concern for both differences and things shared. The notion of world sisterhood might have been a strategically useful polemical device, but among intellectuals and others there was an early scepticism about its reality (Oakley and Mitchell 1976: 10–13). The notion of some solidarity was exciting and inspiring when it took the form of all-women groups and conferences. Today, such groups and events are taken for granted. For women then it was a revelation to be in a hall or room filled entirely with women and where only women were the organisers and speakers. Previously, women had no choice but to assist in male-dominated meetings, whether trade unions, political gatherings or academic seminars. All-women meetings had up to then been insignificant or associated with organisations which reified women as servicers of men. But by the early 1970s, all-women seminars were seen as dangerously subversive by some academics. For example, at one university postgraduates were not permitted to use the official premises for women-only seminars. Thus the marginality of women's issues was spatially reinforced.[1]

The women in the Liberation Movement differentiated themselves from the earlier generation of post-suffrage 'equal rights feminists' who sought integration within the prevailing system. By contrast, the Women's Movement confronted and celebrated gender differences. They questioned the assumption that women should fit into existing institutions as honorary men. The private, they argued, could no longer be separated from the public. Sexual relations, domestic labour, childcare and family structures were subjected to new political and theoretical scrutiny. The discussion of sexual experience had been smothered by the postwar 1950s ideology of the monogamous family and conflation of sexual pleasure with reproduction. Consciousness-raising groups in both the USA and Britain focused on personal relations, pursuing ways in which the personal could be seen as political (Rowbotham 1990). Other themes included notions of motherhood, relations with men and awareness of sexed bodily functions. Rowbotham, inspired by de Beauvoir, pointed to the problems implicit in rationalism, liberal feminism and Marxism which had treated women as merely human:

> The general cover of human-beingness camouflaged both the anatomical differences between men and women and concealed the manner in which the notion of the human being is male-defined in all forms of existing social organisation – including the revolutionary party. In fact this defensive denial of actual difference left the way wide open for a crude and mechanical reduction of feminine potential to the body. It was easy for the anti-feminists to determine a woman by her anatomy because the feminists persisted in ignoring that her anatomy existed at all.
>
> (Rowbotham 1973: 10–11)

Special emphasis was placed by the Women's Liberation Movement on recapturing the body. *Our Bodies Ourselves* (1976) and *Woman's Body: An Owner's Manual* (1977) were key texts. Women wanted knowledge about themselves which was bodily grounded.

In order to counter the Western ideological invisibility of the female genitalia, Western women experimented in self- and mutual examination with the speculum, an instrument hitherto restricted to the medical encounter and the male gaze. Female anatomical self-observation was both empirically informative and symbolically subversive. The well-worn argument about phallic power that the protruding penis 'naturally' lends itself to superior representation, whereas the female genitalia is 'naturally' invisible, was challenged by the new feminists who instead suggested that the perception of the biological was recognised as ideologically selective. The tamed and domesticated portrayal of the female genitalia, women argued, was a historically and culturally specific obliteration, rather than anything essentially anatomical. Artists like Judy Chicago, in the co-operative work *The Dinner Party*, reinstated women's genitalia as aesthetic and as celebratory, highly visible objects. Mary Kelly, to public journalistic furore, framed behind glass and exhibited as art form a month's supply of her used Tampax at the Institute of Contemporary Arts in London. Thus the usually hidden parts of feminine bodily identity and experience were brought to the public gaze.

Feminist scholars in other disciplines subsequently examined Western representations of the body. Walters' (1978) re-examination of the nude male in art raised questions about masculinity. The male body from Greek statues, through Leonardo and Michelangelo, she argued, has been taken as the norm against which the female body is deviant. Given that the male body is the taken-for-granted centring of existence, those who live in such bodies, including male anthropologists, may not be stimulated to be puzzled about them.

Consistent with this renewed curiosity in the sexed body was the search by Western feminists for alternative femininities in other cultures. Again I use the term 'femininity' on the understanding that it is culturally constructed and neither universal nor innate. It was important to consider evidence from beyond the West. Such an enterprise has a long tradition and has other political parallels. Bloch (1983) has lucidly suggested that Marx and Engels, drawing on others' writing, used pre-literate societies as a rhetorical device to argue that there were alternatives to capitalism, i.e. things could change in future if the study of the past showed fundamental differences from the present. Marx and Engels painted an idyllic inverse of capitalism in 'primitive' societies where allegedly mother right, sexual freedom, and a form of communism existed with neither private property nor class conflict. The rhetorical use of other societies had populist implications in that Marx and Engels also wrote texts for a popular readership, e.g. *The Manifesto of the Communist Party*.

Evans-Pritchard (1951) noted comparable uses of non-Western societies by Western religious theorists as a covert critique of the theorists' own society and religious ideology. Nineteenth-century theorists of primitive religions and of the origins of religion in general were often writing in a context where it was awkward to question the truth of the dominant Christian religion, so they safely transposed their debates to the study of the 'other' and 'primitives'. By demonstrating the multiplicity of beliefs elsewhere, it could be suggested that Christian theology was not an inevitable universal.

Male theologians, with the strategic advantage of the pulpit for a non-academic congregation, were also read beyond the academy and monastery.

Similarly, through the quest for answers outside the West, the androcentric academic restrictions on the discussion of gender relations, women's experience, their sexuality and reproductive practice were open to subversion or debate in wider popular circles. If Western women could find utopian solutions or alternatives elsewhere, there would seem to be hope for change in their own society. Some popularist Western women writers have, in the same tradition as class politics and theological debates, used or imagined non-Western examples to offer alternatives to the Western gender status quo. But they were less easily absorbed into mainstream academic theories. This is in part because both writers and readers were of the subordinate gender and because the women writers' theoretical and methodological approaches rarely emerged from the 'malestream'. They were writing either from outside the discipline or from its margins. They were not always in a position to update their arguments in the light of current theoretical debates within the discipline. They had to appeal over the heads of the academy. In some instances, as in two examples I discuss below, other cultures were used to re-legitimate Western systems.

In the postwar period there had already been some signs of a demand for answers from women readers for critical discussion about gender relations and aspects of sexuality, reproduction and childcare. De Beauvoir's *The Second Sex* (1949) is an important example of a text which was read and absorbed by thousands of women through the anti-feminist 1950s and for decades later and yet was condemned and belittled by mainly establishment male reviewers of all political leanings. Even the author was surprised by the enthusiasm of the response from her otherwise invisible female readers who wrote to her in huge numbers. They said that the book had changed their lives (Okely 1986). The dialogue between the woman writer and women readers was conducted outside the academy. In this massive and scholarly work (see chapter 9, this volume), de Beauvoir addressed such issues as women's subordination, its possible causes, sexuality and the sexed body. Whereas the women readers looked for identifications with themselves, her largely generalised account was read as unseemly self and sexual exposure by François Mauriac, the novelist. In a letter to a writer at *Les Temps modernes*, he wrote: 'Your employer's vagina has no secrets from me' (de Beauvoir 1965: 197). This tells us more about the culture of the male gaze than the writer's anatomy.

De Beauvoir gave an unusually negative and provocative view of maternity and childcare (Okely 1986). She was writing against the prevailing postwar Western ideology which represented women primarily as housewives, stigmatised or obliterated women's extra domestic employment and which sentimentalised maternity. Despite the fact that a large number of women did have such employment, albeit part-time, women were exhorted to look to a husband for financial support. Questions as to their subordination within this contract were not up for debate. Only de Beauvoir raised them for her silenced women readers.

In contrast, the Women's Liberation Movement of the 1970s also focused attention on parenting. Since full employment had brought greater numbers of women into the labour force, increased numbers of college-educated women were faced with decisions of maternity in conjunction with extra-domestic employment and/or careers. This greater number of educated women readers looked for answers both within and outside their own cultures.

With some notable exceptions, social anthropology in Britain and the West had ceased to problematise the subordination of women and the construction of gender relations. It was generally taken for granted that women in non-Western societies were subordinate. The silence about comparisons with Western examples indicated some complacency in the Western anthropologists' own society (chapter 10, this volume). After the granting of the franchise to women, it was presumed that all Western gender relations were peaceably complementary and that women were 'equal but different'.

SEXUALITY, THE FIELDWORKER AND THE MALE GAZE

The constraints on the study of sexuality, menstruation and childbirth across cultures can in part be explained by the dominant masculine gender of the fieldworker. Male anthropologists, enjoying gendered privileges and academic power in their own society, were unlikely to be concerned with making connections or contrasts in gender relations their major focus of investigation elsewhere.

The character of anthropological fieldwork, entailing daily proximity, compounded the constraints. With the increasing professionalism of the discipline at the turn of the century, and the practice of participant observation fieldwork replacing armchair speculation and reliance on secondary sources, social anthropologists were keen to emphasise the objective scientific nature of their studies. Since sexuality in exotica was both popularly and academically interpreted as of sensational interest, anthropologists wished to distance themselves from amateur travellers' tales in which primitive peoples had been treated as objects of sexual voyeurism for Western readers.

The anthropologist was faced with an immediate dilemma of how to research and write about the intimate topic of sexuality which would not have remained hidden during the long-term immersion of participant observation. If in addition, anthropologists have ever engaged in individual sexual relationships with 'the other', they have been loath to record, let alone consider, the implications in print. Such encounters, rather like much of the generalised topic of sexuality, have been confined to whispering in corridors or bar room boasting (see, by contrast, Abramson 1993; Kulick and Willson 1995).

Like many of his subsequent students, Malinowski wished to distance himself from speculative stereotypes about primitive behaviour. Earlier accounts had included presuppositions of primitive promiscuity and other tantalising inversions of the visitors' own morality. Sexuality and bodily matters were seen as subjects which risked sensationalism. Nevertheless, Malinowski was ambivalent. He played along with popular voyeurism in his melodramatic choice of title *The Sexual Life of Savages* (1929), despite the fact that a great deal of its contents was devoted to kinship, marriage and mortuary rites.

Malinowski was considerably handicapped as a male enquirer and in many instances tries to overcome this. Nevertheless his text does not usually problematise his masculine perspective. The sections on childbirth devote considerable space to the mainly absent men rather than the presence of women (1932: 194–5). His *Diary* (1967) explicitly reveals his major pre-occupation with women as sexual objects for his repressed desire (see chapter 2, this volume). When writing of seduction, the reader, both male and female, is drawn into his description of women as 'the fair sex' (1932: 257). While seeming indifferent to women's views of menstruation, Malinowski is at pains to inform the reader that men are not repelled by menstrual blood and that women washed daily in the public water hole. Men did so also (ibid. 144). At key junctures he inserts himself into the text in case his knowledge of 'the fair sex' appears to be first hand: 'I am told that girls at the time of their first menstruation are tattooed round the vagina' (ibid. 257). He feels compelled to find convoluted explanations for 'the undiscriminating way in which young and handsome boys will sometimes fornicate with old and repulsive women'(ibid. 289). The reverse is not a matter for query, pre-sumably because unions between 'old and repulsive' men and 'young and handsome' women are viewed as natural among the Western bourgeoisie. His text can now be read as a classical example of the male gaze.

Although Malinowski convincingly encouraged an approach which privil-eged the everyday rather than the sensational and exotic, if not the erotic, women's experience was not seen as part of what he called 'the imponder-abilia of everyday life' (Malinowski 1922). Women's beliefs about menstru-ation, pregnancy and childbirth could have been seen as ethnographically important, yet they were marginalised.

Endless debates had arisen within anthropology as to whether sexual intercourse was understood by the 'natives', including the Trobrianders, to be connected with reproduction. Subsequently, Leach (1969) questioned whether Malinowski's material on the Trobrianders' alleged ignorance was nothing more than a public ideology. The Trobrianders' public denial that sex before marriage ever brought pregnancy could have been investigated in other practical ways. The reference to abortion magic suggests that preg-nancies before marriage might have been systematically terminated by additional physical interventions, to which magic was an accompaniment.

Although Malinowski (1922: 168) denies the widespread practice of abortion, he is not in a position to prove this. The extent to which 'the natives' whom he questioned were female is often unclear. I suggest that he systematically underestimates the Trobrianders' need to conceal abortion from a white man, given the powerful censorship which missionaries had already imposed upon sexual customs (ibid. 218) (Okely 1975b).

Malinowski's (1929) sensationalist title may have been addressed to a wider readership, but it had negative repercussions within the academy (MacClancy 1993). At Cambridge University, the library copy was locked away after publication and only made available to postgraduates after special written permission from the appropriate professor (private communication, E. Leach). Thus even this limited and somewhat androcentric study of sexuality was considered too controversial for scholarly enlightenment and further research within the academic canon. Decades later, it was an inadequate source for the understanding of women's bodily and sexual experiences in another culture.

WOMEN AS SUBJECTS OR OBJECTS

Up to the late 1970s (for exceptions see S. Ardener 1975b), and generally until the late 1980s, sexuality, if ever broached in the British anthropological academy, was more likely to be seen from masculine perspectives. Just as in Malinowski's texts women were less likely to be seen as subjects, and more likely as objects, so the same can be found in Lévi-Strauss. His celebrated discussion of a difficult childbirth (Lévi-Strauss 1967) concentrates on the role of the male shaman rather than the experience of the mother in labour. There was little study of women based on their accounts, interests and experience, in relation to sexuality and other issues. Edwin Ardener, in a now much-quoted passage, noted that:

> At the level of 'observation' in fieldwork, the behaviour of women has, of course, like that of men been exhaustively plotted . . . . When we come to that second or 'meta' level of fieldwork . . . that social anthropologists really depend upon to give conviction to their interpretations, there is a real imbalance. We are for practical purposes in a male world.
>
> (E. Ardener 1975: 1–2)

In some rare cases, especially in the work of the numerical minority of women anthropologists, women were treated as subjects or as active agents; their specific experience and standpoint explored. Kaberry (1939) (see chapter 10, this volume) and Richards (1956) were among these exceptional examples. Nevertheless, even Richards' innovative focus on girls' initiation rites excluded the voiced experience of the neophytes. Douglas has never explicitly identified herself with feminist issues, but her attention to daily practicalities associated for example with hygiene (Douglas 1966) reveals an eye for the detail of practices often associated with 'feminised' experience, such as domestic cleaning.

Earlier, Margaret Mead's (1928, 1935, 1949) pioneering work on aspects of gender identity, adolescent sexuality and childcare was pilloried for her popular and proselytising style. She was marginalised. 'Instead of making what she perceived as the male world of academia her focus, Mead made a conscious decision to centre her professional life at New York City's American Museum of Natural History, where she remained for almost fifty years' (Yans-Mclaughlin 1989: 252). Few of the questions she raised about gender issues were followed through in the years following her publications.

Within the anthropological academy, these questions had to await the renewed enthusiasms and delayed effects of the Women's Movement upon social anthropology and a new generation of mainly women researchers (Rosaldo and Lamphere 1974; Reiter 1975; S. Ardener 1975a). These pioneering edited collections entirely from women (with the exception of E. Ardener 1975) were mainly by researchers without tenured positions. Rosaldo and Lamphere, it was said, were encouraged to waive their royalties, as it was suggested that the book would have only limited circulation. The articles in these pioneering volumes raised preliminary questions from the margins of the discipline.

Although these publications have subsequently been read and referred to widely both within anthropology and across disciplines, and have been frequently reprinted, they neither reached nor were addressed to a popular readership. In the long run, their theories and ethnographies have percolated through other more popularist texts. Earlier, it was the less theoretically innovative books outside academia which reached the wider readership.

GENDERED INSTITUTIONS

While institutionalised androcentricism at the apex of the discipline may still exist, its implications in the 1970s were especially acute. Gender issues were being raised in the then ferment of feminist political circles, but anthropology was initially somewhat detached from these concerns. The tendency to universalise from only masculinist gendered perspectives (and from middle-class heterosexual ones) may in part be explained by the predominance of men at the research level. As social anthropology expanded as an under-graduate degree subject, it attracted a predominance of women students. This sex ratio continues to be reflected in most of the social sciences and the arts or humanities. Unlike science, where the majority of both staff and students are male, in the majority of other disciplines, women students outnumber men, but again staff and the research elite are predominantly male. A specific example is available in British social anthropology.

A study (Barker 1978 and Caplan 1978) in the 1970s over five years of the three main colleges at London University (the London School of Economics, University College and the School of Oriental and African Studies) teaching social anthropology revealed that 60 per cent of those gaining 'bachelor' degrees were women. Of those gaining 'master's' degrees, 52 per cent were women. From then on, the gender proportions were reversed: of those gaining doctorates, only 36 per cent were women, while 64 per cent were men. Among research staff, only 23 per cent were women (Caplan 1978: 547). The percentage of women anthropology lecturers was less than 10 per cent and in the mid-1970s there was only one woman as full professor of social anthropology in the entire United Kingdom. This was consistent with the overall invisibility of women in *all* subjects, i.e. science and the arts, as well as the social sciences in the mid-1970s:

> The proportion of university teachers who are women drops . . . to 9 per cent . . . women academics tend to be concentrated in the lower grades . . . only 1 per cent of professors are women.
>
> (Blackstone 1976: 207)

The reversal in gender proportions from undergraduate to research and professional practitioner is replicated in the relationship between reader and writer. The majority of the readers of key anthropological texts have tended to be female, while the majority of the anthropological writers have been male. Undergraduate enthusiasm for the study of social anthropology and other cultures has been found to be disproportionately among women.

When in the early 1970s women readers, both inside and outside the anthropological academy, sought alternative gendered information about other cultures, anthropology was not in a position to elucidate. Anne Oakley's *Sex, Gender and Society* (1972), a scholarly and multidisciplinary overview which had scoured the available anthropological literature, was the nearest to answering questions about the construction of gender in other cultures. Significantly, it had emerged from a doctorate in sociology, where she had also found that women took 'the insubstantial form of ghosts, shadows or stereotyped characters' (Oakley 1974: 1).

Popularising writers were not always engaged in original nor in-depth research. Detached from current theoretical debates within anthropology, the popularist presentation of other cultures has had a tendency to slide un-critically into the eclectic and monocausal tradition of Frazer's *Golden Bough* (1900). Information in this mode is presented as cumulative titbits, often strung together with little theoretical analysis, except speculation about a single ancient origin. The reader is invited to respond with a series of silent 'fancy thats'. Alternatively, there may be appeals to mystical unintellectual-ised universalisms and Jungian archetypes.

Popularisation of potential themes for or from anthropology are not neces-sarily written in an easily accessible format and style. The publications may, in the tradition of Frazer, be replete with extensive detailed descriptions and extracts from others' research. It is likely that the theoretical underpinning is based on long-familiar assumptions and that the main arguments have polem-ical potential.

SUBORDINATION AND EVOLUTION AS POPULARIST ISSUES

A woman's contestation of male domination in evolution emerged as a riposte to Morris' (1967) androcentric and populist account. In *The Descent of Woman* (1972) Elaine Morgan, a playwright and journalist, with no known qualifications in anthropology, argued that *Homo sapiens* had evolved from the sea and that once females were dominant. Influenced by a marine biologist, Alister Hardy (Morgan 1972: 30), her utopian reconstruction of the past had similarities with feminist science fiction. Given the ground swell of new feminist interest, the text found its way into a first year course on physical anthropology at an English university in the late 1970s. It was a popularist route to engaging female students with sociobiology rather than with feminist social theory.

Another text which re-assessed gender hierarchy, the question of women's subordination and its possible causes was provided by a woman anthropologist who had worked for years on the margins. While the few women anthropologists (Rosaldo and Lamphere 1974; Reiter 1975) with a first tentative toe-hold in the academy were debating the causes of women's subordination, without being able to point to an egalitarian or matriarchal past, Evelyn Reed offered the vision of an ancient and universal matriarchy. *Woman's Evolution* (1975) was the product of over twenty years of research. The extent to which it was produced outside debates in institutionalised social anthropology is exemplified by her uncritical comments on 'some savage groups in modern times' who 'still fail to make the distinction' between themselves and animals (ibid. 274). Lévi-Strauss' influential *Totemism* (1963) seems to have passed her by. Similarly, Reed revealed a pre-Malinowski theoretical perspective which still sought to explain customs in terms of their origins and as 'decayed forms' or as 'a vestige of its more ancient symbolism' (Reed 1975: 260).

Reed's work appealed to women readers outside contemporary anthropology as a massively detailed *Golden Bough* of women's activities in pre-literate societies. Certainly, Engels was being re-read sympathetically by the Women's Movement for his early association between gender divisions and the mode of production (Delmar 1976). Nevertheless, to the new generation of women anthropologists Reed's thesis was considered to be an unconvincing reiteration of Engels' thesis that associated the subordination of women solely with the rise of private property and which argued for a prior existence of gender equality. In Reed there are claims for an original matriarchy. So detached was Reed from the academy, that she found herself out of tune with the emerging feminist anthropologists of the mid-1970s and described them as having been 'brainwashed' when they presented her with evidence of female subordination even in hunting and gathering societies.

At a meeting at Durham University in the late 1970s which I attended, when Reed presented her matriarchal thesis, the response among the non-anthropological women in the audience was close to that of Christian revivalists as they grasped at this vision of a previous matriarchal utopia. Scepticism expressed by both male and female anthropologists was summarily dismissed. Some feminist sociologists on the fringes of the academy then developed her material and amplified Engels. They were invited by liberal male lecturers to address an alternative seminar in Durham.[2]

Reed's arguments were more original and grounded when she challenged popular and androcentric texts which used animal studies to argue that women were naturally subordinate (Reed 1978). The leap from observations and interpretations of animals and insects to Western humans proved highly appealing to many non-feminists. Fatalistic, innate and universalist explanations for domination of some categories of humans over others vied with women's search for non-universalist alternatives in other human cultures, rather than among animals.

Reed's (1978) critique of Ardrey, Lorenz and Morris challenged both the assumptions of innate human aggression and their wholesale generalisations about gender, race and class divisions. Implicitly, in challenging the biological basis to gender difference, she also engaged in notions of the sexed body. Morris, Reed argued, 'pumps sex into his sexist book by devoting many pages to spicy accounts of the private parts and private lives of primate females and the kind of erotic stimuli that move naked apes into their body-to-body contacts' (ibid. 70–1). In this popularist publication by Morris (1967), there is the now familiar voyeuristic treatment of sexuality. Both women and animals are treated as titillating objects for the male gaze and male reader.

Reed challenged the work of popularist writers, who, in contrast to her own training, had very little anthropological education, but who used the label anthropologist to help legitimate their theories. Feminist anthropologists within the academy have subsequently felt free to explore sociobiology and primatology from an alternative and rigorously academic perspective, using the intellectual traditions of anthropology against sexism (Haraway 1989; Sperling 1991). There were also earlier forays (Slocum 1975).

BODILY AND SOCIAL REPRODUCTION

I present three examples which addressed, in a popularised fashion in the mid-1970s, aspects of women's sexuality or bodily reproduction and childcare. All remain in print in the early 1990s.

1 Menstruation

The Wise Wound: Menstruation and Everywoman (1978) by Penelope Shuttle and her partner Peter Redgrove was the authors' first work of non-fiction. They had previously published novels and poetry. Redgrove, with a degree in Natural Sciences, worked as a research scientist and scientific journalist.

They acknowledge the influence of Layard, anthropologist and psychoanalyst (see MacClancy 1986), with whom Redgrove studied in the late 1960s. While strongly Jungian, the work is not classified by the publishers as a psychology text, but is instead located within sociology and anthropology. The links with either of the latter subjects are somewhat tenuous. However, the work aims to answer some of the questions sought from other cultures by women in the 1970s, in this case the search for some universal, pan-cultural meaning to menstruation, 'a blessing or a curse?' (1978: 13). It addresses what is seen as a conspiracy of silence. 'It will, we hope, encourage women to ask these questions themselves, and to begin building up a body of information which is about what women actually experience and not what they are told they should experience by doctrinaire authority' (ibid.).

The authors drew attention to the neglect of writing and attention to 'two of the most basic experiences in human life . . . . Both of these belong to feminine experience. One is the experience of bearing a child, and the child's experience of its mother in being born; and the other is the woman's experience of herself during menstruation' (ibid. 16). They argue that it should be up to a woman herself to determine her 'own labour experience' (ibid. 17) as well as her wishes towards the experience of menstruation. Through the mass of cross-cultural examples, the authors thus appeal to a search for women's bodily self-determination.

As with other texts which appeal to a non-specialist readership, the material is not necessarily simplified. The work is packed with detailed, near-encyclopaedic data, mainly from Western historical sources, folklore and psychoanalytical literature, although hostile to Freud. There are references to anthropologists, especially those of the pre-fieldwork generations, such as Briffault, but also to E. Ardener, Benedict, Buxton, La Fontaine, Skultans (a rare article (1970) on menstruation practices in Britain) and Turner. The ethnographic material in *The Wise Wound* is rarely discussed in a rounded social context, whether or not it was originally so presented in the few anthropological studies cited.

For an anthropologist reader, used to a specific theoretical organisation of empirical material, the text becomes increasingly bewildering with the accumulation of examples. The organising argument, when it can be identified, appeals to universalist assumptions which are thoroughly ethnocentric. The authors look to something beyond the prevailing hegemony of a predominantly technological society. Readers are invited to escape the status quo by affirming an underlying, lost set of beliefs or power. Other cultures are referred to in so far as they support the theme of Western malaise.

The major appeal is to the Western woman reader looking to subjective experience and to her own body for mystical answers to depression, especially that apparently related to premenstrual tension or powerlessness. The prologue is explicitly addressed to a female reader in that the authors suggest: 'This implies a change of attitude towards and a reassessment of *one's* femininity' (ibid. 14, my emphasis).

The underlying assumptions in the text presume a universal and essential 'feminine' and an unproblematised link between all women and the biology of bodily process. Contrary to cross-cultural examples, the authors argue that 'witchcraft is the natural concern of all women . . . the natural craft of all women . . . because witchcraft is the subjective experience of the menstrual cycle' (ibid. 209). The authors assert that a creative process of 'descent and return . . . was learnt by the women from their first menstrual cycle and imparted to their male partners who have taken it for their own and forgotten their teachers' (ibid. 274). Thus the anti-biologism of feminist and Women's Liberation writing was overridden. In the hands of these authors, the resurgent interest in the female body moves from the material to a mystical and ahistorical universalism. While the text makes use of other cultures, the potential answers from social anthropology are largely absent.

The book was marketed for the wider non-academic readership. The cover suggests that it tackles 'a subject that has been forbidden for centuries. It is the first study of its kind, and in unveiling taboos both ancient and modern, it will change the way women – and men – view themselves'. The journal *Psychology Today* (quoted without reference) suggested that 'It could bring about a major change in our understanding of the sexes'.

A quote from the *Observer*, also reproduced for marketing purposes, captures the inherent Frazerian tradition and gives anthropological legitimacy: 'An Aladdin's cave of scientific, psychological and anthropological insights . . . all quite irresistible.'

2 Birth

The study of the experience of childbirth by women called for by Shuttle and Redgrove was addressed by Kitzinger in a number of publications. *Women as Mothers* (1978) made extensive use of cross-cultural examples, in this case to challenge the notion that the modern Western experience was ideal or essential.[3]

The book is presented and 'marketed' as challenging any innateness of maternal instincts. The underlying theme is to demonstrate through multiple cross-cultural examples, that maternity can be different. There are also echoes of Mead in Kitzinger's contrast between cultural practices in America and the 'African bush', in this instance childbirth rather than adolescent sexuality.

Kitzinger was registered for a higher degree in Social Anthropology in the 1960s. She had been inspired by a visit by Margaret Mead who 'validated what I wanted to do' (pc, 1995). She says that she found it difficult for her thesis topic on 'Pregnancy, birth and motherhood in Jamaica' to 'be accepted as a "valid subject"'. Such topics she claims, years later, were regarded 'as female trivia . . . women's networks were not seen as relevant' (ibid.).

Certainly, among the subsequent generation of women postgraduates, of which I was one, the belief, right or wrong, was that topics like childbirth were considered inappropriate for a doctorate. A number of women anthropology postgraduates of the early 1970s both in the UK and the USA (pc, Jane Szurek) felt they had to prove their ability by studying areas and topics classically validated as gender free, or in effect 'masculine'.

There is critical irony in Kitzinger's genderised observations about choices of topic:

> Anthropologists do not write much about birth – possibly because they are usually men and are not permitted to take part in the rituals surrounding labour. They have, however, written so extensively about the disposal of the placenta that one might be forgiven for believing that this must be one of the most important rites in primitive and peasant childbirth.
>
> (ibid. 105)

Kitzinger presents the image of the male anthropologist waiting outside the birth hut to take notes when the placenta is brought out for disposal. I find her observations confirmed in Malinowski's discussion of childbirth. He can write little about the experience of birth, but gives relatively detailed comments on the afterbirth (Malinowski 1932: 195–6).

Kitzinger makes the general point about the anthropological neglect of 'the private world' of women.

> Anthropologists have tended to discuss women as objects involved in transactions between social groups and to see society largely in terms of relations between men, referring to women only when they affect men's behaviour. In Evans-Pritchard's brilliant studies of the Nuer of the Sudan, women come into the books rather less often than cows.
>
> (ibid. 13–14)

Kitzinger is acutely aware of the belittling by the canon of the cultural anthropology of Mead. She quotes Evans-Pritchard's paternalistic comments on the popularising style of *Coming of Age in Samoa* (1928) as follows: 'A discursive, or perhaps I should say chatty and feminine book. . . . Nevertheless, it is . . . written by a highly intelligent woman' (Evans-Pritchard 1951; cited in Kitzinger 1978: 14). In this way, Kitzinger invites the reader to notice the explicit gender-marking of style and author in the male commentary and canon.

That childbirth 'is a cultural act in which spontaneous physiological processes operate within a context of customs' (Kitzinger 1978: 105) is a major organising argument. Given the earlier biologistic texts, and despite the work of de Beauvoir and Mead, this would still have been a relatively novel approach to non-social science readers. As with de Beauvoir before her (see Okely 1986), there is sometimes the tendency towards universalisms (ibid. 80). At the time, they had a didactic worth and appealed to the women readers looking for both similarities and differences with other women (cf. Okely 1986 and chapter 9, this volume). Kitzinger engagingly moves from universalisms to examples selected for their exotic contrast with anything Western:

> In parts of East Africa. . . a woman who is having a long and arduous labour may have her vagina packed with cow dung. It is an act which has significance in pastoral societies where the main economic value is cattle. The dung is meant to encourage the birth of the child by letting it smell how wealthy the father is.
>
> (Kitzinger 1978: 109)

Women as Mothers is consistent with the popularist style of producing a mass of cross-cultural examples, often extracted from the total ethnographic context. The experience of maternity is examined chronologically, commencing with an awareness of the Women's Movement within which there was 'ambiguity in the approach to motherhood. It represents for some a biological trap . . . and for others an opportunity for achieving something which a man manifestly cannot do' (ibid. 47). The examples confirm women's ambivalences, adding a cross-cultural dimension to the then Euro-American ethnocentricity of some feminist texts.

In contrast to other popularist texts, there are some references to the few anthropological texts about and by women anthropologists at the time, e.g. du Boulay (1974), Rosaldo and Lamphere (1974), Ortner (1974) and Woolf (1972). But in the mid-1970s, especially for a woman then writing on the fringes of the anthropological academy, there was little opportunity for an overall theoretical perspective. The sociologist Anne Oakley's (1972) anti-biologistic discussion of maternity and use of cross-cultural examples is not referred to. This is another indication of the isolated context then of feminist social scientists.[4]

The cover of *Women as Mothers* draws attention to the current malaise:

> At a time when mothers in the West feel their role as an increasingly challenged and difficult one. . . . Sheila Kitzinger shows that maternal behaviour, far from being inborn and unchanging, is a direct response to the society the mother lives in. . . . Conception, pregnancy and childbirth itself are surrounded by quite different kinds of ritual and expectation.

Kitzinger's text lived up to the popularist expectations of the time. Other cultures were seen to provide critical alternatives for Western women readers.

3 Childcare

Liedloff's *The Continuum Concept* (1975) addressed a need to examine other cultures for utopian answers to questions about childcare in the industrial or post-industrial capitalist West. Again, the legitimacy of anthropology is invoked in this publication and, like Shuttle and Redgrove, the author has no qualifications in the discipline. The Penguin paperback classifies the work under sociology and anthropology. Quotes of approval from five men include professionals such as Leboyer and the psychiatrist Storr, but no anthropologists. Connections with anthropology are invoked simply because tropical forest Indians as an exotic Other are the object of study.

Liedloff's career as university dropout, artist and poet who turned down the offer to model for Dior, is vicariously appealing to the general woman reader. On a trip to Florence, she met two Italians by chance who invited her to Venezuela to hunt for diamonds. After such an expedition and acquaintance with some Tauripan Indians, she was inspired to spend more time with the latter.

She focused increasingly on their childcare. She describes the Indian practices and identifies the 'in-arms phase' when, until babies can crawl, they are in continual physical contact with the mother. There are some detailed observed incidents of the Indians' daily life in relation to children. But these are detached from an ethnography of the total context. The Indians, who have machetes, are persistently described as Stone Age. The presumption is that they have had no independent history and that they are vestiges of early 'Man'. The Indians are represented as having no hang-ups, no word for work, no competitiveness. Their rituals are described ethnocentrically as follows:

> Ritual is another form of relief from the burden of choice-making. One's mental state is very like that of an infant or another species of animal. During the ritual, especially if one has an active part, such as dancing or chanting, the organism is run under a flag far older than that of the intellect.
>
> (1986: 136)

The text is full of evolutionists' theories and uncritical comparisons with primate behaviour, more specifically with the occasional monkey whom the author had as a pet in the woods. Lorenz' theory of 'imprinting' by geese makes its appearance. There is no awareness that other non-Western cultures may have a multiplicity of different forms of childcare. Although some comparisons are made with another group, these Indians are not compared with other non-Western groups elsewhere in the world. It is implied that they are the embodiment of all non-Western others.

The main advice transposed from the tropical forest is that Western mothers should continuously hold their babies during the 'in-arms phase':

> Once a mother realises that seeing that her baby is carried about for the first six or eight months will ensure his self-reliance . . . even her self-interest will tell her not to spare herself the 'trouble' of carrying him while she is doing her housework or shopping.
>
> Once a mother begins to serve her baby's continuum (and thus her own as

a mother), the culturally confused instinct in her will reassert itself and reconnect her natural motives.

(ibid. 155, 156)

Liedloff has to answer the problem of women's work outside the home. The mother is exhorted not to do so: 'Very often these jobs are a matter of choice; the mothers could, if they realised the urgency of their presence during the baby's first year, give up the job in order to avert the deprivations which would damage the baby's entire life' (ibid. 156). There is no suggestion that fathers could be a substitute. Where mother 'must work', babysitters are advised to hold the baby on their laps while watching television or doing homework. Again, it is presumed that all carers, even a grandparent, should be female.

There are some quite forceful directives:

Holding a baby while doing housework is a matter of practice. . . . Dusting and vacuum cleaning can be done mainly by one hand. Bedmaking will be a little more difficult, but a resourceful mother will find a way. . . . Cooking is largely a matter of keeping one's body between the cooker and the baby when there is danger of splashing.

(ibid. 156–7)

There is no awareness of the problems a mother might face if she has to watch over other children, perhaps toddlers, at the same time.

In contrast to the new feminist concerns to describe and to make visible domestic activities as exploited unpaid labour (Oakley 1974), Liedloff lumps cooking and cleaning with 'walking and talking with friends' and advises mothers: 'It would help immeasurably if we could see baby care as a non-activity. We should learn to regard it as nothing to do' (Liedloff 1975: 157). Baby care is reduced to nappy changing and breast feeding. Bathing the baby can apparently be done alongside the mother.

Whereas Kitzinger had pointed to the ambivalences in the Women's Movement towards the institution of motherhood, Liedloff is uncompromising towards any new ambivalence or challenge to the status quo. Not only are mothers made to feel guilty for working outside their home, but their time and personal space must be entirely baby centred. A new more refined perfectionism is asked of mothers in the name of the natural. The female body which gives birth is now to be linked without a break for several years to the growing baby. The father's body is not recruited likewise for care. Liedloff's ideal mother depends entirely on the earnings of a husband who, whether in that role or as a father, is largely absent from her text and programme. Here the mother's bodily and economic autonomy is subordinated entirely to the infant and to the male earner.

In effect, the main themes and messages of the book resurrect the 1950s Bowlby thesis (1951) that mothers should remain at all times with their offspring. Bowlby is one of the few writers referred to at length (Liedloff 1975: 80–1). De Beauvoir's resistance (1949) to maternity and critique of domestic labour is unmentioned. The gender division of labour is never questioned. Predictably, the language has no self-consciousness of gender. The baby is always described as male. Thus the elementary questions of the new feminism and existing gender scholarship are passed over. The primitive Other is used selectively by Liedloff to reaffirm the Western patriarchal nuclear family. Any women readers' search for alternatives to gender asymmetry re-exposed by the Women's Movement is answered by a new orthodoxy disguised as a liberation from modern capitalism.

CONCLUSION

In the late 1960s and the early 1970s, gender divisions were challenged by the Women's Liberation Movement. The so-called Swinging Sixties, with greater sexual licence, were experienced ambivalently by women who began to question the extent to which they were being treated as objects rather than subjects. Women began to investigate the political in the personal, to seek for specificities in sexed bodies, and experiences which might be associated with their gender. Consciousness-raising groups encouraged the recognition of similarities as well as possible differences. There was a curiosity about female bodies, female heterosexualities, maternity and childcare. If alternatives might be found in other non-Western cultures, what was once thought to be natural could be unmasked as contingently social and cultural.

Social anthropology was not in a strong and informed position to provide the ethnography and answers to these questions, either within the academy or for a popular readership. First, such genderised areas had hardly been studied by the mainly masculinist academic hegemony. Women anthropologists at post-doctoral level and with academic power were a tiny minority and had not been encouraged to examine genderised issues. Secondly, any gender research in progress was understandably addressed to the academic community. Feminist anthropologists had to legitimate their research in erudite language and presentation. The long-popular Frazerian tradition of presenting bits and pieces from other cultures, out of total ethnographic context, was no longer the theoretical priority within the discipline. Some women experimented with this on the fringes of the academy.

Shuttle and Redgrove drew on aspects of anthropology as incidental adornment to their arguments. Eurocentric Jungian universals were the organising principles to their varied historical and non-Western examples. The 'Feminine' was understood as pan-cultural and universal. The unproblematised biological facts of menstruation among females was appealed to as a source of mystical power. The varying cultural perceptions and constructions of the female physiology were not addressed. The woman reader, in a time of cultural change and critique in the 1970s, was encouraged to see menstruation and aspects of female bodies as an escape from worldly powerlessness.

Kitzinger, with postgraduate experience in social anthropology, by contrast used the many examples of maternity from other cultures to show its cultural rather than any essentialist biological context. She treated the reader as female and invited her to think about alternatives. Both implicitly and explicitly, there was a critique of the technologised and dominant Euro-American view of birth. Her agenda was non-directive, in contrast to that of Liedloff, whose use of one non-Western culture resulted in a reaffirmation of the Western patriarchal nuclear family, in conjunction with new bodily constraints upon a mother. The example of Liedloff reveals how critical questions raised by the Women's Movement were also open to re-appropriation by the prevailing Western ideology. Moreover, the gender of the writer does not guarantee any specific gendered standpoint. It cannot of course be presumed that any woman anthropologist may be an expert on or even interested in gender (E. Ardener 1975). But a critical mass of women anthropologists in positions of academic and intellectual authority has innovative consequences.

Subsequently, feminism has had greater influence within social anthropology. Whereas in the 1960s or 1970s, women anthropologists had to conceal their feminist or gender interests from examination and appointment boards, since the late 1980s, the concept of gender has almost become gentrified.

Despite some contributions in Britain and the USA in the 1970s by a few women anthropologists (La Fontaine 1972; Paul 1974; Faithorn 1975; Rubin 1975; S. Ardener 1975b; Okely 1975a, and chapter 4, this volume; Hastrup 1978; Hirschon 1978; Callaway 1978), it was only in the late 1980s that sexuality and the related experience of women as sexual and reproductive subjects have been recognised as academically acceptable topics.[5] Questions of sexuality and gender in reproduction are now the subject of new, fertile research: e.g. Caplan (1987) and to some extent Ortner and Whitehead (1981). Martin's (1987) detailed monograph exposes as culturally specific and androcentric Western medical textbooks on menstruation, reproductive organs and the management of birth. Detailed anthropological texts on menstruation cross-culturally have emerged (Buckley and Gottlieb 1988; Gottlieb 1990; Marcus 1992). Strathern (1992) has unravelled the legal presumptions in reproductive technology showing them to be ethnocentric rather than scientifically neutral.

Sexuality, the gendered body, the gendered division of labour and an attention to gendered voices and experiences, masculine and feminine, are now part of some academic agendas. None the less, there are areas of sexuality which remain controversial, as women and some men have extended their anthropological gaze to masculine sexuality, especially heterosexuality (Arnold 1978; Hart 1994; Cornwall 1994).

There continues to be a popularist demand for overall and daring overviews, something which anthropologists, trained in micro-studies, have been reluctant to attempt. Consequently, the ethnographies of anthropologists may be raided, especially when approaching the ever-sensationalist areas of sexuality. Greer's dense and mass-marketed tome on sex and fertility (1986)[6] invited readers to consider alternative non-Western forms of birth control and female circumcision from a culturally relativist perspective. Greer, like her cohort of feminists now confronting middle age, found a paucity of literature on yet another taboo subject of women's sexuality: the menopause (Greer 1991). Here there is less use of cross-cultural material, partly because even the earlier reporters of exotic erotica lacked any consideration of this topic. This absence of material is possibly because menopause has been thought to be about the loss of female sexuality, not just fertility, and therefore only of concern to the subjects who experience it, rather than to those male subjects who perceive women primarily as sexual objects.

In the context of the 1990s in a different political and economic climate, popularist demands from women readers about other cultures will inevitably have changed. The extent to which women wish to popularise gendered, anthropological research from within the discipline remains open to question. In any case, gendered research continues to be affected by institutional structures. Even in the 1990s, the majority of undergraduates, whose task it is to read the academic publications, are largely female, yet women researchers relative to men are still grossly under-represented, and the proportion of women in university positions in British social anthropology remains minuscule. Women, whatever their research interests and standpoints, are still not writing half – let alone the majority of – academic anthropological texts.[7]

NOTES

1 The professor, who had escaped the LSE, saw no contradiction in being a member of All Souls College, whose privileges were exclusively for males. The seminars at Queen Elizabeth House led eventually to the founding of the Centre for the Cross Cultural Studies of Women.
2 The one woman sociologist in the department, Ruth First, joined me in scepticism. Her pioneering work and political struggle, which eventually brought her assassination, embraced the analysis of sexuality and racist, gender and class divisions in apartheid South Africa.
3 In the late 1970s, I found it a useful addition to my course reading list.
4 Oakley's *Sex, Gender and Society* (1972) was published under the auspices of *New Society* rather than via academic publishers.
5 Moore's overview (1988) does not address questions of sexuality and the body.
6 It was hailed by Fay Weldon in *The Times* as one of the greatest books of the twentieth century, to be compared to Marx's *Das Kapital*.
7 Julie Marcus puts it more starkly: 'Today, the major arguments within the discipline of anthropology remain arguments among men and about men, arguments about the matters men consider important; those matters remain those of the past-relations between men' (1992: viii).

REFERENCES

Abramson, A. (1993) 'Between autobiography and method: being male, seeing myth and the analysis of structures of gender and sexuality in the eastern interior of Fiji', in D. Bell, P. Caplan and W. J. Karim (eds) *Gendered Fields*, London: Routledge.

Ardener, E. (1975) 'Belief and the problem of women', in S. Ardener (ed.) *Perceiving Women*, London: Malaby Press.

Ardener, S. (ed.) (1975a) *Perceiving Women*, London: Malaby Press.

—— (1975b) 'Sexual insult and female militancy', in S. Ardener (ed.) *Perceiving Women*, London: Malaby Press.

Arnold, K. (1978) 'The whore in Peru', in S. Lipshitz (ed.) *Tearing the Veil*, London: Routledge and Kegan Paul.

Barker, D. (1978) 'Women in the anthropology profession – 1', in R. Rohrlich-Leavitt (ed.) *Women Cross-Culturally: Change and Challenge*, The Hague: Mouton.

Beauvoir, S. de (1949) *Le Deuxième sexe*, trans. H. Parshley, Paris: Gallimard.

—— (1965) *Force of Circumstance*, Harmondsworth: Penguin.

—— (1972) *The Second Sex*, Harmondsworth: Penguin.

Blackstone, T. (1976) 'The education of girls today', in J. Mitchell and A. Oakley (eds) *The Rights and Wrongs of Women*, Harmondsworth: Penguin.

Bloch, M. (1983) *Marxism and Anthropology*, Oxford: Clarendon Press.

Boulay, J. du (1974) *Portrait of a Greek Mountain Village*, Oxford: Oxford University Press.

Bowlby, J. (1951) *Maternal Care and Mental Health*, World Health Organisation.

Buckley, T. and Gottlieb, A. (eds) (1988) *Blood Magic: The Anthropology of Menstruation*, Berkeley: University of California Press.

Callaway, H. (1978) '"The most essentially female function of all": giving birth', in S. Ardener (ed.) *Defining Females*, London: Croom Helm.

Caplan, P. (1978) 'Women in the anthropology profession – 2', in R. Rohrlich-Leavitt (ed.) *Women Cross-Culturally: Change and Challenge*, The Hague: Mouton.

—— (ed.) (1987) *The Cultural Construction of Sexuality*, London: Routledge.

Cornwall, A. (1994) 'Gendered identities and gender ambiguity among *travestis* in Salvador Brazil', in A. Cornwall and N. Lindisfarne (eds) *Dislocating Masculinity*, London: Routledge.

Delmar, R. (1976) 'Looking again at Engels's *Origin of the Family, Private Property and the State*', in J. Mitchell and A. Oakley (eds) *The Rights and Wrongs of Women*, Harmondsworth: Penguin.

The Diagram Group (1977) *Woman's Body: An Owner's Manual*, London: Paddington Press.

Douglas, M. (1966) *Purity and Danger*, London: Routledge and Kegan Paul.

Evans-Pritchard, E. (1951) *Theories of Primitive Religion*, Oxford: Oxford University Press.

Faithorn, E. (1975) 'The concept of pollution among the Kafe of the Papua New Guinea highlands', in R. Reiter (ed.) *Toward an Anthropology of Women*, New York and London: Monthly Review Press.

Frazer, J. (1900) *The Golden Bough: A Study in Magic and Religion*, London.

Gottlieb, A. (1990) 'Rethinking female pollution: the Beng case (Côte d'Ivoire)', in P. Reeves Sanday and R. Gallagher (eds) *Beyond the Second Sex*, Goodenough, Phil.: University of Pennsylvania Press.

Greer, G. (1986) *Sex and Destiny: The Politics of Human Fertility*, New York: Harper and Row.

—— (1991) *The Change*, London: Hamish Hamilton.

Haraway, D. (1989) *Primate Visions*, New York: Routledge.

Hart, A. (1994) 'Missing masculinity? Prostitutes' clients in Alicante, Spain', in A. Cornwall and N. Lindisfarne (eds) *Dislocating Masculinity*, London: Routledge.

Hastrup, K. (1978) 'The semantics of biology: virginity', in S. Ardener (ed.) *Defining Females*, London: Croom Helm.

Hirschon, R. (1978) 'Open body/closed space: the transformation of female sexuality', in S. Ardener (ed.) *Defining Females*, London: Croom Helm.

Kaberry, P. (1939) *Aboriginal Woman: Sacred and Profane*, London: Routledge and Kegan Paul.

Kitzinger, S. (1978) *Women as Mothers*, London: Fontana.

Kulick, D. and Willson, M. (1995) *Taboo: Sex, Identity and Erotic Subjectivity in Anthropological Fieldwork*, London: Routledge.

La Fontaine, J. S. (1972) 'Ritualization of women's life-crises in Bugisu', in J. S. La Fontaine (ed.) *The Interpretation of Ritual*, London: Tavistock.

Leach, E. (1969) 'Virgin birth', in *Genesis as Myth*, London: Cape.

Lévi-Strauss, C. (1963) *Totemism*, Harmondsworth: Penguin.

—— (1967) 'The effectiveness of symbols', in *Structural Anthropology* vol. I, London: Allen Lane.

Liedloff, J. (1975/1986) *The Continuum Concept*, London: Duckworth/ Harmondsworth: Penguin.

MacClancy, J. (1986) 'Unconventional character and disciplinary convention: John Layard, Jungian and anthropologist', in G. Stocking (ed.) *Malinowski, Rivers, Benedict and Others*, Madison: University of Wisconsin Press.

—— (1993) Introduction to *Popularising Anthropology*, J. MacClancy and C. McDonaugh (eds), London: Routledge (in press).

Malinowski, B. (1922) *Argonauts of the Western Pacific*, London: Routledge and Kegan Paul.

—— (1929/1932) *The Sexual Life of Savages*, London: Routledge and Kegan Paul, 1932 edition referred to in text.

—— (1967) *A Diary in the Strict Sense of the Term*, London: Routledge and Kegan Paul.

Marcus, J. (1992) *A World of Difference: Islam and Gender Hierarchy in Turkey*, London: Zed Press.

Martin, E. (1987) *The Woman in the Body*, Boston: Beacon Press.

Mead, M. (1928) *Coming of Age in Samoa*, Harmondsworth: Penguin.

—— (1935) *Sex and Temperament in Three Primitive Societies*, Harmondsworth: Penguin.

—— (1949) *Male and Female*, Harmondsworth: Penguin.

Moore, H. (1988) *Feminism and Anthropology*, Cambridge: Polity Press.

Morgan, E. (1972) *The Descent of Woman*, London: Souvenir Press.

Morris, D. (1967) *The Naked Ape*, New York: Dell Publishers.

Oakley, A. (1972) *Sex, Gender and Society*, London: Temple Smith.

—— (1974) *The Sociology of Housework*, London: Martin Robertson.

Oakley, A. and Mitchell, J. (eds) (1976) *The Rights and Wrongs of Women*, Harmondsworth: Penguin.

Okely, J. (1975a) 'Gypsy women: models in conflict' in S. Ardener (ed.) *Perceiving Women*, London: Malaby Press (See ch. 4, this volume).

—— (1975b) 'Malinowski's interpretation of sex and reproduction: a reappraisal'. Unpublished paper for the Women's Anthropology Seminar, Oxford.

—— (1986) *Simone de Beauvoir: A Re-Reading*, London: Virago.

Ortner, S. (1974) 'Is female to male as nature is to culture?', in M. Rosaldo and L. Lamphere (eds) *Woman, Culture and Society*, Stanford: Stanford University Press.

Ortner, S. and Whitehead, H. (eds) (1981) *Sexual Meanings: The Cultural Construction of Gender and Sexuality*, Cambridge: Cambridge University Press.

Phillips, R. (1976) *Our Bodies Ourselves*, London: Simon and Schuster.

Paul, L. (1974) 'The mastery of work and the mystery of sex in a Guatemalian village', in M. Rosaldo and L. Lamphere (eds) *Woman, Culture and Society*, Stanford: Stanford University Press.

Reed, E. (1975) *Woman's Evolution: From Matriarchal Clan to Patriarchal Family*, London: Pathfinder.

—— (1978) *Sexism and Science*, New York and London: Pathfinder.

Reiter, R. (ed.) (1975) *Toward an Anthropology of Women*, New York and London: Monthly Review Press.

Richards, A. (1956) *Chisungu*, London: Faber and Faber.

Rosaldo, M. and Lamphere, L. (eds) (1974) *Woman, Culture and Society*, Stanford: Stanford University Press.

Rowbotham, S. (1973) *Woman's Consciousness, Man's World*, Harmondsworth: Penguin.

—— (1990) *The Past is Before Us*, Harmondsworth: Penguin.

Rubin, G. (1975) 'The traffic in women: notes on the "political economy" of sex', in R. Reiter (ed.) *Toward an Anthropology of Women*, New York and London: Monthly Review Press.

Shuttle, P. and Redgrove, P. (1978) *The Wise Wound: Menstruation and Everywoman*, Harmondsworth: Penguin.

Skultans, V. (1970) 'The symbolic significance of menstruation and menopause', *Man* 5, 4: 639–51.

Slocum, S. (1975) 'Woman the gatherer: male bias in anthropology', in R. Reiter (ed.) *Toward an Anthropology of Women*, London and New York: Monthly Review Press.

Sperling, S. (1991) 'Baboons with briefcases: feminism, functionalism, and sociobiology in the evolution of primate gender', *Signs* 17, 1.

Strathern, M. (1992) *Reproducing the Future*, Manchester: Manchester University Press.

Walters, M. (1978) *The Nude Male*, Harmondsworth: Penguin.

Woolf, M. (1972) *Women and the Family in Rural Taiwan*, Stanford: Stanford University Press.

Yans-Mclaughlin, V. (1989) 'Margaret Mead', in U. Gacs, A. Khan, J. McIntyre and R. Weinberg (eds) *Women Anthropologists: Selected Biographies*, Illinois: University of Illinois Press.

Chapter 7

Girls and their bodies

The curriculum of the unconscious

This is a popularist introduction to chapter 8 which gives the wider ethnographic context of the gendering and class acculturation of some female bodies.

I can still remember a great deal about my years from nine to eighteen at an English boarding school in the fifties. But only now, as an adult and social anthropologist, can I analyse the experience. What I say about the 1950s may be relevant to girls' bodies at other times and other cultures once subjected to British colonialism, and in some instances regardless of class.[1]

Both public boarding school boys and girls are educated away from towns, from other social classes, from home and family, and normally from members of the opposite sex. Each gender has a contrasting future, although they unite in marriage. Males are generally educated for power, and females less explicitly for dependence. The powerful marry the dependent, who give birth to legitimate heirs. Like the disease of haemophilia, power may be transmitted through females but is only manifest in males.

Today, less emphasis is placed on the girl's biological virginity, but her social virginity must remain intact. Ideally a public school girl should eventually marry a man of the same 'background'. Despite the possibly greater use of higher education by upper-class girls since the sixties, such accomplishments may become merely a new cultural dowry, rather than the means to independence.

But I remember an earlier time when, with thirteen O levels and while working for four A levels, I was advised against university by the school authorities. It was suggested instead that I make use of my A levels in art and French, by training as a designer of corsets and lingerie for a famous company in Switzerland. Exuberance was to be sublimated and strapped in whale bones and elastic. Scholarship would be lost in lace.

Such concern for 'bodily containment' was central to the girls' boarding school. The training of the child's body is a 'curriculum of the unconscious'. A system of beliefs or principles can be implanted by bodily training because, as the French theorist, Pierre Bourdieu (1977), has suggested, the body is treated as a 'memory', which is not easily obliterated by conscious thought. Bodily lessons may be taught without the pupils' intellectual collaboration.

But the body and its feelings may resist, as the following example shows. Our school reports contained a section headed 'Physical Culture' which was subdivided into 'gymnastics, games, deportment and swimming'. Under gymnastics and games, an entry for my sister read: 'Does not exert herself at all, so has made no progress.' Another term read: 'Can stand and move well but is inclined to droop. Has ability but lacks the concentration to make good use of it.' Yet the same sister gyrated and rocked whenever possible to the music of Elvis Presley; so obsessively that her friends paid for her membership of the Presley fan club. Nothing arrived in the post. Weeks later, my sister was summoned to the headmistress, who opened a drawer full of the offending literature which she intended to destroy. When my sister asked if she might be allowed to keep one picture, she was rebuked in the following terms: 'You are fit only to dance at Hammersmith Palais!'

The choice of a stigmatised working-class institution was apt. For, in the 1950s, Elvis came as a vulgar force to rock our refinement. He represented the tabooed proletarian phallus which, as with any phallus, was explicitly denied by our schooling. His greased coiffure, echo-chamber vowels and sequined legs mocked English men in tweeds and brown (not blue) suede shoes. Those furtive dormitory jives to Radio Lux were our bodily rebellions, however comical they seem today.

There were other bodily restrictions. Independent movement beyond the school grounds was rarely permitted for the girls. Only the five or six prefects were ever allowed out alone and into town. The other girls walked at set times in crocodile, or in threes, away from the town, which they entered perhaps twice a term under escort. Movement within the grounds was also strictly regulated. The timetable dictated each girl's exact location. Rules forbade running and talking in passages at all times. The awesome stillness and silence in girls' schools, in contrast to boys' schools, have often been noted by visitors.

The girls' bodily posture was constantly reviewed. At all times the pupils were to sit, stand or walk erect, chin up, back straight and shoulders well back. The games mistresses, as guardians of the girls' bearing and movement, wielded considerable power. Girls were scrutinised at meals, in chapel and in 'roll call'. The fear was to be poked unexpectedly in the back by a bayonet finger, when a girl lolled forward. There were good and bad deportment marks, and cups to be won. The ultimate approval by the authorities was indicated by a red felt badge embroidered with the word 'Deportment', and sewn on the left side of the tunic.

The matron held dominion over the girls' bodily appearance and health. Uniform was checked, finger nails inspected. Hair which touched the back of the collar had to be cut, because longer hair hinted at sexuality. Illness tended to be treated as social malingering. The patient was isolated in the sick room and forbidden books, wireless and visits. Whether the symptoms were flu, nausea, a high temperature, lassitude or headaches, solid foods were generally banned. The only bodily intakes would be tea, Bovril or plain water, sometimes for days on end. I would hallucinate and imagine I could smell burnt toast. When each girl's temperature approached normal she had to eat her first food of cornflakes sitting over a sick bucket, alongside other desperate inmates.

Matrons hovered over the girls' nightly sleep, although not like the angels sung of in hymns. Being found out of bed or talking 'after lights out' brought the punishment of detention on Saturdays. Our reclining posture was also observed. Girls were not to lie on their backs with knees bent. Thus was sexual shame to be instilled.

Figure 7.1 The author and friend after First Communion with hands chastely placed.
Source: Bridget Okely.

Figure 7.2 The author and friend outside school: hands loose, legs apart.
Source: Edward Stanford.

Male bodies were rare intrusions in the school grounds. Two elderly men visited for a few A level classes. Having retired from teaching boys, they were cultural eunuchs, considered safe for girls. Other males seen about included two non-resident gardeners and the boilerman; the shadows of a stigmatised class. The girls found a peripatetic phallic symbol in the headmistress's male dachshund, who sat on her lap at the centre of the school photograph. The daily absence of men did not mean feminist potential, since men were explicitly recognised as superior.

The school chaplain was the guardian of the girls' spiritual body and disembodied soul. The presence of males in the girls' religious ritual symbolically affirmed the continuity of patriarchal rule. Only men could preach to us. Women just gave us 'rows' (strict talkings-to). The chaplain prepared the girls for their *rite de passage* into Anglican adulthood. Our confirmation gave us the right to take and eat the body, and drink the blood of our male god. Until the 1990s, only males were given the power of 'laying on of hands', and of consecrating and bestowing the sacred bread and wine. In a culture where women are seen as sexual objects and reduced to handmaidens, they cannot be permitted to stand as exposed bodies at the altar, and in a position of power.

At our confirmation, we neophytes were clothed as virgin brides in white coats and white veils; a British purdah. The girls' bodies were properly covered, as they knelt for the bishop's touch on their veiled heads. A photograph of my best friend and me (figure 7.1), after our First Communion, shows us unconsciously assuming an ideal pose, with our hands protectively placed on the lower body. Another photograph (figure 7.2) shows us out of school one weekend the same year. The pose is different. In our smuggled home clothes we stand with hands loosely by our sides and legs well apart.

The day before our confirmation, the profane body had already been broached in a separate ritual. The neophytes walked unaccompanied, on this unique occasion, from the school grounds to the local church. Here we were to write down all our sins in special notebooks with printed questions on each page. One question was, 'Have I defiled my body?' So unspoken was the topic of sexuality in the public sphere, that I didn't know what it meant. I thought it might be squeezing spots. We read out our sins to the school chaplain or the local vicar. Tears rolled as I confessed to cheating once in a Latin test and to disliking some of my custodians.

After absolution, we returned to the school and handed our notebooks to the boilerman, who committed them to the eternal flames of the school boiler. Thus the man at the lowest end of the class structure intervened to deal with our impurity, while the bishop, at the apex, a member of the House of Lords, gave us purity and access to the faith of the majority of the governing elite. None of this we found peculiar or funny. Body and soul were committed to this sacred event. One fear was that it might be the 'wrong time of the month' and that we might offer an unclean body to the bishop and Christ.

In this ceremony led by men, our impotence as non-men was effectively confirmed. The girls could not identify with the elusive bishop and his phallic crook, nor with the male body on the cross. The Virgin Mary's veiled head and unmarked body never featured on the altar, but below it and to the side. Our reception into the Anglican communion simultaneously separated us from other peoples and races, in this year of the Suez crisis and the Hungarian uprising. Our veiled progress up the aisle was the dress rehearsal for a future marriage, and for the day of first savouring the one man's flesh.

In contrast to the tradition of boys' public schools, girls are not controlled by the threat of corporal punishment. The girl's body remains fully clothed and untouchable. This apparently more humane treatment coincides with a system which entails greater intervention in the inmates' lives. Psychological exposure replaces immediate physical pain. From infancy, girls are expected to be, and are made, more modest and self-effacing than boys. So a public 'stripping' as an individual wrongdoer is all the more threatening. For example, in my school a girl might be made to stand while everyone else remained seated. There were many variations of this public punishment. The individual miscreant so treated became a conspicuous bodily shape, as if a cut-out from a group photograph. The more the girls complied with the ideals of modesty and invisibility, the more terrifying any public exposure. Alternative humiliations were used; for example, the matron would make a deviant girl sit under her surgery table as, with full refinement, she consumed tea and scones above.

The school uniform elaborated an invisibility of the body. Female curves were skilfully concealed by the tunic's shape. Two pairs of knickers were obligatory. This double layer symbolically shielded virginity. The unsexing of the female body was also observable in the uniform's ill-assorted male traits: school ties, lace-up shoes, blazers and striped shirts. The girls were dressed as if imitating men, whom they could and should never become. The uniform contradicted the demand that they appear 'feminine' upon leaving school. A feeling of impotence is doubly felt if male bodily apparel (like the phallus) is represented to girls as the unattainable ideal. After school, the girls would cast off their ambiguous clothing, along with any ambitions independent of men.

Sport is the body's playground. Whereas the games favoured in the girls' boarding curriculum impose artificial limits on the girls' potential, those in boys' schools tend to develop the body's potential. This gender bias is found also in state schools and is continuous. Sports exclusively for males include rugby, football and boxing.[2] Those mainly for females include netball, lacrosse and hockey. The last two are sometimes played by boys, but alongside at least one of the male sports. Tennis and occasionally cricket are played by both sexes. In my school, games were compulsory every day. They included netball and hockey, with tennis and rounders on limited occasions.

Differences between the male and female sports indicate different bodily experience. Certain characteristics of male sports are absent from the sports permitted for females. Rugby demands physical contact between the players. The arms and whole body are used as weapons. Players are expected to throw themselves and their opponents to the ground. Neither physical contact nor such use of the body is permitted in girls' sports. This kind of bodily behaviour among women is so taboo that the Greater London Council for years banned public displays of female wrestling.

Both rugby and football require vigorous kicking of the ball, and thus the opening and raising of the legs. Females must never kick balls, lest perhaps they kick the other kind. Females who raise and kick the leg are seen, in the dominant male ideology, to be metaphorically exposing their genitals. This movement, without a target, is institutionalised in the titillating can-can. In a faded photograph from school (figure 7.3), I am posing with three friends

Figure 7.3 A tentative and tabooed raising of the leg.

in a 'Tiller Girl' line. One leg is slightly raised in a mock can-can. This tentative inversion of the correct boarding-school girl stance provokes a coy grin from another girl, with legs locked together and both feet grounded.

In the public and state school sports curriculum generally, the 'weaker sex' is made weaker, being forbidden aggressive and defensive use of the legs, arms, feet and body. However, manual dexterity is encouraged in handling, 'dribbling' and 'cradling' the ball. Speed in running is thereby inhibited. Cricket and tennis, played by men, also demand manual dexterity, but such skills are acquired by men in addition to the other skills. These games are permissible for females because they lack the characteristics of exclusively male sport.

Although lacrosse and hockey pitches may be of a size comparable to those for rugby and football, movement for females in that space is always encumbered by holding a stick in both hands. Rugby and football players can at times run free and fast, hurtling through space. Even the rugby player's flight is not greatly impeded by holding the ball. For females, only in netball is movement free of a stick, but it is restricted within the smaller space.

When contrasting the exclusively male with the mainly female sports, we find that schoolgirls must limit their expectations in use of space, speed, bodily attack and defence. They are left untouched, with feminine dexterity and an eye for detail. For boarding-school girls, the greater restrictions encountered and learnt on the hockey and netball pitches are similar to the restricted movements enforced within school grounds.

Ballet and dance are alternative forms of exercise where girls need not necessarily feel that they are failed men. In my school, these had to be paid for as extras, and were compulsorily combined with ballroom dancing. Here, the quickstep and waltzes gave the sole institutionalised physical contact between persons. The girls, as surrogate man and wife, experienced a tactile premonition of adult life.

Ballroom dancing again reflects the opposing gender ideals. The male fittingly leads the female, who walks backwards into the future. She is entirely dependent on the male's vision of the path ahead. If her partner is a poor dancer, she is helpless to improve his performance.

As in other aspects of schooling, feminine dependency is learnt in the body.

NOTES

1 When I presented this to the Women's Inter-Congress of the IAEUS in Delhi 1978, a number of upper-class Indian women found echoes from their own boarding schools, originally established by the British.
2 Since the mid-1980s some women's rugby and football teams have emerged. But these and many other sports are still male dominated, as any TV sports programme or newspaper section demonstrates.

REFERENCE

Bourdieu, P. (1977) *Outline of a Theory of Practice*, Cambridge: Cambridge University Press.

Chapter 8

Privileged, schooled and finished

Boarding education for girls

THEORETICAL AND METHODOLOGICAL QUESTIONS

The public school has moulded a large proportion of the dominant male elite in British society, as well as their wives and mothers.[1] It has also had a wider influence and has affected, albeit elusively, the alternative state form of schooling. While we find considerable research into public schools for boys,[2] there is little serious investigation of the girls' schools, nor indeed of the larger topic of gender differentiation in education.[3] It is assumed either that girls' boarding schools are replicas of those for boys, or that they are of peripheral importance. The male and female institutions are not analysed as parts of one system. In addition to the studies of boys' schools, we have a plethora of autobiographies by men, while little comparable information exists from women, since few achieve the status which calls for an account of themselves.[4]

Statements about the educational achievements of 'the middle class' have tended to conceal their gender bias. Certainly some middle-class girls attend schools, boarding or day, of high academic quality, which encourage independent careers for their pupils. But there are other middle- or upper-class girls who are denied this, and *precisely because of their class*. The development of a distinct class consciousness is seen as more important than scholarship and achievement for them, as are beliefs which maintain the boundaries of their class. The girls are protected for a future marriage contract within an elite whose biological and social reproduction they ensure. They have no economic and political power independent of males such as their fathers, and later their husbands and sons. Born into a privileged and powerful elite, the women learn to live ambitions only vicariously through men.

The girls' school may be, invisibly, a preparation for dependence, while the boys' school is more visibly a preparation for independence and power. Some of the lessons of a girls' boarding school carry uncertainties, or are inapplicable in later life. There is greater continuity for boys who, for example, are not confronted with the marriage–career dilemma which, for girls, becomes a source of conflict within their identity as female. In the boys' education, self-confidence, the experience of leadership and ambitious expectations are what count. Paradoxically, academic qualifications may not be crucial for public school boys who, even if they do not progress to university, often move into lucrative and prestigious occupations not made available to their sisters with possibly equal potential. The girls' expectations are circumscribed by marriage.

The boys' and girls' educations are not symmetrical but they are ideologically interdependent. That considered female is partly defined by its opposite: that which is considered to be male. The characteristics of one institution are strengthened by their absence in the other. Qualities primarily reserved for one gender will have a different meaning in the institution for the opposing gender. The two educations are also linked in practice since, in adulthood, individuals from the separate institutions will be united in marriage, for the consolidation of their class. As members of the same social class the girls and boys may share similar educational experiences, but as members of different gender categories some of their education may differ. This aspect is also considered below. Little emphasis is placed here on the academic curriculum and the transmission of knowledge associated with it. Instead attention is paid to the kind of instruction received in contexts other than the classroom lesson, but which is nevertheless integral to public school education.

The ethnographic material for this preliminary enquiry is largely autobiographical, my main informant being myself. Only these resources are explored fully here. In due course they may be synthesised with accounts by other former residents of boarding schools, including those giving the perspective of the staff, which, of course, will be quite different. Subsequent comparative research will necessarily reveal a diversity of experiences and understanding. Many women will have enjoyed their boarding schools, especially those who fulfilled the aims of that education. But for some, including myself, it failed to teach its terms. If my sister and I had learnt our lessons correctly, it is unlikely that we should have gone to university. The extent to which my boarding school is 'typical' of its time, the 1950s, or is similar to any such institution years later, cannot be examined here.[5] Obviously there will be considerable variations and changes.

I deliberately confront the notion of objectivity in research by starting with the subjective, working from the self outwards. The self – the past self – becomes a thing, an object. Yet this past creates and governs the present and future. Even social anthropologists who usually study other cultures are led back from the other to the self. Indeed Pocock (1973, 1975) has suggested that there is a need to explore the totality of one's 'personal anthropology' and its consequences in order to be able fully to perceive others.[6] This interest in the subjective is no doubt strengthened by my being female and brought up so. Women's language of experience is often distinctly personal, but the general implications are always there to be found. We must therefore explore the abstractions contained in our anecdotes.

A word on the epistemological status of the autobiographical. It is retrospective – unlike a diary which is the record of the present. There will be a loss of memory. Some forgotten experiences may nevertheless affect the narrator unconsciously. The past will have become distorted. Misunderstandings will be revealed later if accounts of events are cross-checked with others who were present at the time. But their information will also be skewed. The accuracy of childhood events may, however, be less important than the child's perception of them. They may have important repercussions in later life, some of which may be contrary to the conscious intentions of instructors and parents. The validity of autobiographical material is no different from many presentations by social anthropologists based on data gathered from informants during their fieldwork. The former is merely one account of what is believed to have existed, whereas the latter often include several autobiographical accounts which have been collapsed into one version.

I am concerned with what I believed happened. My information is based on nine years as a boarding school girl in the 1950s and on all the subsequent years of retrospective analysis. Participant observation (methodologically crucial to social anthropologists) is perfectly split. In the study of childhood a temporal split between participation and observation is special, and in some instances unavoidable, because children cannot articulate their experiences in the language of adults. Only after childhood can it be thus expressed. When young we found the school world the reality, the norm, the only rationality. That was its power. My mother has often said since, 'But why didn't you tell me?' We, my sister and I, could not discriminate that which now seems bizarre. Whenever I inwardly questioned aspects of this education, I thought myself mad, and identified with the mad and isolated, for example, Nijinsky, Van Gogh and other heroes of Colin Wilson's *The Outsider* (1956).

THE GIRLS' BOARDING SCHOOL

Boarding academies for ladies existed in the eighteenth century, offering certain 'accomplishments'. But most of the now famous girls' public schools were established at the end of the nineteenth century and later, long after the boys' public schools were founded. Even in the 1920s and 1930s many middle- and upper-class girls, for example Jessica Mitford and her sisters (Mitford 1977), were kept at home to be taught by governesses, whereas their brothers were sent away to school. My mother had a governess until the age of sixteen. Her five enjoyable terms at the school I later attended were a release from a somewhat claustrophobic home and gave her a chance to meet other girls. Her brothers went to boarding school at an early age, but her younger sisters never went to school.

The girls' public boarding schools may have been depicted as a new freedom and advance in women's education, but there were important class interests. Pauline Marks has noted that in 1898 in England, 70 per cent of girls in secondary education were in private boarding schools 'often in towns where grammar and high schools had empty places'. The advantage of the schools they attended was their social homogeneity: 'eligibility for marriage and not the content of their daughter's education remained the dominant concern of middle-class parents' (Marks 1976: 189). These observations are relevant to at least one girls' boarding school in the 1950s.

Even though both private and state schools have been affected by various reforms, including sometimes the principle of equality of opportunity for women, they have failed to resolve a persistent dichotomy, the choice for the future for girls between a career and marriage with motherhood. This is reinforced by a sexual division of labour which, both inside and outside the home, perpetuates women's relative economic dependence and insecurity, whatever their social class, and whether married or single. Educational reform alone cannot resolve this. Its confused policies have alternated from an unrealisable attempt at assimilation of female education into the male model, to an emphasis on teaching the qualities supposedly required of women as wives and mothers; other skills being regarded as secondary (cf. Marks 1976: 185–9).

It is not surprising that the dilemma between a career and marriage scarcely arose in a middle-class and relatively undistinguished boarding school such as mine. Ideally, marriage was the ultimate vocation. Without records of the stated intentions of my teachers, I reconstruct these from remembered incidents. Some slogans remain: we were 'fortunate to be receiving a good education', and we believed it. Yet if there was academic intent, this was not borne out by the girls' performance, since the majority left after taking a few GCE O levels. Out of a class containing up to 35 girls, six or less remained to take sometimes a single A level – an accomplishment which simultaneously prohibited university ambition. There is no memory of the word equality. The pattern after school tended to be a year at a private domestic science or finishing school, preferably in Switzerland, and progress to an exclusive secretarial college. The ideal was to be a debutante, before making a 'good marriage'. Another respectable vocation was nursing, and then only at select London hospitals. Teachers' training was *déclassé*. Whereas work as a private secretary or nurse offered contact with a man of the right social class, teaching did not. Few, if any, of the girls entered occupations comparable to their brothers'.

Scholarly achievements and higher education were, nevertheless, reserved for a few girls,[7] possibly marked as vocational spinsters. These had also to conform to the school's ideas of good conduct. Academic proficiency did not guarantee encouragement.

With thirteen O levels and while studying for four A levels, I was summoned to the senior mistress. She declared I would be 'selfish to go to university, *even* Aberystwyth', thereby depriving a worthier person of a place. She suggested a career which would make use of my A levels in French and Art – by training as a designer of corsets and lingerie for a famous company in Switzerland.

SEPARATIONS

The British boarding school is marked by its forms of separation from urban culture, from other social classes, from family and home, and from the opposite sex. Anthropologists have devoted much attention to *rites de passage*, ceremonies associated for example with birth, adulthood, marriage and death. In the transition of persons from one status to another, a frequent element is the separation of the individual (socially, spatially and temporally) from 'normal life' and from the community at large. In some initiation rites marking the transition from childhood to adulthood, the neophytes are grouped together, separated from the village, perhaps in the forest, and subjected to painful physical experiences, such as circumcision. They are instructed by selected adults in the sacred mysteries of their culture, by the use of special songs and sacred masks. Their pain is mingled with drama and beauty. They return with new knowledge and are reintegrated. A lasting bond is created between the neophytes who shared the same terror. The boarding school can also be seen as a *rite de passage* from childhood to adulthood.[8] The separation from 'normal' life lasts many years. Although separations exist for both boys and girls, the differing consequences for each sex will become apparent.

1 Geographical and cultural

British public schools nowadays are almost invariably set in rural areas, distant from urban concentrations, the threatening proletariat and metropolitan culture. Originally the boys' public schools were not so organised. But from 1850 they were increasingly concentrated in large buildings, and some were moved out of London, and 'set in large houses, cut off by great oceans of land from the outside world' (Gathorne-Hardy 1977: 103–5). The girls' schools followed suit. Apart from the efficacy of isolation and its greater control, the choice of the countryside was consistent with the current British belief that open spaces and fresh air improve moral, as well as bodily, health.

Our instructors never initiated us into nature's beauties, but only marched us through the landscape, two by two. Yet nature in the form of wild scenery was a fortuitous compensation. This was the only sacred knowledge acquired – from the downs, pine trees, woods and the uncontrollable south coast sea. Nature with its lack of discipline confounded their rules. It nurtured our souls.

Compared to boarding school boys, it seems that girls are permitted even less contact with the world outside the school grounds.[9] For us, the nearby town was banned, taboo, except for perhaps a termly shopping trip under strict surveillance and with our few shillings handed out on Saturdays. We retained our coppers for Sunday chapel collection. Money found on us on any other days brought the severest punishment. Thus we were withdrawn from commerce, from earning and purchase.

We left the grounds about twice a week in 'crocodile' on set rural routes, skirting the town. Over-fifteens could go out for 'walks in threes' on certain days. Parents came and 'took us out', perhaps once a term. Written contact from and to the outer world was overseen. Outgoing letters not to parents were placed in unsealed envelopes for checking, incoming mail was examined, steamed open, even confiscated in some cases.

> My sister was crazy about Elvis Presley. Her friends paid for her subscription to the Presley fan club. Nothing arrived. Weeks later, the senior mistress summoned her and showed her the pile of Presley literature. My sister was told, 'You are fit only to dance at Hammersmith Palais!' The papers and pictures were destroyed.

Presley, sexually insinuating, was part of that proletarian culture from which we were to be protected. Yet even tamer forces threatened. Except for the *Illustrated London News* and *Punch* in the library, comics and magazines were banned, even *Woman's Own*, which we read secretly in the lavatory, where its torn pages were hung by matron for wrapping our dirty sanitary towels. All personal books had to be checked and signed by staff. Our storage drawers and our mattresses were searched for any offending literature which might have come from that far, urban world. Like the neophytes, the girls were bound together as partners in pain, or we detached ourselves in shared humour, and laughed at our custodians.

2 Class

Geographical seclusion was matched by our separation from all other social classes in the strange English hierarchy. Parents of middle- or upper-middle-class children demonstrate a desire to protect them from any classes below, and from contamination in what were euphemistically called the 'local' schools. Families may see themselves as randomly scattered and without sufficient contact with others of the same class pretensions, thereby risking inter-class familiarity. The boarding school solves the technical problem. Offspring are concentrated with their kind and simultaneously separated from others. That is the meaning of 'exclusive' when applied to these institutions. When the children are home for the holidays, their parents can control their friends and contacts.

The children in such schools don't need to be told they are different and superior, since they are able to perceive it, learn it, know it for themselves. The children are isolated from any alternative life and the ways of others become the more alien. Stereotypes take form. We despised the grammar school children we had to encounter at county music competitions. They were unknown, frightening and inferior, and the males of course were unmarriageable. Henceforth we could never treat anyone from another 'background' as equal. The differentiation was epitomised in the 'accent'. Here we received support from the dominant ideology of the larger society of which we were a necessary ingredient. The children in a boarding school pool their parents' accents. Differences in a minority of girls in my school, such as the few scholarship girls, were ridiculed and mimicked until repressed. The public school accent, just as the pronunciation of any language, must be constantly reinforced through childhood. Our inner ears or class tuning forks were sensitised by years of sounds in words. If the school teaches nothing else, it stamps the child with a way of speaking and the awareness of deviation. Style spoke before content. We need only utter a few words – any assortment – to mark ourselves. The consequences of our separation would go for ever with us when reintegrated into British society. The accent is a sign and a weapon.

Along with our accents went a pooling of prejudices and values, and ways of eating and moving – even our handwriting conformed. When I arrived, aged nine, from my Lincolnshire school, my ornate looped writing had to be unlearnt; it was too proletarian. A distinct set of manners was acquired.

Many years after leaving, I met an old school friend who commented on another former inmate who appeared to have slipped down the class ladder: 'She wrote to me on lined paper. I know when a friendship has to stop.'

We were taught that we could give charity but never receive it, thus defining precisely our class position:

A dormitory mate, whose parents were abroad, asked her relatives to forward a parcel of discarded holiday clothes. Several of us shared out the luxurious dresses, skirts and sweaters. The parcel had aroused the curiosity of the authorities. We were summoned, rebuked for 'accepting charity' and bringing shame on our parents, then ordered to repack and send the items to an East London mission. I managed to conceal a skirt and pair of shoes in the recesses of the games corridor until the end of term.

3 Family and home

Ironically the fifties witnessed the popularity of Bowlby's claims that early separation from mothers would produce unstable children. The arguments were extended to schoolchildren of working mothers. The cry went up of 'latch-key' children. It was really directed at working-class mothers. The upper middle classes continued to despatch their children from home, depriving them of affection though guaranteed twenty-four-hour custodial care. In some cases boarding school has been justified as the solution after divorce or widowhood. The loss of one parent is thereby compounded by separation from the other.

Unlike prison or Borstal, we were there because our parents loved us. Prisoners and Borstal offenders know they are incarcerated in order to suffer for their own misdeeds. Their relatives and parents may lament and oppose their sentences. Even if the parents of a Borstal offender assisted the authorities, it would be apparent that they had failed as parents or rejected their offspring. The trick for us at boarding school was that we were not ostensibly there as a punishment. We could not take responsibility for what our unconscious might tell us. Parents were wholly in collaboration with our fate. The school song made us declaim: 'It is well understood/We are here for our good/So our parents/And mistresses say/And I fancy that we/Are inclined to agree, /Though we mean it/A different way.' After each verse, the refrain concluded: 'Your lot's not a bad one at all./ NOT AT ALL!' The last line was shouted – one of the few occasions when the girls were encouraged, and indeed expected, to raise their voices.

The boarding school can appropriately be defined as a 'total institution' (Goffman 1968). The holiday intervals with parents are part of a continuous moral universe, since the parents are responsible for boarding their children and demand that they succeed there. Accepting, conforming and surviving can be a duty to the parents whose financial contribution is translated as love and sacrifice for the child's greater good. Whereas Borstal offenders may be able to nurture revenge against the establishment which sentenced them, public school children dare not think through the ultimate blame upon their parents. The 'double bind' is complete.[10] In contrast to Borstal inmates' attempts to escape, running away from school can only be an emotional appeal to the parents who made the initial decision and may merely send their child back.

We were orphans but did not know it. Ironic that each child was encouraged to have a collection box in the shape of a house – a Dr Barnardo's home. Here we placed our pennies for the 'real orphans'. 'Family Favourites' on the Sunday radio fascinated us. We unconsciously identified with the messages sent between relatives apart. Our separation meant, indeed, the loss of a personal relationship with any adult. The ratio of staff to child within the school made it technically impossible. Moreover, at least from my experience, the demands of the institution overrode even the memory of family relationships. For individuals facing the crisis of the death of a parent or relative few, if any, allowances were made.[11] Misbehaviour arising from these circumstances was punished. We defied the rules to comfort our friends in the dormitory at night.

Denied personal access to adults, we were also constrained in rigid peer groups. Friendships, even prolonged encounters, were not permitted between persons of different forms – since they threatened the rigid hierarchy with its ascending privileges and status. Only love could undermine it. Friendships between different ages were deviant and passionate, though rarely expressed in physical terms. For the authorities such relationships were seen as a dangerous emergence of sexuality and of course perversion. There were strict regulations also on intimacy between equals. No two girls were ever allowed to be in the bathroom, lavatory or small music rooms. Thus any loving relationship possible was taboo. Two girls were actually expelled, allegedly for mingling their blood from cut wrists and swearing friendship on the Bible.[12]

There appears to be a difference in the age when boys and girls in England are sent away from home. Boys are more likely to be boarded before eleven or even eight years of age (Lambert 1975: 35), while girls are more likely to be boarded from eleven or later (Ollerenshaw 1967: 128–9; Wober 1971: 44–5).[13] A minority of us were younger when we joined our school. This difference between boys and girls may have consequences for each gender's responses and expectations in adult relationships. I suggest tentatively that boys seem to be required to repress 'childish' emotional dependence sooner, and thus more violently, than girls. Boarding for a 'prep' school boy entails an early severance from the mother and her emotional power, and absorption into a future where authority is vested in men. The fearsome school matron is no mother substitute. In other societies, male initiation rites express most dramatically this break with the mother. For the girl who may be at home longer, intimacy and identification with the mother become clearly established. It is at the onset of puberty, when her social and biological virginity must be protected, that she is sent from home and the local school. By contrast, a boy's virginity is of little or no consequence. Thus both boys and girls are separated from home and parents, but not always for the same reasons.

4 Gender

Along with the hierarchy of class, another major division of British society is the segregation of the sexes. For girls, separation from boys and men will have meaning and consequences not symmetrical to that of boys in single-sex schools. Compared to the boys, girls are subjected to greater restrictions and less autonomy.[14] Female adolescence, if not childhood, is socially prolonged in such schools, for this is a dangerous time for girls who are sexually mature, but considered too young for a marriage contract. This is especially true of a girl of a wealthy class, since her prospective spouse must be well established in his occupation, and have property, either transmitted or acquired. So the boarding school offers safe segregation for girls from males of all social classes. Ollerenshaw (1967: 29) hints at this:

> Some parents and headmistresses feel that there is advantage for some girls in their being withdrawn during the school day or at boarding schools for the school term from the emotional turmoil of relationships with boys so that they may develop poise and self confidence.

Boys, it will be argued, are likewise segregated from females,[15] and are deprived of heterosexuality. Unlike girls, however, they are not separated from the vision of political power. Indeed, separation from women and the domestic sphere consolidates patriarchy. By contrast, girls in a boarding school are deprived of both heterosexuality and education for power, our glimpse of which would always be vicarious, would always be through males. Like the disease of haemophilia, as Helen Callaway once said, power can be transmitted through females but is only manifest in males. In schools such as mine, we were separated from those destined to monopolise certain political and economic spheres – those who were to acquire lucrative occupations and earn our living for us. Our own exclusive education, unlike theirs, was not for a career.

The school consisted almost entirely of females – the Head, matrons, teaching and domestic staff – most of whom were resident. The males usually seen within the school grounds can be listed:

the school chaplain;
two non-resident gardeners;
the boiler-man;
two elderly retired male teachers, for German and English A levels, who visited perhaps one day a week;
the part-time tennis coach who appeared in my last two summer terms;
the headmistress's male dachshund.[16]

The majority of girls directly heard the voice of only one male, that of the chaplain. On Sundays we occasionally had a visiting preacher. If we were lucky enough to have a wireless we could hear male voices transmitted from the outer world. Yet men lurked somewhere, unseen. The Board of Governors consisted almost entirely of men – for example, a lord, a Tory MP, JPs and bishops.[17]

Men were directly involved in our most important initiation rite, our confirmation within the established Church of England – giving the right to partake of the body and blood of our male god (who had a peculiar British flavour). The day before the laying on of hands by the bishop (the supremely visible male authority) we neophytes had to retire, not to the school chapel, but to the local church – where we had to write down all our sins in a notebook which had printed questions on each blank page. One question was, 'Have I defiled my body?' I didn't know what this meant. I thought it might be squeezing spots. After filling in our books, we then read our sins to the chaplain. We were given absolution and returned to the school to give the notebooks to 'Arold the boiler-man, who committed them to the eternal flames of the school boiler. (In earlier years the girls burned their notebooks on the hockey pitch.) Thus the man at the lowest end of the social hierarchy dealt with our impurity. The equally inaccessible bishop at the top, a member of the House of Lords, gave us purity and access to the sacred – the faith of the majority of the governing elite – while we were veiled in white, as if at a dress rehearsal for our future weddings within that elite.

The bishop's address at my mother's confirmation in 1933, in the chapel where I would also be initiated, included the following:

> You all know Mr Baldwin. About a year ago he said, 'I did what I believed to be right and I will always stick to what I believe to be right.' That exactly expresses what you and I will be trying to do. . . . A year ago I was standing by a grave . . . the inscription was very short: 'Douglas Haig, Field Marshal. . . . He trusted in God and tried to do right.' I don't think that you could have anything more splendid said of you. . . . Suppose I go back a long way and quote you a man every Englishman and woman is proud of and it is Francis Drake . . . Drake said to his ship's company, 'Let us show ourselves to be all of a company' (not a bad motto for a school) 'and let us not give the enemy cause to rejoice at our decay or over-throw.'

Parts of the bishop's address were more religiously inspiring, but hypnotically entangled with lessons about male politicians and British colonial history. Similar examples occurred in the 1950s.

Famous men, not women, were to be our heroic models. The school was divided into four cosmological 'houses', not represented by buildings but as groups of girls competing for cups in sports, conduct, drama, deportment – but not academic performance. The houses were Shackleton, Scott, Living-stone and Rhodes, after male explorers and chauvinists of the colonial kind whom we, as Penelope to Ulysses, could never imitate. We could only marry and beget these kinds of men and the bishop's heroes. Aspirations were stimulated which were simultaneously shown to be impossible for women to attain. Our impotence was confirmed. Even our classrooms were named after male, not female, writers: Shakespeare, Cowper, Kingsley (not Brontë, nor Eliot, certainly not Wollstonecraft). The choice of famous men indicates how completely an alternative, potentially revolutionary, female ideology was suppressed.[18]

With no heroines with whom to identify, heroism was always located in the mysterious 'other', from which we were to choose just one man as spouse. The male/female category was not learnt and created by observable opposition, as was possible for those in mixed schools or living at home, but by an absence or omission. There was no way either to become as men, or to find an independent female way. Our lives and potential were presented as those of failed men. We knew and learnt that women were beneath men in that hierarchy in which we ourselves believed. Only a male could confirm us, preach to us. Marriage offered the only release from this multiple separation. Without a husband, we knew we could not maintain our financial hold in the class system, however exclusive our accent and manners. Our privileges were at the mercy of men.

We learnt this also from the teachers. An exclusively female community does not necessarily have feminist aspirations, nor do its custodians provide models of ideal independence. The majority of our teachers were unmarried[19] and, apart from a few proud and self-sufficient ones, they presented themselves as victims of misfortune – so many tales of fiancés killed in the war – perhaps to justify self-confessed failure. They did not teach us to emulate themselves. We recognised our teachers as of a lower social class, some by their accents. In so far as the girls upheld beliefs in their exclusive background, they could not easily identify with women who came from the stigmatised state schools. Wober's data on girls' boarding schools in the 1960s confirm that only a minority of staff had themselves been boarded, the majority, 63.6 per cent, had been to day school (Wober 1971: 40). Women from boarding school do not wish to return there as teachers, because the desired destiny of most was a marriage which excluded a career. The same is not the case for men. Lambert's study of boys' public schools notes that: 'Most teachers . . . come from social groups which correspond to their pupils. . . . Over 70 per cent of staff in public schools were themselves educated at public schools and about 10 per cent of them were educated in their own schools' (Lambert 1975: 54). Thus the boys can more readily identify with their teachers.

CONTAINMENT AND POWERLESSNESS

It is sometimes said that girls' boarding schools are more 'homely' than boys'. Certainly there were feminine touches for us (the rose garden, the floral curtains and coloured bedspreads) and the main building was more a country house than a utilitarian edifice. Wober (1971: 282–3) notes the visual beauty of the girls' boarding schools and seems almost to justify them in the name of that beauty. But within homely or domestic quarters life may still become oppressive. We longed for love and approval from these substitute parents, our custodians, but they were not mothers with relaxed affection and visible femininity. Nor were they like fathers, for we saw how they deferred to male visitors. Girls, in contrast to boys, were addressed by their first names, a practice which states, among other things, that surnames were merely passing premarital stamps of identity. The use of the personal name may not reflect kindness though it speaks of intimacy, which in the boarding school is not reciprocated between the child named and the adult namer. Some intimacy facilitated greater control. Privacy could be thus invaded. Further research is required into variations between male and female boarding schools in the extent of control exercised. From the evidence now available, it seems that girls are more rigidly confined within the precincts of the school and subject to greater control (cf. Gathorne-Hardy 1977: 241, 246). Ollerenshaw (1967: 20) hints at the demands made by the invisible fathers who delegated control of their daughters. The girls' schools 'had to establish the academic capabilities of women . . . with the approval and support of Victorian parents – in particular Victorian fathers. Rules of behaviour and deportment were therefore strict.'

The ethnography of the school I describe includes the limitations on the girls' movement in space and time, and on their sounds and speech. Movement *beyond* the school grounds was minimal. Only the five or six prefects could ever go out alone. Control *within* these boundaries was infinitely detailed. The focus on minutiae demanding all our concentration impeded the thought of, reduced the possibility of, bolder action. What counted as crime for girls may seem petty, especially when compared to the misdemeanours of boys. But its very triviality affirmed the pervasiveness of control. For instance, to be 'out of bounds' was almost unimaginable. It rarely occurred, and carried the risk of being expelled. Our triumphs were less dramatic, although meaningful to us – when on a 'walk in three', for example, taking the lift instead of the many steps from the beach, and having the pennies to pay for it. (I still have that lift ticket in my album.)

At any time of the day and night, any day of the week, our exact location was ordained. Summer alone gave free range of the garden in the limited play periods. Otherwise we traversed the grounds on set paths to outhouse and games field. Within the buildings, we moved along the corridors to specified rooms. Rules established that each location, such as dormitory, dining room and common room, were out of bounds when the timetable demanded our presence elsewhere. As we moved according to the lines of the timetable, we could neither hurry nor linger:

No running in the passage
No talking in the passage

were cardinal rules.

Just as space, so was time subjected to a changeless grid. An electric bell rang at half-hour intervals, or more often. There was no unorganised time for doing what we wanted or going where we wanted, even at weekends. No way to decide for ourselves the next move. After lessons our prep was supervised: often seventy silent girls sat in one long room. We had no private studies. One of the very few times when the girls were not within sight of an adult was 'after lights out' in the dormitory. The punishment for talking or being found out of bed was therefore the severest. We defied the invasions of our privacy which surveillance implied by hiding in the lavatory or bathroom. I would climb on to the roof at night. A former inmate confessed that she even went for moonlit walks in the grounds. The constraints on space and time were further compounded by the rules imposing silence during the ten or so hours between lights out and the morning bell, also when lining up and entering the dining room, moving from chapel to 'roll call', indeed in all passages and inevitably in lessons. Not only were our words limited, but at all times sound was abated.[20]

Not being expected to choose, to decide and to make statements, the girls had to exercise extreme self-discipline, especially when they complied with orders which seemed either small-minded or incomprehensible. The notion of 'character' was contrasted favourably by our instructors with 'personality' – a negative trait because it carried the notion of individuality. Leadership of sorts was expected from seniors, not charisma, but the ability to lead others into a conformity to maintain a status quo predetermined by adults.

In contrast, in boys' public schools, seniors and prefects assume dictatorial powers, including the right to inflict corporal punishment, to have 'fags' (junior boys as servants) and to establish rules. They thus acquire near-adult authority before they leave school. Cyril Connolly (1961: 194–5) has compared the position of senior boys at Eton to 'feudal overlords'. Lambert describes how, in the 1960s, the boarding pupils at the top of the boys' public school hierarchies exercised 'more real power over others than sometimes the junior teachers . . . and many other teachers in day schools'. Day pupils did not experience 'this dual training in responsible authority on the one hand and obedience on the other' (Lambert 1975: 241). For girls, obedience rather than authority is emphasised. Present evidence suggests that girls' prefect power is weak compared to that of their male counterparts. Certainly the fagging system is non-existent. Wober (1971: 78) found that girls gave low priority to being a prefect, and that houses in girls' schools were rarely residential entities 'with separate authority and privilege systems' (ibid. 116). The vertical social grouping found in boys' schools coincides with the extensive supervision of juniors by seniors. The horizontal social grouping of girls coincides with the reduced authority of seniors over juniors.[21]

In girls' schools, authority is placed beyond both the pupils and teaching staff in a single individual: the headmistress.[22] This is described by Gathorne-Hardy (1977: 241–4) as 'the dictator headmistress tradition'. The position of the headmistress in my school appeared extremely powerful. Even the school magazine was edited by her. The staff had some authority, but the girls always had to defer to both staff and head. The seniors had no powers to initiate rules, they could not even give out 'bad marks' in the punishment system. The responsibilities of the 'junior sergeants', 'sergeants', 'sub-prefects' and 'prefects' consisted mainly of keeping the other girls silent in the passages and when lining up for meals, serving out the food at each long table, and reporting misdemeanours to staff. The head girl – the most coveted station for a pupil – performed mainly symbolic functions. When the entire school filed in silently to the dining room, she stood in the passage in a focal position raised four inches in a doorway. She announced the 'notices' after lunch (usually timetable changes). At the end of 'roll call' she marched out first to the military music. She helped the headmistress put on her MA gown in the vestry before daily prayers. At Sunday evensong she held the cross, processing before the chaplain. She sat on the headmistress's right at lunch on high table – her confidante, a ritual handmaid, but no innovatory leader. She had 'character', usually also an ability at games, and academic mediocrity. The closest description of this ideal type is provided in Angela Brazil's *The Nicest Girl in the School* (1909: 20–1).[23]

PUNISHMENT BY EXPOSURE

In boys' schools, punishment includes the cane – often wielded by other boys. Paradoxically the girls abdicate more freedoms without the terror of corporal punishment. How are they controlled when there is this apparently greater leniency? Foucault (1977) has demonstrated how direct and spectacular attacks on the body by public torture and execution before the eighteenth century were replaced by the more 'humane' methods of imprisonment. These controls were more effective because they entailed intervention in every aspect of the criminal's existence. Girls, too, are controlled not by material and metonymic weapons upon the flesh, but through intangible and metaphorical routes to the soul.

The system of punishment plays on the behaviour expected of girls, among whom self-control and self-negation take special forms. From infancy they are made modest, passive and withdrawn compared to boys. The pattern is already set before school, but there it is exploited, reinforced and elaborated. I use again the ethnographic example of my boarding school. The required behaviour, and that which brought the precious reward of non-interference, included modesty, deference and submission. After a misdeed, part of the punishment was a 'row' from a member of staff and later the house captain. Humility, an apologetic stance, downcast eyes – possibly tears of defeat – were the correct forms. Any appearance of pride or dignity provoked further rebukes. Self-defence was rebuked with 'Don't answer back.' The 'right attitude' was rewarded, in that the girl was permitted to merge into the group. Our 'total institution' had all the elements which Goffman (1968: 29) has described as 'stripping', by which he means loss of personal identity. Here we see a closed circuit. The more a girl successfully complied with and internalised modesty, humility and the invisibility of the self, the more devastating the threat of their opposites.

We were given a number, useless, but printed on name tapes and stamped in nails on the soles of our shoes. But there was a worse kind of 'stripping' than that described by Goffman for us: being exposed before others as deviant, and regaining individuality as wrongdoer. Both formal and informal methods of punishment had this common ingredient – public exposure, or individual visibility. To be picked out and stared at was to be stripped as naked, with feminine reticence denied. This threat seems recurrent in girls' upbringing.[24] Control in our school was maintained not by the ultimate threat of cane marks but by disembodied conduct marks engraved on the collective mind. Whereas there was only one reward for good conduct, a 'good housemark', our crimes were minutely subdivided (cf. Foucault 1977: 98). Running or talking at the inappropriate place or time and other vaguer acts of 'insolence' earned a 'disobedience' mark (or 'disso'). The slightest delay brought a 'late' mark. 'Order' marks were given for the misplacement or loss of items like uniform or books, and for offences so trivial I cannot remember. Untidiness, even poor darning, brought a 'bad housemark'. We were bound in spiders' webs of fine rules and constraints until spontaneity seemed to be a crime. On the last morning of each holiday I would lie in bed wishing that I could foresee and avoid all my future misdeeds, for their consequences were frightful.

The stage was set at daily 'roll call' where, in the presence of the entire school and staff, a girl with a 'disobedience', 'order' or 'late' had to announce the mark instead of saying 'present'. Hearts thumped as names came nearer. After a disobedience the headmistress would always ask, 'What's that for?' and the girl would have to detail her crime. While the rest of the school was sitting cross-legged on the floor, she might be asked to stand up and repeat her crime loud and clear. This public confession was also a symbolic variant of the public execution, with its necessary witnesses among whom fear of a similar fate would be generated. At 'fortnightly marks' the headmistress would read out the percentages of each girl's academic performance in the preceding weeks. We learnt that obedience and good conduct were inseparable from and superior to the intellect and academic knowledge. From our total percentage received for classwork, two points were deducted for a disobedience and one point for a late or order. The term culminated in 'Marks and Remarks' where every girl received a conduct comment, again read aloud by the headmistress to staff and school. Ideally it was 'good', but terrifying if different and among the few like 'a poor term', 'Jane resents criticism', or worse. After this ordeal a girl might weep as I did, in the lavatory.

Conduct marks were given textual form, emblazoned in a public record of crime or obedience. In the main passage at the chapel entrance, for all to see, were four boards, one for each house (Rhodes, Livingstone, Scott and Shackleton). A large sheet of paper bore the name of each house member at one edge, with columns marking each day and week of the term. A 'disso' earned a black cross, as did a bad housemark. A 'late' or 'order' brought a nought, a good housemark a vertical stroke. Every week ended with an additional column and an individual square, for painting according to individual conduct. The house colour (red for Rhodes, yellow for Livingstone, blue for Shackleton and green for Scott) was painted in for 'good' or 'normal'. There were different intermediate gradings for bad conduct, the squares being half-white and half-coloured, or all white, or half-white and half-black, in order of severity. The worst was a completely black square with the word 'disgrace' printed alongside. Thus the performance of each girl for each week of the term was mapped and open to scrutiny by everyone. The black squares generated the most curiosity and excitement and the recipient would be picked out wherever she went. At the end of term, the house with the best score in conduct would be awarded the school 'house cup', so each deviant knew the multiple consequences of her misbehaviour. A miniature cup was awarded by each captain to the 'best' girl in the house.

Informal methods of exposure were also used by staff and senior girls. A girl who talked and who failed to respond to the sergeant or prefect while lining up for the dining room was made to stand in the main passage, her back turned, not seeing those who filed past, but conspicuous to all. A miscreant might be ordered to stand in the aisle of the dining room, or made to stand up at her table throughout a meal while the entire school sat eating. The final humiliation was standing on high table, again with back turned, but abjectly visible. One matron would punish a girl by making her sit under the table in the surgery, while she had afternoon tea above.

Thus we were punished by the very terms they demanded of us. If modesty were not pre-existent or not enforced, exposure would be no terror, but instead would call for the bravado so often found among boys. The girls who rejected modesty, submission and shame were impervious to exposure. Only deprivation (such as detention on Saturday after tea and no weekend sweets) might work for them. For one, it was whispered, the slipper was used; the corporal punishment was resorted to because she behaved as a boy. Such girls were eventually expelled. For the rest of us, the more successful our conversion, the more we eliminated individuality, the more terrifying the punishment for any deviation. We were both rewarded and punished for our complicity.

In some contexts public exposure occurred without opprobrium and in pride. Like the duties of the head girl, they were mainly in ritual, in chapel. Girls would be chosen as servers at Holy Communion and for the daily Bible reading from the chapel lectern. They could speak with authority while reading the Holy Word, God's word, not mouthing their own. Here we could expose ourselves, for we were clothed in righteousness, especially on Sundays when our heads were covered by a blue veil, and we were muffled and purified. Prize-giving demanded a brief public walk, before disappearance back into the crowd, protected by the mass applause. Such exposure was different. First, because there were many prize-winners and second, because prizes were rewards for conformity. Some rewards in the form of privileges such as promotion to sergeant, sub-prefect or prefect, came with age, combined with the 'right attitude', and were welcomed. Indeed, not to be promoted with your age group meant further exposure (for instance, having to line up and sit with younger girls in the dining room). Your state of promotion, or lack of it, was doubly visible, in the felt embroidered badges of authority sewn on the uniform, and in games team membership. There were no badges for academic achievement or intelligence – that which celebrates individual and original thought, and which can subvert.

THE BODY: SUBJUGATED AND UNSEXED

The concern with demeanour and carriage is one aspect of a total view of the body which reflects the extent of the institution's invasion and the ambivalences of its intentions. Mauss (1936) has discussed the ways different societies, groups and forms of education make use of the body. These may change over time and there are individual variations. Mauss isolates three factors: social, psychological and biological.

> In all the elements of the art of using the human body, the facts of education are dominant. . . . The child, the adult, imitates actions which have succeeded and which he has seen to succeed among persons in whom he has confidence and who have authority over him.
>
> (Mauss 1936: 369)

In the girls' boarding school, the pupils must acquire such movements. They may give the longed-for anonymity, as well as conspicuous selection as a team member. Within our school there could be no 'natural' movement which might contradict what the authorities considered correct. 'Bad' ways we had learnt elsewhere had to be changed. We did not merely unconsciously imitate movements and gestures, we were consciously made to sit, stand and move in uniform ways. We were drilled and schooled, not by those in whom we had confidence, but by those who had power over us. Our flesh was unscarred, yet our gestures bore their marks.[25] Even when outside the classroom or off the games field, we were to sit, stand and walk erect, chin up, back straight, shoulders well back. At table when not eating, our hands were to rest in our laps. During the afternoon rest period, matrons ordered us not to lie on our backs with knees bent. The games mistresses watched girls at meals, at roll call and in chapel, and would award good and bad 'deportment marks', recorded on a chart, and with house cups. If you were consistently upright you won a red felt badge, embroidered with the word 'Deportment'. This, sewn on your tunic, was a sign of both achievement and defeat. Our minds and understanding of the world were to reflect our custodians. With no private space, we could not even hide in our bodies, which also had to move in unison with their thoughts.

The authorities observed accurately the language of the body. However much a girl might say the right things, do and act within the rules, and however in order her uniform may be, her general carriage, her minutest gesture could betray a lack of conviction, a failure in conversion. I remember (after yet another term's anxious waiting for promotion) being called to the headmistress who said that I needed to improve my 'attitude' before I could be made a sergeant. I was baffled because I thought I had successfully concealed my unorthodoxy. I had said and done what appeared to me to be in order. But they must have seen through me, just by the way my body spoke. It also had to be tempered. I eventually won my deportment badge, and then soared from sergeant, to sub-prefect, to prefect. But my conformity over-reached itself; the games mistress took me aside and said I was now sitting and walking too stiffly, too rigidly. I was becoming conspicuous again.

Eventually the imitating child becomes the part. To survive in a place which beats down diversity, the victim has to believe in the rightness of his or her controller. Children and adolescents are most vulnerable, their minds and growing bodies may be permanently shaped. Apparently insignificant details such as bearing and posture are emphasised because, to use Bourdieu's words, the body is treated 'as a memory'. The principles of a whole cosmology or ethic are 'placed beyond the grasp of consciousness, and hence cannot be touched by voluntary, deliberate transformation' (Bourdieu 1977: 94). At an Old Girls' meeting, I talked with an old form-mate who had tried to train as an opera singer, but who could never breathe deeply enough. She spontaneously laid the blame on her schooling – her chest had, as it were, been too rigidly encased, and later she couldn't free herself, couldn't project her voice. In our bodies, we carried their minds into the future.

The presence of corporal punishment in boys' schools and its absence in girls' schools indicates differing attitudes to bodily display and contact, and possibly a differing consciousness of sexuality. Connections have been made between the childhood beatings of English males and their adult predilections for flagellation in brothels.[26] Although our deportment was continually viewed, our corporal modesty nevertheless stayed intact. In punishment, the girls were fully clothed and untouchable. In this sense, our bodies were invisible, anaesthetised and protected for one man's intrusion later.

As skeletons, we were corrected and straightened, ordered to sit and stand in upright lines. As female flesh and curves, we were concealed by the uniform. Take the traditional gym slip – a barrel shape with deep pleats designed to hide breasts, waist, hips and buttocks, giving freedom of movement without contour. My mother wore such a tunic. Previously women wore clothes which revealed the 'hourglass' shape, but one made rigid and immobile by 'stays' or corsets. From the gym slip of the 1930s, we had graduated to the tunic of thick serge ('hop-sack' we called it), without pleats, but again skilfully flattening the breasts and widening the waist. While my mother's legs had been hidden and desexualised by thick black stockings, we wore thick brown ones, 'regulation shade', and called them 'bullet-proofs'.

In those days before tights, our movements were further constrained lest we expose our suspenders beneath our short tunics. There was no risk of any greater exposure. We had to wear two pairs of knickers – white 'linings' and thick navy blue baggy knickers complete with pocket.[27] For gym we removed our tunics and any girl in linings only was shamed and punished. In summer the navy knickers were replaced by pale blue ones.

A friend still recalls being given a 'disobedience' for doing handstands and, unknown to her, exposing her knickers to a nearby gardener. She was told only to say 'for handstands' at roll call.

Thus her unmentionable exposure was effectively treated by psychological exposure. For games, our shorts concealed the existence of a split between the thighs. Two deep pleats in front and back made them like a skirt, but one which did not lift and reveal the thighs or buttocks as we ran or jumped. The lower abdomen retained its mystery.

This was the fifties when the dominant female fashion meant long full skirts. Yet our tunics had to be 'three inches above the knee when kneeling' (note the supplicant pose), even for girls aged seventeen years. I have been informed by a girl at another boarding school in the 1960s, when the mini-skirt symbolised fashionable femininity, that her tunic had to be '*touching the floor when kneeling*'. Thus the girls' schools demand the opposite to the notion of sexuality in the world outside. Our appearance was neutered. Our hair could not touch the backs of our shirt collars; in effect we were given the male 'short back and sides'. The crucial inspection time was the daily march-past at roll call. The dilemma was whether to bend forward and be rebuked for 'poking' the head (and not marching in the male military fashion) or whether to straighten up and risk being summoned for mutilation by the hairdresser. We were caught between conformity to the school, and saving our female sexuality as symbolised by longer hair.

The girls' uniform also had strange male traits: lace-up shoes, striped shirts, blazers, ties and tie pins. Unlike some of the boys' uniforms, ours was discontinuous with the clothes we would wear in adulthood. To us the school tie had no significance for membership of an 'old boy network'. We were caught between a male and female image long after puberty, and denied an identity which asserted the dangerous consciousness of sexuality. Immediately we left school, we had to drop all masculine traits, since a very different appearance was required for marriageability. Sexual ripeness, if only expressed in clothes, burst out. The hated tunics and lace-ups were torn, cut, burnt or flung into the sea. Old girls would return on parade, keen to demonstrate their transformation from androgeny to womanhood. To be wearing the diamond engagement ring was the ultimate achievement. There was no link between our past and future. In such uncertainty our confidence was surely broken.

EXERCISE: GAMES AND MARCHING

Bodily exercise of a distinct kind competed with and usually triumphed over academic study. For 220 girls there were two hockey pitches, six netball courts converted for tennis in the summer, along with two grass courts, a gymnasium and a swimming pool. The library, an old glass conservatory, half the size of a netball court, with three entrances linked to the main buildings, was little more than a draughty passageway. The games mistresses enjoyed at least equal and, in some cases, higher status than the academic staff. Boys could admire and model themselves on athletes. The games mistresses, however, even more than the academic staff, presented a model we were not willing to emulate either at the time, or after leaving school – the boyish hair style, shorts, aertex shirt, muscular unstockinged legs and sandals on all occasions. Games were compulsory every weekday. On Saturdays those girls selected for teams played in matches, while the rest of us took our compulsory exercise in walks. The timetable also demanded gym lessons twice a week, and those whom the games mistresses decided had flat feet or round shoulders devoted evenings to 'remedials' (stretching, balancing on tip-toe, or hanging on rib stools).

Pressure of exams meant no release from the daily obligation to play hockey or netball in winter and spring, and tennis, swimming and rounders in summer. Sometimes I would bandage my ankle and dare to put my name on the 'non-players' list, hoping no one would confer with my matron – the final authority on my bodily health.[28] Then I would lie on the cold lino under my bed, secretly reading. Before 'walks in threes', we would stuff books in our knickers so as to study in the fields. After 'lights out' we would revise for A levels in the lavatories or in lit passages off the matron's beat. Knowledge and academic success were acquired by stealth.

It can be argued that physical exercise is essential, that youthful energy must be unleashed and directed. This does not explain the special form our exercises had to take. They were not merely to satisfy physiological needs, but another route to the mind. Those traditional 'female' accomplishments, dance, ballet and riding, at which we could excel as women, and which some of us preferred, were 'extras' to be paid for above the basic fees and then only available one hour a week. Games, on the other hand, were compulsory and free. We marched as soldiers out of roll call but alternative movement to music was absent from the official curriculum. Our gymnastics were not of the modern kind, feminine and flowing, but instead freakish masculine jerks. Hockey and netball captured mind and body, because they concentrated group mentality, required whistle-blown attention, and imprinted rules on the imagination.

In many cultures, the right and left sides of the body, like the hands, are used to represent symbolic and social oppositions (Hertz 1960). The right is given pre-eminence and may be associated with order, legitimacy and the male, while the left can be associated with disorder, disruptive forces and the female. In our school, the games and deportment badges were sewn on the left, while the badges of authority, including those with a male military idiom, e.g. 'sergeant' and house 'captain', were sewn on the right side of the tunic.

Aptitude in the gym was indicated on the left by a miniature shield bearing the word 'Drill'. The red fire-fighter's ribbon hung from the left shoulder while the 'fire captain', the authority holder, sewed her badge on the right. Swimming abilities, usually demonstrated by proficiency in life-saving exercises, were marked on the left. There were no badges for music and dance. In this way, the potentially destructive forces of fire, water, the female body and movement were clamped with maximum control and minimum expression.

Popular images of the girls' boarding school sometimes give important hints of the ambivalence and contradictions in these institutions. Ollerenshaw (1967: 21–2) refers to the image of St Trinian's, with its 'whisky-swigging, hockey-stick-hacking, little horrors', and that of 'seminaries for nice girls where daughters can be safely locked up for the greater part of their troublesome teenage years'. She concludes that no girls' school fits either image. I suggest that elements of both may be found together in the institution. On the games field we were expected to show a certain aggressive muscularity which in no way undermined the simultaneous demand that we be chaste and feminine.

There are indeed certain male and female sports. Those exclusively for boys include rugby, football and boxing. Those mainly for girls include netball, hockey, lacrosse and rounders. Tennis, swimming and sometimes cricket are found in both. The association of 'hockey-stick-hacking' with girls sometimes elicits laughter. Apparently incongruous for females, hockey is yet considered insufficiently masculine to count as a major sport for British boys,[29] and is absent or marginal to the basic curriculum.

What differences exist between male and female sports? First, rugby permits the use of the arms as weapons to hold or push opponents. Boxing depends on an even more forceful drive and punch of arms and fist. In the rugger 'scrum' the players are obliged to cling to each other. There are 'running tackles'; and the players throw themselves at each other. Netball, rounders, hockey and lacrosse do not permit holds and pushes with the arms, fists or body. If you knock or hold an opponent this is a 'foul'. As in the punishment system, there is no bodily contact. The only institutionalised body contact in exercise at our school took place in ballroom dancing lessons (paid for as an 'extra'), or during the Saturday evening dances. In those quicksteps and waltzes, the partners were surrogate man and woman, permitted the one tactile premonition of adulthood.

Other differences between male and female sports concern the use of the legs, feet and hands. The aggressive use of the legs (kicking, and thus opening or raising the legs forward to expose, metaphorically, the genitals) is not permitted for girls. They must not touch the ball with the foot, must not kick any male ball. Modesty is retained.[30] Thus the 'weaker sex' are made weaker, being forbidden aggressive and defensive use of the arms, legs and feet. All the female sports demand manual dexterity in throwing, catching, hitting, 'dribbling' (hockey), or 'cradling' (lacrosse) the ball. This inhibits speed in running. Rounders is freer in some ways in that players can hit and swing with the full force of their bodies, with both arms raised. Sports, like cricket and tennis, played by men also, demand some manual dexterity, but these, tennis more especially, are permitted for women because they have none of the characteristics of the exclusively male sports discussed above.

Although rugger, football, lacrosse and hockey pitches are of comparable size, movement for girls in that space is at all times encumbered by holding a stick. The rugger and football players can at times run free and fast, hurtling through space. Even the rugger player's flight is not greatly impeded by embracing the ball. For girls, only in netball is movement permitted free of stick, but restricted within the smaller space, and the player holding the ball is rendered immobile. The proximity of lines and many players require delicate avoidance within what amounts to a cage. I understand more clearly now why I would gaze out through the wire mesh of the netball court, repeating Shelley's words:

Oh, lift me as a wave, a leaf, a cloud! . . .
A heavy weight of hours has chained and bowed
One too like thee: tameless, and swift, and proud.

Despite the rationale for games as being for exercise and development, netball was experienced by me as an endeavour to domesticate, slow down and humiliate us. In the girls' games speed is reduced, the body peculiarly controlled or burdened. When playing hockey or lacrosse, an intermediary was required between our feet and the ball, between our arms and the ball, between our bodies and the opponent. Off the games field the limited, aggressive skill we had acquired was useless without our tools. We were rendered powerless, impotent without our substitute phallus.

Gathorne-Hardy (1977: 251) notes that a girls' game 'however well done, looks unconvincing'. He suggests that girls are more sensitive than boys to purposeless activities, and that games reinforce the contradiction whereby girls are educated to be like boys and then expected to be subservient to them later. He examines neither the gender differentiation in games nor their form, whereas I suggest that the contradiction is embedded in the rules of the games and enacted and reaffirmed in each performance. The girls' bodies are extended and constrained in this choreography of their future which they learn unconsciously in legs, arms, hands, feet and torso. The girls' games when contrasted with those for boys affirmed our impotence in speed, attack and defence, leaving us with feminine dexterity and an eye for detail. While our school song acknowledged the greater restrictions on noise from girls, it strove to assert an equality which we couldn't achieve, which couldn't exist:

So we jog day by day
On our life's pleasant way
And although we don't make such a noise,
There are things I can name
Such as playing the game,
We can do them as well as the boys.

Success was circumscribed, for to be truly female, we were not to develop masculine muscles. In any case, we knew that hockey, lacrosse and netball, unlike football, rugger or boxing, rarely penetrated the adult sports pages and radio. Tennis, being a mixed game, and one we could continue most easily after schooldays, was not systematically coached unless, like dance lessons, we paid for it above the main fees. Generally we were trained in games we could neither continue, nor identify with, when grown.

We also marched: daily at roll call and as the major event of Sports Day. For weeks of the summer term we practised on the hockey pitch, while the games mistress gave orders through a megaphone. On the final day we were decked in tunic and clean striped shirts, with white ankle socks and tennis shoes. A hired van blared out recordings of military bands, playing especially the compositions of J. P. Sousa. A shape resembling the Union Jack was chalked on the pitch and we travelled along its lines, dividing, redividing, crossing and regrouping. The parents, staff and honoured guests (the prize-giver was usually the headmaster of a boys' prep school) and the rejects from the marching watched from a raised bank. This was all very exhilarating, but again we were being exercised in an unfeminine accomplishment to be abandoned after leaving school. Only men did national service and marched in the forces.[31] That straight-shouldered gait with swinging arms and regular footwork would have to be discarded, indeed unlearnt, as feminine step took over. We would only need it for country walks and following the hounds. Just as hockey hinted at impotence, so did the mode of marching. Instead of thumping our heels first on the ground, we had to point our toes; the feminised fall of the foot. Our attack was gently broken. Moreover we landed on the sound-dead turf of the hockey pitch; no noisy thrill of tarmac. Beneath the military music we heard only the rustle of our skirts and starched sleeves.

CONCLUSION

There are similarities between the girls' boarding school and that for boys: the separation from urban life, from economic production and members of other social classes, from parents and home, and the separation by gender. In this preliminary analysis I have concentrated on some of the differences for girls concerning the choice of heroic models, the degree of control over pupils, the distribution of authority between adults and pupils, forms of punishment, the approach to the body and the types of movement permitted in the games curriculum and the like. For girls, important discontinuities may be found between school and what is realisable in later life. The presentation to girls of models of achievement generally associated with men undervalues any which might be associated with women, and conveys male dominance as inevitable. The girls' school, without corporal punishment, may para- doxically be stricter than that for boys, and allow its pupils less self- determination. Indeed, power may be exercised more completely over girls precisely because it is not visible as physical force. I suggest that in so far as alternatives are not emphasised, the girls are prepared mainly for economic and political dependence within marriage,[32] whether or not this is the intention of the authorities. The differences between the education of boys and girls are important indicators as to how within the same social class each gender is socially defined and culturally reproduced. In this chapter, I have taken as an example a type of education usually regarded as privileged, but the analysis may be relevant to other girls' schools without such pretensions.

NOTES

1 The terms 'public' and 'independent' refer to private fee-paying schools in the UK, in contrast to wholly state-maintained schools. In 1965 only 2 per cent of girls in the thirteen-year age group in the United Kingdom were in independent public schools (Ollerenshaw 1967: 13).

2 See Lambert 1975; Honey 1977 and Gathorne-Hardy 1977.

3 See Blackstone 1976: 199.

4 Wober's *English Girls' Boarding Schools* (1971) was a pioneering study but limited in scope. The data are based on only twenty weeks of fieldwork in twenty- three schools, using questionnaires. It is significant that the terms of the original grant for the larger research project by Lambert (1975: 5) on boys' schools specifically excluded girls' schools. Gathorne-Hardy's (1977) research is largely devoted to boys' schools. His two chapters on girls' schools offer some imaginative, although sometimes erratic, observations. There has been a revival of interest in the fantasy literature on girls' boarding schools (Cadogan and Craig 1976; Freeman 1976). Angela Brazil, the major pedlar of illusion, never attended such an institution as a participant member. Inevitably, crucial aspects of boarding school experience do not surface.

5 When I delivered the first draft of this paper at the Oxford Women's Seminar, reactions were mixed. Those who had attended day school were incredulous, while former boarders found many parallels or echoes of their own experience.

6 Cf. Okely 1975.

7 A girl's academic ambitions will also depend on the extent to which she is encouraged by her parents off-stage. Wober notes in his questionnaires among the girls that 'Careers and professions seemed less common as a central focus; instead the emphasis was on "good jobs" ... that would finance the gay pre-marital years, and thereafter serve for part-time or temporary occupation' (Wober 1971: 88).

8 Gathorne-Hardy (1977) found the concept of the *rite de passage* illuminating.

9 Further research is necessary to explore the extent of permitted free movement by individuals beyond the school grounds. Certainly, some of the girls' schools are elaborately bounded by high walls, barricades or battlements to prevent both

intrusion by outsiders (Gathorne-Hardy 1977: 240, 258) and to reaffirm the enclosure of the inmates.

10 See Bateson 1973.

11 The evening after a nine-year-old girl learnt of her father's death, she was told by the matron not to cry lest she keep the other girls in the dormitory awake.

12 Further research might confirm the impression from the literature and other sources that homosexuality is more explicit in boys' schools (Gathorne-Hardy 1977: 171). As in other areas, the differences would relate also to early socialisation, not merely the effects of schooling.

13 Public school boys are literally prepared in 'prep' schools. Lambert (1975: 126) notes that over 80 per cent of all boys in public schools had been to preparatory schools and that 85 per cent of his own sample had boarded in such institutions. Wober (1971: 44) found that only 25 per cent of his sample of girls (the majority of whom arrived at boarding school at eleven or thirteen) had previously boarded in a prep school. Many had attended co-educational schools.

14 See later section, Containment and Powerlessness.

15 There are, by contrast, more persons of the opposite sex in boys' schools, namely the domestic staff, matrons and masters' wives. But 'boys and staff have learned to relegate women to marginal organisational and largely decorative roles' (Lambert 1975: 116).

16 This dog was named after a day of the week, just like Crusoe's Man Friday. A colleague from another girls' boarding school has noted a similar collection of males. Her headmistress had two male dachshunds.

17 Wober recorded that among his sample of girls' schools 'About one-third of the governors were women' (1971: 48).

18 In many schools, girls had to sing 'Forty Years On' which was written specifically for boys and included the inappropriate football chorus (Haddon 1977: 21–2).

19 Even in the late 1960s Wober (1971: 38) found that the majority of teachers in the girls' boarding schools were unmarried and that only a minority had boarded (ibid. 40). By contrast Lambert (1975: 54) records that the majority of staff in boys' public schools were themselves educated in such institutions.

20 Wober found in most cases, no matter at what time one arrived, the schools appeared quiet; girls, if seen, were 'scurrying about . . . whispering' (Wober 1971: 293). Gathorne-Hardy (1977: 244), during his visit to Cheltenham Ladies, noted 'a dead silence . . . a silence more awesome and more indicative of discipline than any bell, 800 girls swished in swift lines down the long, dim, tiled corridors towards the next classroom'.

21 I am grateful to Dr Peter Rivière for drawing my attention to this difference in social structure.

22 It is possible that the extent of authority allotted to girls in boarding schools containing adolescents is similar to that for younger boys in their prep schools.

23 'No one could really call Patty pretty . . . she was neither dull nor particularly clever, only possessed of average abilities, able to remember lessons when she tried hard, and gifted with a certain capacity for plodding, but not in the least brilliant over anything she undertook. She was never likely to win fame, or set the Thames on fire, but she was one of those cosy, thoughtful, cheery, lovable home girls, who are often a great deal more pleasant to live with than some who have greater talents' (Brazil 1909: 20–1).

24 See also women's reluctance to speak or speak audibly at seminars where egoistic panache is demanded.

25 See also Foucault (1977: 135–69) for his discussion of 'Docile Bodies'.

26 Stephen Spender has said of his prep school: 'They might as well have had me educated at a brothel for flagellants' (cited in Gathorne-Hardy 1977: 111).

27 The navy knickers and linings were a feature of many girls' schools (Haddon 1977: 75–6).
28 The matron's dominion over the girl's bodily health and sickness cannot be fully explored in this chapter (cf. chapter 7)
29 E. Hobsbawm remarked (pc) that the various forms of these male sports depend also on the public school. Eton has also its own, like the Wall Game. There are also preferences according to social class and nationality within the UK. But the broad gender differentiation occurs in both public and state schools.
30 In the privacy of the gymnasium, the legs are opened when jumping over the 'horse' or when hanging on bars, but not raised in an aggressive kick. Some kicking motions are permitted when helplessly lying on the floor, with no target.
31 The single annual visit to London by the whole school was to the Royal Tournament; an all-male military display.
32 Since the 1950s the girl's biological virginity may be less important although her social virginity must still be protected. Moreover, greater sexual freedom may not alter a woman's economic and political dependence.

During the late 1970s and the 1980s, after this article was first published, boys' public schools began to admit a minority of girls, especially at the sixth form level. However, gender hierarchy is not necessarily solved. Girls and boys who attended some such schools have informed me how girls were expected to do domestic work from which the boys were exempted. Girls were seen as emotional servicers of boys and felt obliged to underplay their own intelligence. Moreover, within mixed-sex fee-paying institutions, class segregation is reaffirmed.

REFERENCES

Bateson, G. (1973) *Steps to an Ecology of Mind*, Farnham: Paladin.
Blackstone, T. (1976) 'The education of girls today', in J. Mitchell and A. Oakley (eds) *The Rights and Wrongs of Women*, Harmondsworth: Penguin.
Bourdieu, P. (1977) *Outline of a Theory of Practice*, Cambridge: Cambridge University Press.
Brazil, A. (1909) *The Nicest Girl in the School*, London: Blackie.
Cadogan, M. and Craig, P. (1976) *You're a Brick Angela!* London: Gollancz.
Connolly, C . (1961) *Enemies of Promise*, Harmondsworth: Penguin.
Foucault, M. (1977) *Discipline and Punish*, London: Allen Lane.
Freeman, G. (1976) *The Schoolgirl Ethic: The Life and Work of Angela Brazil*, London: Allen Lane.
Gathorne-Hardy, J. (1977) *The Public School Phenomenon*, London: Hodder and Stoughton.
Goffman, E. (1968) *Asylums*, Harmondsworth: Penguin.
Haddon, C. (1977) *Great Days and Jolly Days*, London: Hodder and Stoughton.
Hertz, R. (1960) 'The pre-eminence of the right hand', in *Death and the Right Hand* (trans. R. and C. Needham), London: Cohen and West.
Honey, J. R. de S. (1977) *Tom Brown's Universe*, London: Millington.
Lambert, R. (1975) *The Chance of a Lifetime?*, London: Weidenfeld and Nicolson.
Marks, P. (1976) 'Femininity in the classroom: an account of changing attitudes', in J. Mitchell and A. Oakley (eds) *The Rights and Wrongs of Women*, Harmondsworth: Penguin.
Mauss, M. (1936) 'Les Techniques du corps', in M. Mauss (1938) *Anthropologie et sociologie*, Paris: Presses Universitaires de France.
Mitford, J. (1977) *A Fine Old Conflict*, London: Michael Joseph.
Okely, J. (1975) 'The self and scientism', *Journal of the Oxford Anthropology Society*, Michaelmas term: 171–88.

Ollerenshaw, K. (1967) *The Girls' Schools*, London: Faber and Faber.
Pocock, D. (1973) 'The idea of a personal anthropology'. Unpublished paper given at the 1973 ASA Conference.
—— (1975) *Understanding Social Anthropology*, London: Teach Yourself Books, Hodder and Stoughton.
Wilson, C. (1956) *The Outsider*, London: Gollancz.
Wober, M. (1971) *English Girls' Boarding Schools*, London: Allen Lane.

Chapter 9

Re-reading *The Second Sex*

Though de Beauvoir's study now reads differently both for her past and her new readers, the earlier reading cannot be easily jettisoned. The book is part of some women's personal history and part of the history of feminism. This double reading, then and now, is the rationale for my selection of certain themes for a critical discussion. I have used the ink markings in my original 1961 copy as a guide to the earlier reading.

De Beauvoir's central section on mythology proved startling and evocative to a young woman like myself in the early 1960s. Today, thanks partly to anthropology and to feminists' interrogation of the subject and greater awareness of race and class, it is easier to recognise that de Beauvoir's generalisations fit neither all cultures nor all women. Women readers whose experience in no way approximated that of de Beauvoir were undoubtedly sceptical long ago. From the myths, I have selected for critical discussion those concerned with the female body and sexuality: matters which women now feel freer to talk and write about. With reluctance and for reasons of space I have had to exclude my discussion of de Beauvoir's critique of five male authors (Okely 1986: 80–9).

In the decade since the mid-1970s, a number of women have been concerned to consolidate a theoretical approach to feminism. While the attempt to find the 'origins' or 'first cause' of women's subordination has been largely abandoned, greater emphasis is now placed on explanations for women's continuing subordination and the conditions which could change it. As part of this enterprise, feminists have re-examined Marx and Freud. De Beauvoir's interpretation of these two theorists therefore requires comment. Her extensive debate with biological explanations is of continuing and crucial relevance since the resurgence of sociobiologism in the last decade. The implications of the biological difference between males and females have provoked debates both within feminism and outside it. Considerable space is therefore devoted to various biological explanations and a closer reading of de Beauvoir's text.

My general comments on volume II of *The Second Sex* invite the reader to place her detailed ethnography of women's lives in a specific context. From this volume, I have selected de Beauvoir's discussion of early childhood which contrasts with her more generalised comments on psychoanalysis and social influences in volume I. Inevitably the record here of a re-reading has to be selective and cannot do justice to de Beauvoir's enterprise of encyclopaedic proportions. In volume II de Beauvoir does not make use of statistical or in-depth social science studies of women; the latter appeared in strength only from the late 1960s. Instead she draws on the representation of women's experience from psychoanalysts' case studies and literature, especially that written by women. Parshley, the American translator, a zoologist, has tended to retain the evidence from the former and cut the latter.[1] The other major source for de Beauvoir is personal observation and experience. Insights into the young girl were drawn both from her own past and the many years of teaching in girls' lycées. De Beauvoir sometimes gives examples of friends and acquaintances to back up her argument, making use of the 'continual interest' which she and Sartre had had for many years in 'all sorts of people; my memory provided me with an abundance of material' (de Beauvoir 1968: 196). Her autobiographies in fact reveal how restricted her acquaintance was with people outside café society and the bourgeoisie.

De Beauvoir has in part done an anthropological village study of specific women but without the anthropological theory and focus. Her village is largely mid-century Paris and the women studied, including herself, are mainly middle class. There are almost no references to working-class urban women and only rare glimpses of rural, peasant women who still made up the majority of French women at that time. There is just one striking discussion of the burden of the peasant woman in postwar France in the history section (1972: 165). Despite this hidden subjectivity, her observations and her recourse to historical, literary and psychoanalytical documentation raise questions beyond the local study. A paradoxical strength is the hidden use of herself as a case study, and it was one to which many of her women readers intuitively responded. Although in the text she never uses the word 'I' in a personal example, when we examine her autobiography (1959) written nearly ten years later, we can see the link between her own experience and some of her generalised statements about the girl and woman.

MYTHS AND IDEOLOGY

The discussion of the myths which surround 'woman' is the core to volume I. As with her treatment of other aspects, its strength lies in its focused description rather than in any convincing explanation or first cause of women's subordination. Some later feminists have read the section only for an explanation of women's subordination and thus missed its accumulative impact (see, for example, Barrett 1980).

Whether or not she has been misread and simplified, ideas from this section are frequently referred to by feminists and others. De Beauvoir's words hold the imagination by pointing to powerful symbols of 'the feminine' and either explicitly or implicitly challenge their truth. Her description is not neutral, but accompanied by a mocking value judgement. Certain repetitive themes in different ideologies about women are systematically collected together, but de Beauvoir is most convincing in the treatment of Western culture. Her description reminds the reader of a long tradition of the 'earth mother' and the 'eternal feminine' which, she argues, while purporting to be laudatory towards woman, is thoroughly dehumanising. The myths which present woman as a powerful symbol mask her effective powerlessness. De Beauvoir's women readers could learn that Western myths which were so often said to be complementary to themselves were only mystifications; that is, they served to mask the truth of women's objective subordination and oppression.

The opening pages try to link the myths of the feminine to general existentialist concepts which de Beauvoir has refined by introducing a gender difference. 'Man' needs 'Others' to affirm his existence and to break away from immanence. He engages in projects to achieve transcendence. The female is used by the male as this 'Other' and she remains the object; she never becomes the subject. De Beauvoir does not convincingly explain why 'woman' never becomes the subject, she merely asserts this, yet she described a painful truth of her time.

There are oblique references to Hegel's 'master–slave dialectic', although she does not always bother to name him. She develops Hegel's ideas by contrasting the position of the slave with that of woman. Whereas in Hegel's view the slave is able also to see himself as subject or 'essential' in his struggle with the master, de Beauvoir asserts that woman is in a worse position because she does not see herself as subject and cannot, unlike the slave, ever see the master (man) as inessential. Whereas the slave can supersede the master, apparently woman cannot supersede man by the same means. In de Beauvoir's view, woman cannot reach the necessary consciousness for emancipation. It is this use of Hegel which later feminist theorists (e.g. Craig 1979) have teased out of de Beauvoir's text in their analysis of her underlying theoretical position. If woman is deprived even of the potential victory attained by a slave, then it seems that de Beauvoir's message is that woman can never win freedom for herself, except perhaps by some independent change in society and the 'master' male.

If indeed de Beauvoir's Hegelian theory is taken as the major if not sole message of *The Second Sex*, then it would seem that all she is saying is that woman's subordinate state is fixed. But few of de Beauvoir's readers were aware of such embedded theoretical implications. Today it is certainly important to make explicit de Beauvoir's theoretical underpinnings; however, it should not be concluded that these were the key contributions to a past feminist reading of *The Second Sex*.

In contrast to de Beauvoir's preceding examination of biology, psychology, economics and history, the section on myths explores a process whereby women's subordination is continually reaffirmed or 'overdetermined' through ideology. Whether or not de Beauvoir is offering these ideas about women as causes or consequences of women's subordination, she should be credited for pointing to recurrent aspects of the myth of woman, especially in European culture. De Beauvoir sharpened scepticism in her reader.

That woman is the 'Other' is devastatingly stated:

> Since women do not present themselves as subject, they have no virile myth in which their prospects are reflected; they have neither religion nor poetry which belongs to themselves in their own right. It is still through the dreams of men that they dream. It is the gods fabricated by males which they adore.
>
> (1949: 235)

> The representation of the world, like the world itself, is the work of men; they describe it from the point of view which is theirs and which they confuse with the absolute truth.
>
> (1949: 236)

Whereas de Beauvoir's comments on much of European Christian ideology are fairly systematic, her tendency towards generalisations is very misleading when she strays into cultures in another time and space. De Beauvoir selects from social anthropology cross-cultural examples which confirm her argument and avoids reference to the many available counter-examples. To be fair, she does attempt some broad distinctions between Islam, Graeco-Roman culture and Christianity. But otherwise, random cases are plucked from India, Egypt and Oceania, with only occasional counter-examples.

Indeed, the text oscillates between a defiant angry declaration that woman is always 'Other' and a subdued acknowledgement that this view of women may be eclipsed by the presence of some non-female idols in the course of history (1949: 234). For example, under dictatorships, woman may no longer be a privileged object, and in the 'authentic democratic society' advocated by Marx, de Beauvoir observes there is no place for 'the Other'. This recognition of broad differences is modified when she notes that Nazi soldiers held to the cult of female virginity and that communist writers like Aragon created a special place for woman. De Beauvoir hopes that the myth of woman will one day be extinguished:

> The more that women affirm themselves as human beings, the more the wondrous quality of the Other will die in them. But today it still exists in the heart of *all* men.
>
> (1949: 235; my emphasis)

This last sentence reveals her continuing need to conclude with a pan-cultural generalisation.

While she is ambivalent as to whether woman as 'Other' is a true universal, she states that 'the Other' is itself ambiguous. It is evil, but 'being necessary for good' it returns to good. Woman embodies 'no fixed concept' (1949: 236). In this way, de Beauvoir can explain the apparently conflicting fantasies which women are believed to embody for men. One of these myths is the association of woman with nature. There is a double aspect to this. Nature can be seen as mind, will and transcendence as well as matter, passivity and immanence. On the one hand nature is mind, on the other it is flesh. As evidence for the latter view of nature de Beauvoir looks back to the classical Greek scholars (for example, Aristotle), who asserted that only the male principle is the true creator, while female fertility is merely passive; that is, that woman is the passive earth while man is the seed.

De Beauvoir's examination of classical European writers was helpful to both Western and non-Western women in exposing the mystification of 'woman' in a long-standing tradition. It was harder for de Beauvoir to look beyond the traditions of her own culture, especially when she had to rely on less accessible sources for a view of nature elsewhere. She offered some examples from India which compare the earth to a mother, but random selections do not prove the universality of any such principle; moreover, her example from Islamic texts where woman is called a field or grapevine (1949: 238) is an image from agriculture not wild nature. The two are certainly not the same.

Despite these errors, de Beauvoir systematically outlines a dominant European tradition which, since the eighteenth century Enlightenment, sees nature as inferior to culture (see Bloch and Bloch 1980). Her suggestions about women and nature have stimulated anthropologists to think about the association (E. Ardener 1975). De Beauvoir's link between women and nature is not as absolute as some of her successors have tried to make it (Ortner 1974). More recently, anthropologists have given examples from other cultures which challenge any pan-cultural generalisation (McCormack and Strathern 1980). For example, Olivia Harris (1980) has argued that Indians of the Bolivian Highlands equate the married couple with 'culture' and unmarried persons with 'nature'; the nature–culture opposition is thus not linked simplistically to a gender opposition.

As elsewhere, de Beauvoir proceeds through the stages of a woman's life. Here, they are examined in the light of external ideology rather than of a woman's concrete experience. Women as a group may comply with and internalise these beliefs as if they were 'natural'. Whereas de Beauvoir tries to suggest that much of the ideology is universal, it was in fact her revelation that this was mere belief, mere myth, which was so powerful to her early readers. In so far as Western women were indoctrinated to believe that they might represent 'mother earth', the 'eternal feminine', erotic temptress or virgin purity, de Beauvoir dismantled these images. Some of us could recognise apparently individual fantasies about ourselves as part of an overarching tradition made outside us, not born with us; the fantasies were historical, not fixed. The problem for us was how to throw them off. Non-Western women, by contrast, gained a novel critical perspective of Western ideology which was seen even more as one to reject.

In searching for the basis for certain ideas and myths of 'woman', de Beauvoir seizes upon woman's capacity to gestate. Her approach is rooted in the European Cartesian tradition which separates mind from body. Man apparently would like to be a pure Idea, absolute Spirit, but his fate is to be trapped in the 'chaotic shadows of the maternal belly . . . it is woman who imprisons him in the mud of the earth' (1949: 239). De Beauvoir compares the womb to 'quivering jelly which evokes the soft viscosity of carrion' (1949: 239). 'Wherever life is in the making – germination, fermentation – it arouses disgust . . . the slimy embryo begins the cycle that is completed in the putrefaction of death' (1972: 178). These extraordinary references to viscosity and slime echo Sartre's (1938, 1943) extensive discussion of viscous substance and some of his own personal disgust with aspects of the sexual body (see de Beauvoir 1981).

In aiming to deconstruct the myth of the feminine, de Beauvoir thus naively reproduces her male partner's and lover's ideas about the female body, while possibly deceiving herself that these are objective and fixed philosophical truths. As in her discussion of biology, she is on dubious ground in suggesting that bodily parts inevitably arouse the same feelings (of disgust) in all individuals and all cultures. She is implying it is 'natural' to look at 'nature' in a specific way. In fact she reveals the extent to which she has internalised both the views of her own culture and the extreme reactions of Sartre.

Her problematic assertions are compounded when she makes unsubstanti-ated generalisations about primitive people's attitudes to childbirth. In her text such people are an undifferentiated lump and she repeats a clichéd belief that their attitudes to childbirth are always surrounded by the most severe taboos. It is interesting to be informed that childbirth in a number of different societies is subject to elaborate ritual; the danger comes when de Beauvoir implies either that taboos vary according to an evolutionary 'progress' or that attitudes to birth are unvaried. De Beauvoir asserts that all the ancient codes demand purification rites from women in confinement, and that gestation always inspires a 'spontaneous repulsion' (1949: 240).

De Beauvoir thus falls into the trap of suggesting that gestation is naturally and universally disgusting. Her evidence about so-called primitives is suspect, first because even 'taboos' do not necessarily reflect disgust, and second because a people's cultural treatment of childbirth is linked to differences in descent, marriage and kinship systems and control over offspring. De Beauvoir's assertion that disgust at gestation is spontaneous speaks more of herself and her own time. Today I can criticise de Beauvoir for her suspect generalisation about humanity's spontaneous psychological reactions to the physicality of childbirth, but some twenty years ago I underlined it.

De Beauvoir makes similar sweeping statements about menstruation. She maintains that in all civilisations woman inspires in man the horror of his own carnal 'contingence'; she reminds him of his mortality. This, according to de Beauvoir, is confirmed by an assertion that everywhere before puberty the young girl is without taboo. It is only after her first menstruation that she becomes impure and is then surrounded by taboos. De Beauvoir then offers a random collection of menstrual 'taboos' from Leviticus, Egypt, India, nineteenth-century Britain and France to support this suspect generalisation.

In the 1950s and 1960s this made interesting reading, but it is perilously close to an old-fashioned type of anthropology, exemplified in Frazer's *The Golden Bough*, in which customs are lumped together for their superficial similarity, although in fact they are meaningless when torn from their different contexts. By contrast, a few detailed examples of menstrual taboos in specific cultures are more informative for placing them in context. De Beauvoir (1949: 243–6) does indeed give three such extended examples, but these are excluded by Parshley.

In de Beauvoir's view, the taboos associated with menstruation 'express the horror which man feels for feminine fertility' (1949: 247). This emphasis on 'horror' is little different from the now discredited view that primitive people's rituals are merely a response to 'fear'. Today, after a wider anthropological reading on these menstrual 'issues' across cultures, I can criticise de Beauvoir's explanation, but I have also to recognise that in 1961 I underlined that single sentence above. Both female writer and reader identified with a myth that woman's body and blood inspired horror and believed it as fact, not fiction. Thus neither de Beauvoir nor the female reader escaped the myths of her own culture.

The myths associated with virginity and the drama of defloration are also discussed by de Beauvoir in terms of psychological fear. Sometimes, de Beauvoir vaguely suggests that customs surrounding defloration have 'mystical' causes, as if this were sufficient explanation. De Beauvoir is at the mercy of outdated European explanations for ritual, partly because any systematic study of rituals associated with women had to await a feminist anthropology. (See chapter 6, this volume.)

In recent decades, anthropologists have looked at rituals associated with menstruation, virginity, defloration, pregnancy and childbirth and the connections between a group's specific control over women's sexuality or fertility and the material context. In some societies menstruation will be merely a private event and without ritual taboo. In some cases childbirth and the arrival of a new member to the group will be publicly significant and so marked by ritual elaboration or specific taboos (see La Fontaine 1972, and chapter 4, this volume).

De Beauvoir's discussion of the control of women's sexuality and reproduction cross-culturally is in places thoroughly misleading, but in its time it told us about some of the strongest taboos in a specific Judeo-Christian culture, if not class. In 1961, as a virgin, I underlined in painful recognition her psychological explanation as to the relative importance of virginity:

> Depending whether man feels crushed by the forces which encircle him or whether he proudly believes himself capable of annexing them, he either refuses or demands that his wife be handed over as a virgin.

> (1949: 250)

In the 1980s the Western bourgeois demand for a virgin wife has all but disintegrated, and *not* because the male has miraculously overcome some innate mystical fear. Changes in attitudes towards female virginity coincide with changes in attitudes to sexuality and marriage and even advances in the technology of birth control. In the early 1960s, as a virgin, I could not see that the bourgeois cult of virginity depended only on the social and historical context. In those days, de Beauvoir's critical discussion of virginity had maximum impact precisely because she mistakenly argued that it was widely valued in a variety of cultures. Today, we may be more concerned to point to the many counter-examples in order to argue, as she intended, for alternative freedoms. There is a demand for specific case studies rather than broad and inaccurate generalisations.

Inevitably the author's own culture was the most closely observed. It is therefore not surprising that de Beauvoir should suggest that the most disturbing image of woman as 'the Other' is found in Christianity: 'It is in her that are embodied the temptations of the earth, sex and the devil' (1949: 270). In the margin I exclaimed 'et on m'a fait Chrétienne!' ('And they made me a Christian woman!'). De Beauvoir, the former Catholic, suggests that all Christian literature intensifies 'the disgust which man can feel for woman' (1949: 270), and her examples from modern male writers show the continuing tradition. Again, as elsewhere, she presumed this disgust to be universal and innate. Thus she had not fully freed herself of her own indoctrination into Christianity when she asserted that its ingredients were general to all societies. But for the reader of the 1950s and early 1960s, de Beauvoir's selection of Western traditions, when juxtaposed with a splatter of historical and cross-cultural examples, had a powerful effect. Dominant Western beliefs were exposed as of no greater truth than other beliefs and customs.

BIOLOGISM

Those who praise de Beauvoir retrospectively invariably quote the opening sentence of volume II of *The Second Sex*: 'on ne nâit pas femme on le devient':

One is not born, but rather one becomes, a woman; no biological, psychological or economic fate determines the figure that the human female presents in society.

(1972: 295)

The first phrase has been read today by many to mean that woman is socially constructed rather than biologically determined, and de Beauvoir was perhaps most influential precisely because she appeared to challenge biological determinism. However, de Beauvoir's rejection also of economic and psycho-analytic explanations of women's subordination means there is a certain ambiguity here. Her account of the causes gives greater weight to the ideological creation of 'woman' and in turn to women's apparent collusion with or existentialist choice in the matter. Despite de Beauvoir's formal rejection of biological determinism, when the details of her arguments are closely examined, it can be seen that she contradicts any claim that biological factors are irrelevant or arbitrary. Again and again she slips into biological reductionism to explain the primary cause of women's subordination.

In the 1980s, with the renaissance of sociobiology and the enthusiasm for biologically determinist causes for social behaviour and subordination, feminist theories become much more alert to latent biologism. De Beauvoir is also now more vulnerable to a current accusation of biologism when subjected to a closer reading.

First let me differentiate the types of biological reductionism. The crudest kind is that which suggests that sexual/physiological differences mono-lithically dictate the social/psychological and economic differences between male and female. It is useful to distinguish sex (male and female) and gender (masculine and feminine and intermediate categories); sex, rather than sexuality, has been defined as a purely physiological/genetic/biological fact; gender is the social construction, the range of variable characteristics attributed to and acquired by males and females (Oakley 1972). The physio-logical differences in this definition are not considered to have a direct and single causal consequence for gender, because the notions of masculine and feminine *gender* distinctions vary across time and place, historically, cross-culturally and also within the same society, depending on class and ethnic identity. The crudest biological–determinist argument claims that the physio-logical differences in reproductive organs and in fat distribution between the sexes, and the fact that only women gestate, lactate and menstruate, auto-matically account for the different work done by men and women (the sexual division of labour). The physiological differences are said to explain the subordination of women or the so-called complementarity of roles. Strangely, some Marxist feminists have recently fallen into the trap of suggesting that women's singular biology should be considered as the 'material base' to gender divisions (Brenner and Ramas 1984). This is a travesty of the Marxist concept of materialism and has been adequately rejected by Barrett (1984).

Sociobiologists have introduced a more flexible interpretation of biological determinism; namely, that over millennia of evolution, this sexual difference has brought a necessary and highly programmed adaptation in behaviour. Thus each sex is said to be genetically programmed towards certain types of behaviour. Aggression is associated with males while emotional nurturing is associated with females. Given the millennia of programming, this is not changeable. However, sociobiologists have invariably taken very specific Western notions of gender and presumed that all societies are of an 'individualistic', competitive type, as found under capitalism and where sociobiologists consider that competitive aggression is the 'civilising' factor. They then look for such characteristics in animals and ignore anything which does not fit their Western stereotypes. Unlike the sociobiologists, de Beauvoir's tendency towards biological reductionism does not extend to the suggestion that each sex is genetically programmed to behave in specific, rigid ways. However, there are times when she over-elaborates the consequences of the female's capacity to gestate and lactate, using it to explain an inevitable division of labour between men and women.

Another more sophisticated form of biological reductionism is the assertion that *perceived* sexual/bodily differences between males and females will inevitably cause the same ideas and social reactions – that the physical differences inevitably stimulate all societies to make the *same* value judgement, so that one sex, the female, is seen as inferior to another. Thus there is the now-hackneyed argument that because the male genitals protrude this explains why they are valued, and because a woman's genitals do not protrude in the same way this explains why they are undervalued. We should make a clear distinction between the penis – the physical object – and the phallus, the psychic symbol of the penis. It cannot be presumed in all societies for all time that the penis should be seen as the powerful phallus. There is no inevitable reason why a protrusion should be valued and a cavity not. Indeed, even in Western Europe powerful symbolic value is attached to dark or black holes. There is no *inevitable* explanation as to why a hard object – the ideal state for the penis in heterosexual intercourse – should be valued over a soft, wet object, the ideal sexual state for the vagina. These value judgements are deeply embedded in so-called neutral subjects: for example, in academia 'hard' subjects like science are valued over 'soft' data and 'soft' subjects like literature. Despite her declared position, de Beauvoir slides into a secondary biological explanation for women's subordination and the sexual division of labour. In so far as women's subordination is explained by a fixed, unchanging *ideological interpretation* of sexual, physical difference, then it would appear that nothing can ever be changed except through surgery, chemistry and the laboratory. De Beauvoir does not take such a line, but there are double messages in her text.

First, de Beauvoir argues that women's subordination is *constructed* both from the outside by the dominant set of beliefs and from the individual's collusion, if she, the woman, fails to choose otherwise. This subordination of women is, according to her celebrated quote, not determined by any biological, psychological or economic 'destiny'. The sentence 'one is not born but rather becomes a woman' cannot be considered as a materialist explanation, which emphasises external conditions.

De Beauvoir argues for the construction, albeit only ideological rather than materialist, of the category 'woman'. There is, on the other hand, a second half-hidden and contradictory message which is as follows: De Beauvoir alleges that women's physiology, her body and her allegedly 'special' kind of eroticism explain why she is always identified as the Other, as the object rather than the subject; why, while man can find 'transcendence' in their bodies and sexuality, women are fated to 'immanence'. De Beauvoir suggests that men find autonomy through their bodies but women are less likely to do so: woman is the victim of the species, is enslaved to it. While men in their brief reproductive role can retain their individuality, women come into conflict with the long-term interest of the species. Whereas animals merely repeat and maintain the species, man (not mankind) creates and invents in accord with the transcendent possibilities open to human beings. In contrast to men, women's reproductive role obliges women only to maintain rather than create. Here we see not only a biological reductionism in de Beauvoir, but also a rejection of the creative significance of social reproduction, the upbringing of children – something for which both males and females could be equally responsible.

Today, feminists may gasp at this biologism. It seems like a permanent trap from which we, women or men, cannot escape. We cannot easily change our bodies. However, some radical feminists have, without even de Beauvoir's ambiguity, confused sex with gender and advocated a solution which is consistent with such biologism. Shulamith Firestone (1982), for example, proposes the substitution of test-tube fertilisation and mechanical wombs in laboratories to rid women of biological reproduction. This does not resolve the more crucial long-term problem of the upbringing and care of children, nor does it confront the fact that in a patriarchal society men direct and control the laboratories which in turn are governed by the state.

De Beauvoir's readers in the 1950s and 1960s, and here I use experience as part guide (see also Ascher 1981), reacted favourably to de Beauvoir's account of maternity. They responded to the raw and negative description of the physiological, near animal, burden of maternity which defied the prevailing sentimental view of the maternal instinct, its naturalness and its supposedly unadulterated pleasure. Even though de Beauvoir sometimes falls into the kind of biological reductionism which elsewhere she was trying to attack, the important difference between her description of maternity and that of postwar propaganda lies in the evaluation. De Beauvoir described maternity with disgust, as something degrading and in conflict with the existentialist ideal of individual self-development. It came to us as a revelation that the foetus and infant could be depicted as a parasite of our bodies. Some of us gladly embraced these images of a growing monster in the belly, threatening our identity rather than extending it. We wanted the language to reject maternity and motherhood which then seemed to demand that women retreat to the marital home and nuclear family.

Let us examine in detail some of the evidence of de Beauvoir's inadvertent secondary biologism in chapter 1 of volume I entitled 'The Biological Facts' (1949). Despite her claims that biology is no explanation for women's subordination, de Beauvoir attributes fixed values and inflexible consequences to the biological differences between males and females. Whereas she argues that no symbolic significance can be read into the differences between egg and sperm and conception by ejaculation and implantation into the womb, she nevertheless introduces a value-loaded hierarchy or asymmetry to the act of sexual intercourse, male animal decoration, the genitalia, menstruation, birth, lactation and the menopause. She also collapses the description of non-human mammals into that of humans.

A close reading reveals that de Beauvoir implicitly suggests that either the anatomical differences between males and females inevitably induce *ideas* of subordination or that biological differences are inevitably debilitating for women. Although she distinguishes the phallus from the penis, and already in the 1940s has read and used the French psychoanalyst Lacan, who clarified this distinction and has influenced some later feminists (for example, Mitchell 1974), de Beauvoir still claims that the penis *naturally* provides a 'tool' for transcendent identity.

Early on in the chapter, de Beauvoir asserts that there is no necessity for the body to have a particular structure: 'it is possible to imagine a society which reproduces itself by parthenogenesis (without sexual union) or one composed of hermaphrodites' (1949: 40). When discussing the part of chromosomes, she denies the passivity of the female since both the male and female play an equal part. She ridicules some people's suggestion that since gestation takes place in a stable organism, the womb, women likewise should remain in another stable place, the home (ibid. 47). Fine stuff. De Beauvoir is here arguing against any secondary biologism, but she loses her head when she moves on to vertebrates:

> The female organism is wholly adapted for and subservient to maternity, while sexual initiative is the prerogative of the male. The female is the victim of the species . . . during certain periods in the year . . . her whole life is under the regulation of the sexual cycle.
>
> (1972: 52)

We are gently led by de Beauvoir to apply observations about non-humans to humans. In sexual intercourse:

> It is in birds and mammals especially that he (the male) forces himself upon her . . . . Even when she is willing or provocative, *it is unquestionably the*

male who takes the female. She is taken. In this penetration her inwardness is violated, she is like an enclosure that is broken into.

(1972: 53; my emphasis)

Parshley's use of the concrete image of an enclosure emphasises the physical dimension, missing the person's state of mind. By contrast, my translation of the last sentence emphasises the psychoanalytical resonance in de Beauvoir: 'She appears like an interior state which is violated' (1949: 57). De Beauvoir gives an extremely subjective view of the mechanics of sexual intercourse. According to her, a man's 'domination is expressed in the very posture of copulation'. The man's organ is 'a tool', whereas the female organ is 'only an inert receptacle' (1949: 57). Here de Beauvoir is imposing a value-loaded interpretation on to the biological facts. Yet earlier, she condemns others for a value-loaded interpretation and dismisses some people's assertions about anatomy as just mediaeval symbolism (1972: 46). To describe the vagina as merely an inert receptacle is also to be guilty of limited symbolism.

Moreover, she is guilty of anthropomorphism in introducing experiences of violation and 'interiorities' when commenting on non-human mammals. She makes no distinction between a human who reflects on his or her experience of sexual intercourse and an animal which does not. De Beauvoir states that among almost all animals the male is 'on' the female. She has to find maximum significance in the metaphor. Yet she has not even got her facts correct for non-human primates, since female monkeys do not lie on their backs. Moreover, the latter's half-squatting position, baring their buttocks in intercourse, could in fact be interpreted as aggressive not passive if adopted by humans. Perhaps de Beauvoir is thinking of the missionary pose which has sometimes been argued by Western middle-class men as evidence of male domination, but the speakers merely expose their own gymnastic rigidity and cultural bias. (I recall being given this argument by a Parisian male in 1961, and was too sexually naive to refute him.)

The process of fertilisation is also value-loaded by de Beauvoir: 'The fundamental difference between the male and female' is that the male in ejaculating his sperm 'recovers his individuality'; it separates from the body while a fertilised egg remains in the female. 'First violated, the female is then alienated . . . she becomes in part another than herself' (1972: 54). It could as well be argued that a man is alienated because he is never sure that he has successfully reproduced. De Beauvoir also lights upon the 'magnificent and gratuitous' plumage of the male as a sign of power and individuality. This again is a partial reading both of animals and humans. First, not all male animals are beplumed. Secondly, today, popularist sociobiologists explain Western women's decorative fashions as the result of biological program-ming. These explanations are inconsistent. Bright 'plumage' among women can be interpreted instead as a sign of decorative dependence.

De Beauvoir describes the strong independence of the male animal whose 'urge towards autonomy . . . is crowned with success . . . he leads a more independent life and his activities are more spontaneous . . . it is always he who commands' (1972: 56). First, the non-human male's 'command' is questionable, it depends on interpretation. Secondly, de Beauvoir reveals an existentialist value judgement which privileges autonomy and independence. Later feminists have stressed the values of co-operation and group solidarity for survival and argue that these values may in turn give a greater sense of fulfilment to the individual. Feminist historians and anthropologists have explored the solidarity of groups of women in the past and present, while the consciousness-raising groups and collectives of the Women's Liberation Movement have worked to create and reinforce solidarity.

Puberty for the girl is seen by de Beauvoir as a crisis because of physiological changes such as menstruation. She neglects to discuss puberty in males, when genital and hair growth and voice change might also be interpreted as a crisis. Her interpretation is arbitrary: 'It is during her periods that she feels her body most painfully as an obscure, alien thing . . . . Woman, like man, is her body, but her body is something other than herself' (1972: 61). She presumes that all women see menstruation as some confirmation of a separation between the self and the body. Yet equally the male seminal flow, especially in wet dreams, could be seen as self/body separation. De Beauvoir's view is governed by the Judeo-Christian perception of menstruation as polluting and threatening. Her focus on the possible pain of menstruation for some individual women can indeed be accepted as a biological fact. The implications, however, are also controversial, and the way society deals with this fact will vary historically (Sayers 1982: 110–24).

A similar emphasis on the pain and physiological risks of pregnancy is made by de Beauvoir. 'Woman experiences a more profound alienation when fertilisation has occurred' (1972: 62). She points critically to the postwar cult of maternity: 'contrary to an optimistic theory whose social utility is all too obvious . . . gestation is fatiguing work which does not offer individual benefit to the woman and on the contrary demands heavy sacrifices' (1949: 66). The pregnant woman's frequent vomitings are seen by de Beauvoir as an indication of the organism's rebellion against the species – which is gradually taking possession of the woman. In a footnote, de Beauvoir acknowledges that she is describing maternity solely from the physiological point of view and adds that 'maternity can be very rewarding psychologically for a woman, just as it can also be a disaster' (1949: 66). Thus any deference to the joys of maternity is immediately negated by the punch line. These passages are heavily underlined in my 1961 copy of *Le Deuxième sexe*. Yet today these same passages provoke anger among a younger generation of feminists.

De Beauvoir declares that there is an incompatibility between the demands of the individual and those of the species. Breastfeeding is described primarily by her as tiring and detrimental to the mother. Women have a hostile element embedded in them: 'it is the species which gnaws at them' (1949: 67). There is no discussion of any sensual pleasure, nor of the beneficial contraction of the womb during breastfeeding. The focus is on the woman as victim.

Although biological determinists of the right have also used the facts of childbearing and lactation to justify women's dependency and subordination, the same facts have been presented rather differently by de Beauvoir. I suggest that only a woman would describe the foetus and infant as a threat to the female adult. No man has to consider pregnancy as a possible experience for himself, although he might think of the *social* responsibility of fatherhood as a threat to his autonomy. To this extent, the different physiologies of male and female have different implications for each sex, but there is no *necessary* reason why a female should see maternity as a threat to her individuality: she could as well feel more complete.

Women's reproductive capacity and experience are continually seen by de Beauvoir as an enslavement. The woman's loss of fertility at menopause, albeit another crisis, is represented as a liberation. De Beauvoir also suggests there are greater instabilities in women, giving a biological or hormonal explanation for their 'hysterical' behaviour (1972: 64). Yet women's hysteria could be seen as the rational disruptive response of the repressed who refuse to accept the dominant language of their 'reasoned' oppressors. Recently feminists have begun to explore how men's apparently lesser ability to cry is linked with the social cult of masculinity.

Throughout this chapter on the biological facts, de Beauvoir slips from an apparently neutral description of the differences between male and female to one which idealises the so-called male qualities. Not only is the male presented as larger and more 'robust' but he is also more 'adventurous' and 'independent', with more 'spontaneous activities'. He is described approvingly as more 'conquering' and more 'imperious' (1949: 60). The male's genital life does not conflict with his personal existence; it apparently unfolds in a continuous way, 'without crisis and generally without accident' (1949: 69). De Beauvoir does not consider the many instances when males do not and cannot live up to her biological ideal, when they *fail* to command or when impotence prevents penetration and reproduction. De Beauvoir's refusal to consider male sexuality and masculinity as problematic occurs throughout her work.

De Beauvoir asserts that among all female mammals 'in no other is enslavement of the organism to the reproductive function more imperious nor more difficult to accept' (1949: 69). This I also once underlined. There seemed no inconsistency to me then between such biological reductionism and my underlined approval of de Beauvoir's concluding argument in this opening chapter. Since my own reproductive function seemed so difficult to accept, it seemed 'natural' that this could be universal. Some recent feminist discussion also finds no inconsistency and applauds de Beauvoir for her consideration of both biology and its social interpretation (Sayers 1982). Yet de Beauvoir's conclusions belie many of the biologically fixed explanations of her detailed discussion. While considering that the biological facts are one of the keys to understanding women, she denies that women have a fixed destiny: 'They are not enough to define a hierarchy of the sexes; they do not explain why woman is the Other; they do not condemn her to remain in this subordinate role for ever' (1949: 70). De Beauvoir also states that the significance of physical strength depends on the varying social context. In passing comments, she suggests that the female regains in maternity another type of autonomy, and that in many cases, even among animals, the male's co-operation is necessary in the care of the young. Finally, she asserts that a society's customs cannot be deduced from biology. Thus, in her general overview she reasserts the importance and variability in the interpretation by human beings of the physiological facts. As it happens, her own interpretation of those facts does not break free of her personal and historical context.

PSYCHOLOGY AND PSYCHOANALYSIS

In the second type of explanation, de Beauvoir attempts to examine an alternative one: from psychology or, in effect, psychoanalysis. Her critique of Freud (Mitchell 1974) is founded on a misreading and misinterpretation of his work, with which she seems to have only a scant acquaintance. Freud is presented by de Beauvoir as saying simplistically that women are doomed to inferiority because of their 'penis envy'. De Beauvoir attributes a biological reductionist interpretation to Freud's celebrated statement 'anatomy is destiny', which could instead be read as a description of society's treatment of the two sexes. Certainly some later psychoanalysts, the post-Freudians, are often guilty of a biological reductionist interpretation, but Mitchell has attempted to argue that Freud was merely describing the position of women in his epoch, in middle-class Vienna, rather than asserting any fixed generalisation. De Beauvoir's distinction between the biological penis and the ideological phallus as well as her emphasis on the different social significance attributed to the two sexes in infancy (volume II of *The Second Sex*) are in Mitchell's (1974) view consistent with Freud's 'real view'.

Ironically, de Beauvoir sets up her Freudian straw man and attacks him with arguments which contradict aspects of her own preceding chapter on biology. In the chapter on psychoanalysis, there is no ambiguity in her critique of biological reductionism. Mitchell suggests that de Beauvoir's misrepresentation of Freud is responsible for a string of misreadings by later feminists (e.g. Firestone 1982), who seem not to have read much Freud at source. Not surprisingly, psychoanalysis was for a while caricatured and reviled by members of the Women's Movement. Yet de Beauvoir made extensive use of psychoanalysis elsewhere in *The Second Sex*, including case studies from analysts as scientific evidence in volume II.

Subsequently, feminists have begun to reinterpret and elaborate ideas from psychoanalysis, looking at the construction of gender within early family relations (for example, Chodorow 1978). Possible sexism in the works of Freud and the French psychoanalyst and theorist Lacan have been confronted. There is disagreement as to whether the power of the phallus is universal and ahistorical (see Mitchell 1974, and Wilson 1980). Infantile sexuality and the concept of the unconscious are recognised as significant determinants and are not necessarily seen as inconsistent with a Marxist–feminist interpretation of women's subordination.

But whether or not de Beauvoir misread Freud, she has consistently denied the existence of infantile eroticism, the lasting effects of childhood relationships and the concept of the unconscious. The latter would contradict her existentialist philosophy which denies the intrusion of any such determining factor on an individual's reasoned ability to choose and change in the spontaneity of the moment. Despite de Beauvoir's theoretical position, I argue that aspects of her fiction and autobiography in fact demonstrate the continuing power of unconscious forces which surface now and then to challenge her rational control (see Okely 1986: chapters 2 and 5).

ENGELS AND ECONOMISM

Having formally rejected biological and psychological explanations for the subordination of women, de Beauvoir attempts to examine an economic one. Her main text is Engels' *The Origin of the Family, Private Property and the State* (1884), without a wider analysis of materialist/Marxist explanations. She concludes that an 'economic' explanation is unsatisfactory and returns to one drawn from existentialism, although with some commitment towards socialism. In 1961 I responded favourably to de Beauvoir's stray remarks like 'the fate of woman and that of socialism are intimately linked' (1949: 98). It is now recognised by de Beauvoir, her admirers and her critics, that such a remark demands something more specific both in theory and practice.

As in the case of her discussion of psychoanalysis, de Beauvoir has a favourable comment for aspects of a Marxist, historical materialism because it recognises humanity not as an animal species but as a historical and changing reality. Human society does not submit passively to nature but rather takes control of it, not through anything subjective and internal, but through 'praxis' (a Marxist term translated by Parshley (1972: 84) as 'practical action'). 'The consciousness which woman makes of herself . . . reflects a situation which depends on the economic organisation of society' (1949: 96). Thus de Beauvoir acknowledges a link between beliefs or ideology and the economic 'mode of production' in a standard Marxist sense. The latter term, whose definition continues to be debated, is used broadly to describe the different forms of organisation, control and distribution of a society's economic resources. Two examples of different modes of production are the feudal and capitalist systems. De Beauvoir then proceeds to reject what is now regarded by many Marxist theorists as a crude 'economism', namely the assertion that everything can be simplistically and directly reduced to an economic cause without intervening factors. Sometimes, when she thinks she is making a critique of Engels, she is in effect attacking classical non-Marxist economics; that is, she rejects a view 'that perceives in man and woman no more than economic units' (1972: 91). A Marxist would surely also agree. She misunderstands both Engels' and others' view of a wider materialist explanation. The notion of the profit-calculating 'economic man' which she attacks really belongs to classical bourgeois economics.

Engels looks at the divisions of the sexes in early history. De Beauvoir appears in this section to accept uncritically Engels' belief, which has since been discredited by most feminist anthropologists, that in earlier hunting and gathering societies there was equality, although a division of tasks between the sexes. She considers that women did productive work like pottery and weaving, but wrongly assumes that they remained at the 'hearth' (1949: 96) while men were out hunting and fishing. De Beauvoir had to depend at that time on the heavily male-biased view of early history. Feminist anthropologists have since obliged the 'experts' to recognise the crucial role of women as gatherers and foragers in hunting *and* gathering societies. Women could hardly accomplish this at the hearth, and indeed ranged many miles from the camp. Moreover, gathering often provided the vital staple food while the meat from hunting could be only an occasional luxury.

Engels explains women's subordination by the advent of private property, which he considers came with animal breeding and agriculture. Women then became property and men demanded monogamy to ensure legitimate heirs. De Beauvoir accepts Engels' description of the changes, but is not convinced by his explanation. The concept of individual ownership, she says, must be preceded by a concept of individual autonomy. This would, however, remain subjective without the practical means to satisfy it in the external world. She then paints a stereotyped Western view of primitive society in which people are allegedly a helpless prey to 'superstitious' beliefs. All is changed, she considers, with the material invention of the bronze or iron tool, but even this is insufficient, for it depends on the *attitude* of the man wielding it: 'an attitude that implies an ontological infrastructure' (1949: 100). Her emphasis on 'the tool' reflects the bias of the early historians who saw the 'phallic tool' as the only mark of culture. She does not consider how or indeed whether the male monopolised the bronze tool. De Beauvoir then offers what she later admits to be an 'idealist' explanation for male dominance; that is, she considers the primary causal factor to be people's ideas rather than any conditions which affect those ideas. In this case, the major explanation lies in man's, not woman's, wish to treat the opposite sex as 'Other'. Enslavement of any kind results from:

the imperialism of the human consciousness seeking always to exercise its sovereignty objectively. If the human consciousness had not included the original category of the Other and an original aspiration to dominate the Other, the invention of the bronze tool could not have caused the oppression of women.

(1972: 89)

Thus she explains male domination unconvincingly as a result of the male's allegedly inherent wish to dominate.

In recent years, a more sophisticated materialist/Marxist approach to the study of gender, as well as of class and race, would also reject the crude economism attacked by de Beauvoir. At the time, she showed minimum evidence of having read Marx and thus her comprehension of materialism was limited. Throughout *The Second Sex*, any attempt to link gender with a class analysis is missing. Years later de Beauvoir confessed that if she were now faced with writing *The Second Sex* her approach would differ:

> I should provide a materialistic, not an idealistic, theoretical foundation for the opposition between the Same and the Other. I should base the rejection and oppression of the Other not on antagonistic awareness but upon the economic explanation of scarcity . . . this would not modify the argument . . . that all male ideologies are directed at justifying the oppression of women, and that women are so conditioned by society that they consent to this oppression.

(1977: 483–4)

However, when de Beauvoir later inserted materialism into a study of another category, the aged (1970), the results are unconvincing (see Evans 1985: 112).

Some feminist theorists, while continuing to reject Engels' hopelessly inadequate armchair anthropology and the assumption that many pre-capitalist societies were marked by equality between the sexes, have none the less been stimulated by his attempt to link changes in the subordination of women to changes in the larger economy or mode of production (see Sacks 1974, and Delmar 1976). In this sense de Beauvoir's idealist critique of Engels and of materialist explanations has subsequently been rejected.

THE EXPERIENCE OF WOMANHOOD

In volume II of *The Second Sex*, de Beauvoir attempts to describe through the various stages of a woman's life how she is *made* feminine. It is at the opening of this volume, entitled 'L'Expérience vécue' or 'Lived experience' (translated misleadingly by Parshley as 'Woman's life today'), that we find the celebrated statement, already partially quoted:

> One is not born, but rather becomes a woman. No biological, psychic, or

economic destiny determines the figure that the human female assumes in the midst of society; it is civilisation as a whole that elaborates this creature, intermediary between male and eunuch, which is classified as feminine. Only the intervention of others can establish an individual as an Other.

(1949: 13)

The last sentence confirms her existentialist explanation that woman is seen as Other; however, de Beauvoir is not very convincing as to *why* this should occur.

Volume II places its arguments in a detailed description of the girl's and woman's actual experience rather than in ideological representations of 'woman'. De Beauvoir gives the impression that this is a description of the experience of all women at *all* times. This suggestion is highly suspect, especially in the light of today's more detailed and solid research, although there are still feminist theorists who take their white, Western and ethnocentric model as universal, with scant regard for other cultures and the specificity of race (Carby 1982). De Beauvoir somewhat defeats her case that woman is made, not born, by resorting to a universalistic language as if 'woman' or 'the young girl' always apparently experienced life as de Beauvoir described it. To be fair, the single-paragraph serving as the introduction to volume II states:

When I use the words 'woman' or 'feminine' I obviously refer to no archetype, no changeless essence whatever; the reader must understand the phrase, 'in the present state of education and custom' after most of my statements.

(1972: 31)

However, this warning still ignores class and race and is quickly forgotten, especially in the translation, where Parshley moves it to the opening of Volume I. Sometimes her generalised descriptions conceal not only a cultural, class and historical bias but also a very personal experience – that of herself. This becomes clearer when passages in her *Memoirs* (1959) are found to echo descriptions of the young girl in *The Second Sex* (cf. Okely 1986: chapter 2). To this extent, de Beauvoir's analysis draws on concrete evidence which has sometimes been overlooked. For example, in a recent study, Mary Evans rightly finds severe limitations in *The Second Sex* in so far as it lacks a material base:

Materialists among feminists have been on much firmer ground in their accounts of sexual relations . . . different wage rates . . . Discrepancies in . . . access to social and political power can all be demonstrated from 'evidence drawn from social reality'.

(1985: 73)

Evans does not, however, notice the concealed ethnography in de Beauvoir, who uses literature and documentary case studies only as illustrations of a pre-existing and coherent account of her own circle and some others. Thus de Beauvoir's text is lacking neither specific evidence nor first-hand fieldwork from 'social reality'; the severity of its limitations lies in what she chooses to observe and to omit. Given that she relies so much on personal experience, she does not or cannot escape her class and cultural entourage, and all the while she remains blissfully unaware of such limits. Part of this is explained by her belief in individual free choice which existentialism emphasises over all wider determinants. De Beauvoir thus feels free to ignore the class and cultural specificity of her relatively privileged circle.

Instead of rejecting de Beauvoir wholesale because she is proved to be merely 'subjective', I argue that it is the very specificity of her material which, in its time, gave the book its appeal, both to those who shared some of her experience and those who did not. Her generalisations, especially in volume II, are grounded in concrete experience, however limited. The vivid detail aroused public hostility and yet privately inspired many white, middle-class women who recognised some parallel experience embedded in her text. It could be read by women of another race and culture as an internal critique of the West, and some of them also found parallels in their own gender or class position. And testimonies of Middle Eastern and Indian women (see Okely 1986: 3–4) record their appreciation of de Beauvoir's mere act of questioning.

Volume II has three major sections. First, 'Formation', which deals with the different stages of the female from infancy to puberty and sexual initiation. De Beauvoir's account of early infancy develops some of the biological and psychoanalytical points raised in volume I, but while more emphasis is placed here on the social and experiential factors which go to create the gender of the child, there are again traces of biological reductionism, despite de Beauvoir's avowed rejection of this.

De Beauvoir offers an explanation for the different gender identities: 'only the intervention of others can establish an individual as an *"Other"*' (1949: 13). She suggests that the child alone would not be able to imagine herself or himself as sexually differentiated. If people notice that a girl even from infancy is sexually specified, this is not because

> mysterious instincts directly doom her to passivity, coquetry, maternity; it is because the influence of others upon the child is a factor almost from the start, and thus she is indoctrinated with her vocation from her earliest years.

> (1972: 296)

De Beauvoir does not support any suggestion that gender identity is significant at a pre-verbal stage.

At some point after weaning, boys are expected to be more independent of the mother than girls. In this sense girls are privileged. The boy is persuaded by the mother or nurse that more is demanded of him because he is superior. This is confirmed through a concrete object: his possession of the penis. To this extent de Beauvoir's argument is that the power given to the penis as phallus is a social not a biological fact. However, now and again she verges on a 'natural' explanation. 'Anatomically, the penis is well suited for this role, detached from the body' (1949: II, 18). De Beauvoir says it seems like a 'natural little plaything, a sort of doll' (Parshley (1972: 299) misleadingly translated doll/poupée as puppet).

Generally de Beauvoir's explicit argument is that a child's different anatomy does not *inevitably* produce a sense of superiority or inferiority. Those feelings are stimulated by the way in which adults encourage the child to think about his or her anatomy: mothers and nurses encourage a boy's pride in his penis, but do not draw attention to the girl's genitals. De Beauvoir rejects both a psychoanalytical theory (be it Freudian or not) of a girl's inevitable penis envy and a castration theory; it depends whether she is already dissatisfied with her situation.

De Beauvoir's ambivalence between social or biological causes is made more explicit when she suggests that the penis, as an external object which can be taken hold of, is a useful means for the boy to project the mystery of his body on to something outside himself. The penis can, she says, be a symbol of autonomy, transcendence and power. Although a little boy might fear castration, de Beauvoir suggests that this is easier to overcome than the vague fear which the little girl has towards her 'insides', a fear 'which often will be perpetuated throughout her life as a woman' (1949: II, 25). De Beauvoir gives a gender twist to the existentialist idea that a person becomes free by projecting herself or himself into transcendent activities by suggesting that only the male can 'naturally' find this transcendence through the body. Again, therefore, we find the hint of anatomical determinism. Apparently the woman's genitals are doomed to be seen only as 'an envelope which is not to be grasped by hand, in a sense she has no sex' (1949: II, 18).

De Beauvoir does not explore the possibility that the female genitals are more than mere absences. The Western, Judeo-Christian tradition has encouraged the perception of female genitals as a blank space, when in fact the mons venus with pubic hair, the labia major and minor, clitoris and entrances could be considered highly visible. They are indeed *made* invisible in much of European sculpture and painting. The female genitals can alternatively be viewed as a voracious mouth rather than as a mere gap. Many Western women have been *made* to treat them as invisible.

The absence of ink marks in the early pages of my 1961 copy of volume II confirms de Beauvoir's statements about the repression of female sexuality; it reflects not only the age, gender, culture and class of the reader but also the epoch. The first recorded contact between author and virgin reader appears when illuminating social statements are made about the construction of sexual shame and gender asymmetry. If de Beauvoir's anatomical discussions elicited anything, it had to be repressed. Today, I can freely and casually take her to task for treating the female genitalia as a blank. In the past, if not today, the male genitals were for many young women also made mysteriously blank; that is, on a conscious level. We were not to know about such things until the wedding night. De Beauvoir's 'forward' discussion of the penis and of little boys urinating seemed vaguely disgusting and certainly threatening to a female product of a single-sex upbringing (see chapters 7 and 8, this volume).

This is not to say that the male genitals and their phallic power were ever denied. They were on display at the Louvre, if only shrivelled and of cold marble. Every now and then they popped out as threats, not sources of pleasure. My first remembered sight of a penis was by courtesy of an immaculate besuited young gentleman, with neat French beard, who leapt into a courtyard off rue Soufflot as my friend Margaret and I descended some stairs towards him. He shook his floppy implement and fixed us with an empty stare. I was numbed. Margaret, thanks to her parents' relaxed approach to nudity, dismissed him with an angry sweep of her hand. The gentleman withdrew. De Beauvoir's adolescent experience of gropers and flashers described in her *Memoirs* (1959: 161) seemed more relevant to me in those days than her psychoanalytical discussions in *The Second Sex*.

Later feminists have, like de Beauvoir, attempted to confront in various ways the symbolic power of the phallus (for example, Millett 1970; Mitchell 1974; Gilbert and Gubar 1979). Some have contested de Beauvoir's received view of the invisibility of the female genitals by celebrating them in life and art (for example, Judy Chicago's *The Dinner Party*) and looking at the experience of other cultures (see S. Ardener 1975, 1987, and chapter 6, this volume).

Some later French feminist writers like Irigaray (1977) have used the female genitals or whole body as powerful sources for an apparently basic feminine identity. De Beauvoir would not be criticised by them for any suggestion of anatomical determinism as such, but instead she would be criticised for having 'internalised' the negation of the female anatomy. These writers lay even greater emphasis on anatomy or the 'essential nature' of the female body and have paradoxically evoked a sympathetic approach from de Beauvoir (Jardine 1979).

Irigaray considers that there exists a hidden, essentially feminine sexuality which derives from the distinct female anatomy and the 'two lips' (Irigaray 1977: 65). Accordingly, women's anatomy gives them a unique erotic experience, and Irigaray builds a theory of language on this. Whereas masculine language has a unity because of the 'singularity' of the penis, for women there are always at least two meanings.

Irigaray and others have in turn been criticised for their 'biologism' by other feminists (Brown and Adams 1979). Thus any traces of biologism in de Beauvoir would not necessarily be seen as grounds for rejection by such writers as Irigaray (cf. Sayers 1982: 169). None the less, de Beauvoir's tendency towards anatomical determinism is ambivalent and contradicts her emphasis on social intervention.

De Beauvoir returns in her argument to the assertion that the penis is valued only because society says so and therefore contests a simplistic suggestion that anatomy is destiny (cf. Mitchell 1974):

> In reality it is not an anatomical destiny that dictates the young girl's attitude . . . . If its [the penis] value is retained . . . it is because the penis has become the symbol of virility which is socially valorised. In this matter the effect of education and surroundings is indeed immense.
>
> (1949: II, 26)

The passivity which is considered part of the ideal 'feminine' woman is not a biological fact, she states, but is imposed by the woman's educators and by society. In this sense she rejects a biological explanation for any apparently fixed 'feminine' character, and is therefore not in tune with some recent radical feminists who support the notion of 'natural' and 'essential' female qualities across time and space.

When contrasting the upbringing of the young girl with the young boy, de Beauvoir gives a devastating description of the little girl's fate. As de Beauvoir moves towards the girl's experience of puberty, menstruation and sexual awareness, the evidence becomes more specific, although disguised as universal. There are illuminating examples from literature, including that of Carson McCullers, but there are also traces of her own experience. The description of a father's reaction to the daughter's first menstruation (1972: 337) echoes evidence from the *Memoirs*. The constraints on bodily movement recall her own. Again there is the tendency, despite her formal denial, to present the girl's responses as universal and therefore programmed by biology or some innate psychology.

After each menstruation, the young girl is alleged to feel 'the same disgust at this flat and stagnant odour . . . of the swamp, and of wilted violets' (1972: 337–8). De Beauvoir explains an adolescent girl's sado-masochistic practices as a way of dealing with this disgust at menstruation and the thought of adult sex. She does not consider that these practices could as well be the sublimation of desires. At other times the young girl escapes into solitude; she becomes 'intoxicated with her isolation' and sees herself as 'different, superior, exceptional'. She makes a promise that her future 'will be a revenge upon the mediocrity of her present life' (1972: 364). There was certainly autobiographical authenticity in this isolation, possibly a state shared by some of her readers in the 1950s and early 1960s. I once vigorously underlined this theme.

An extremely phallocentric view of male sexuality is presented. Apparently the experience of male puberty is relatively simple. Erotic desire is not realised within the young man himself but is projected outwards. 'The erection is the expression of this need . . . he projects himself toward the other without losing his autonomy; the feminine flesh is for him a prey' (1949: II, 130). Although de Beauvoir argued earlier that the significance of the penis/ phallus has its origins in the social context, here she has 'internalised' the primacy of the penis/phallus for man's eroticism.

De Beauvoir offers descriptions of the differing social constraints or freedoms permitted to young girls and boys. She does not consider that these differences would both reflect and reinforce each gender's subsequent attitude to and experience of their sexuality. A languid sensuality of the whole body may be culturally repressed. Margaret Walters (1979) shows how the ideal in Western art depicts the adult male nude as lacking receptive sensuality. If ever passive, the male nude must be heroic in pain, pierced with nails and arrows. Sometimes the active, whole body is portrayed as a giant phallus. These representations are culturally specific and not necessarily a picture of the innate and universal. With life experience, I can make these observations, but as a young virgin I was dependent on the public representations of male sexuality which de Beauvoir unwittingly reflected.

The view of the woman as passive prey in sexual intercourse is confirmed as follows:

> It is through the vagina that the woman is penetrated and fertilised, it only becomes an erotic centre by the intervention of the male and that always constitutes a kind of rape.
>
> (1949: II, 130)

Not yet having been initiated, and deferential to de Beauvoir, the mother/ author and initiator, I underlined that sentence.

De Beauvoir later said that she was wrong to suggest that a girl's defloration was always felt as such and dissociated herself from the more generalised view that sexual intercourse was a rape on each occasion. She was 'shocked' at such an assertion: 'When one says that intercourse is rape, basically one is adopting male myths. That would mean that the male sex organ really is a sword, a weapon' (Schwarzer 1984: 36).

De Beauvoir was herself the recipient of male myths, and some peculiarly close to those of her own initiator and lover, Sartre. Whereas the preceding description of the female sexual organs presents them as near invisible, her subsequent metaphors are vivid and grotesque. Her own disgust, disguised as a universal, combines with Sartre's antipathy towards the raw and viscous, something which de Beauvoir was to recognise as peculiar to him and consistent with his 'refusal of all bodily passivity' (1984: 315–17, 334).

> The female sexual desire is like the soft palpitation of the mollusc. While man has impetuosity, woman has only impatience; her expectation can be intense without ceasing to be passive; man dives upon his prey like the

eagle and the hawk; woman waits like the carnivorous plant, the marshes in which insects and children are swallowed up. She is absorption, suction, vent hole, humus, pitch and glue, a still summons, insinuating and viscous.

(1949: IIk, 148)

The chapter on sexual initiation ends with pleas for mutual generosity, reciprocity and an end to the conditions which perpetuate women's inhibitions, all of which I vigorously underlined. Thus de Beauvoir's apparent message that a girl's sexual disgust with herself was somehow innate was not always read that way. There were in any case instances where the female reader might not see her own experience; for example, I did not see menstruation as the revolting thing she described; it was a joyful blossoming into womanhood and possible fertility in those early days. Our reading was selective, for there was sufficient material into which we could read our own conditions and de Beauvoir's polemic invited us to change them.

The passages on heterosexual relations were treated as textbook information to cloistered middle-class girls, if not to others. The public taboo against pre-marital sex in that epoch was accompanied by greater censorship of film and print. D. H. Lawrence's *Lady Chatterley's Lover*, the works of Burroughs and Miller, were still banned in Britain in the early 1960s – something which feminists might now see as a mixed blessing. Both the pornographic and less exploitative publications were unavailable. The mood was one of secrecy and repression. The public discussion of sexuality in schools was confined to animal reproduction; that of human sexuality was reserved for medical experts. When confronted with a woman's text, some readers took de Beauvoir's descriptions of sexual intercourse as the truth and as future guide. My double or triple ink lines agree with the most questionable assertions . . . for example, that after intercourse the man becomes an integrated body, separate and preoccupied with the mundane – 'he wants to sleep, take a bath, smoke a cigarette, go out in the fresh air' – while the woman apparently wants to prolong the carnal contact (1949: II, 162; 1972: 417). Subsequent life experience and more public discussion deny these observations which merely reflected de Beauvoir's own. De Beauvoir was considered especially outrageous by her critics for having discussed lesbianism, and although some of her uninformed readers considered that she had, however clumsily, 'normalised' lesbianism, her discussion is inadequate and sometimes a caricature of relations between women. For example, de Beauvoir reiterates some of the stereotypes of 'butch' or 'male' roles in lesbian couples. In those days, the subject was so taboo that, despite or because of my previous residence in a single-sex boarding school, not one word is underlined of that chapter.

The second section, 'Situation', deals with the circumstances and roles allotted to adult women, usually in terms of their relationship with men: for example, the married woman, the mother, the prostitute and the mistress. De Beauvoir's autobiographies again reveal the first-hand sources for her descriptions of these different adult experiences of women. In the case of the wife or the kept mistress, she writes from observations of other women in her circle. The polemic and value judgements do, however, come from a personal stance; her rejection of marriage, maternity, housework and the role of economically and emotionally dependent mistress. De Beauvoir's details about marriage find echoes in her observed experience of her mother, but again this is not made explicit. In the subsequent book about her mother she reveals: 'Her case alone would be enough to convince me that bourgeois marriage is an unnatural institution' (1969: 32). Her lengthy discussion of abortion, as opposed to childbirth, at the opening of the chapter on 'The mother' continues to provoke anger. This was indeed her experience of conception. Years later, in the 1970s, she joined a public demonstration composed entirely of women who confessed to having had an illegal abortion.

The third section, 'Justifications', includes examples of women who seem to be both victims and guilty of 'bad faith' by colluding in their subordinate state. They are the 'narcissist', 'the woman in love' and the 'mystic'. Some show the worst excesses of masochistic self-denial or deluded self-adoration. There are some individuals in her autobiographies, especially Louise, apparently maddened by love (1965: 167–79), who reappear in different guises throughout her work, whether as a general 'type' in *The Second Sex* or as a character in her fiction: Paula in *Les Mandarins* (1954), for example. The theme of the rejected mistress, mad and masochistic, in these three forms – in documentation, theory or fiction – worked best for some novice feminists like myself as a general, theoretical category in *The Second Sex*. If left only in her autobiography or fiction, these women might have appeared merely as chance individuals, without any import for the study of women in general.

This possibility is confirmed by the contrasting attitude of another middle-class white woman of my generation. Whereas she devoured de Beauvoir's early novels and autobiographies, she deliberately avoided *The Second Sex*, not because it was heavy going, but because she wanted to distance herself from any generalised theories about women. She could not accept any overall description of women's subordination. Instead, she preferred to identify herself with de Beauvoir's individual examples of a 'free', intellectual woman: Françoise in *L'Invitée* (1943) or Anne in *Les Mandarins* (1954). In this way, she distanced herself from the 'failed' middle-class women whom she saw around her, and continued for a time to believe that women could achieve anything through individual effort. Today, she rejects this type of analysis.

The final section of volume II, 'Towards liberation', devotes considerable space to de Beauvoir's notion of the independent woman and provides the inspiring alternative to the preceding degraded and depressing pictures of women. Its positive inspiration, like other sections, is still not separate from a forceful description of ways in which women's independence is suppressed. At the outset, de Beauvoir declares that the kept woman – wife or courtesan – is not enfranchised of the male because she has in her hands a ballot sheet. . . . She still remains in the position of vassal . . . it is through work alone that she is guaranteed concrete liberty.

(1949: II, 521)

Here de Beauvoir makes the mistake of overlooking unpaid domestic labour and defining work as only that which is paid, although elsewhere in the volume she devotes considerable attention to the labour of housework. She also underestimates the servitude of most women's external employment. Here, in contrast to the preceding sections, de Beauvoir focuses explicitly rather than covertly on the condition of the middle-class woman, with or without a career. The connection between her observations and her own position is less ambiguous. Again, her autobiography reveals some of her sources. The conflicting pressures and problems facing a woman are minutely documented: for example, the demands of outward conformity to a masculine model within the workplace, the pressures to hide intelligence and determination behind a 'feminine' mask, the restrictions on 'sexual adventures' and the incompatibility between a career and marriage or a long-term partnership. The woman is still expected to be 'a true woman . . . a good housekeeper, a devoted mother such as wives traditionally are' (1972: 703). Since de Beauvoir is herself an unusually privileged example of independence, her evidence and polemic here can only be relevant to a minority of women at the apex of a Western class hierarchy. For it is still the case that the external employment which de Beauvoir advocated for all women would, for the majority, mean wage labour in exploitative conditions rather than a fulfilling 'career'.

In the section on independence, de Beauvoir exposes most clearly the reasons for her stand against maternity:

There is one feminine function that is actually almost impossible to perform in complete liberty. It is maternity . . . having a child is enough to paralyse a woman's activity entirely; she can go on working only if she abandons it to relatives, friends, or servants.

(1972: 705)

Thus her biologically based description of maternity (in the opening pages of volume I) which weighs a woman to the earth, and roots her in immanence because she merely maintains the species, is implicitly modified here by de Beauvoir's description of a specific context. If the problems of maternity can be explained by the *social* organisation of childcare rather than by innate biological differences, then they are also amenable to change.

A younger generation of feminists will recoil from the negative view of motherhood. The section on the independent woman may be dismissed because it is concerned with the dilemmas faced by a middle-class woman who has chosen to reject maternity. De Beauvoir did not adequately explore any suggestion that men should share childcare. Whereas in the 1950s and 1960s rejection of or delay in maternity was identified by some middle-class women as a feminist stance, today maternity is explicitly reintegrated within feminism, although it may not be easier in practice. This second volume of *The Second Sex* still offers a rich ethnography of some women's experience. Many of de Beauvoir's observations continue to touch upon key questions even in changed times. Some aspects have subsequently become the subject for specialised studies; for example, a girl's education, female sexuality, marriage, maternity, housework, prostitution and romantic love. De Beauvoir's concluding discussion on the independent woman affirms that this ideal state is as yet impossible, but she does discuss the kind of equality which liberation should entail. It is interesting to see how she attempted such liberation in her own life (see Okely 1986: chapters 2 and 5).

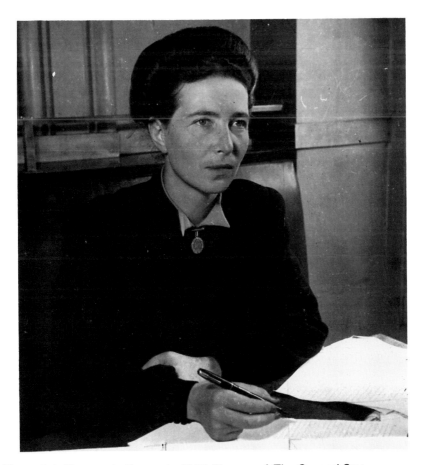

Figure 9.1 Simone de Beauvoir, 1947: The era of *The Second Sex*.
Source: Hulton Deutsch Collection.

NOTE

1 For a discussion of the scandal of the distorted and heavily cut translation see Okely 1986: 53–4. Where I refer to the French edition (1949), the translations are my own. All references are to volume I, unless specified as 1949 volume II. References dated 1972 are from the English translation where I consider that they are reasonably accurate.

REFERENCES

Ardener, E. (1975) 'Belief and the problem of women', in S. Ardener (ed.) *Perceiving Women*, London: Malaby Press.
Ardener, S. (1975) 'Sexual insult and female militancy', in S. Ardener (ed.) *Perceiving Women*, London: Malaby Press.
—— (1987) 'Notes toward a female iconography', in P. Caplan (ed.) *The Cultural Construction of Sexuality*, London: Tavistock.
Ascher, C. (1981) *Simone de Beauvoir: A Life of Freedom*, Brighton: Harvester Press.
Barrett, M. (1980) *Women's Oppression Today*, London: Verso.
—— (1984) 'Rethinking women's oppression: a reply to Brenner and Ramas', *New Left Review* 146.
Beauvoir, S. de (1943) *L'Invitée*, Paris: Gallimard.
—— (1949) *Le Deuxième sexe*, vol. I *Les Faits et les mythes*; vol. II *L'Expérience vécue*, Paris: Gallimard.
—— (1954) *Les Mandarins*, Paris: Gallimard.
—— (1959) *Memoirs of a Dutiful Daughter*, Harmondsworth: Penguin.
—— (1965) *The Prime of Life*, Harmondsworth: Penguin.
—— (1968) *Force of Circumstance*, Harmondsworth: Penguin.
—— (1969) *A Very Easy Death*, Harmondsworth: Penguin.
—— (1970) *La Vieillesse*, Paris: Gallimard.
—— (1972) *The Second Sex*, trans. H. Parshley, Harmondsworth: Penguin.
—— (1977) *All Said and Done*, Harmondsworth: Penguin.
—— (1981) *La Cérémonie des adieux*, Paris: Glassimard.
—— (1984) *Adieux – Farewell to Sartre*, London: André Deutsch.
Bloch, J. and Bloch, M. (1980) 'Women and the dialectics of nature in eighteenth-century thought', in C. McCormack and M. Strathern (eds) *Nature, Culture and Gender*, Cambridge: Cambridge University Press.
Brenner, J. and Ramas, M. (1984) 'Rethinking women's oppression', *New Left Review* 144.
Brown, B. and Adams, P. (1979) 'The feminine body and feminist politics', *M/F* no. 3.
Carby, H. (1982) 'White woman listen! Black feminism and the boundaries of sisterhood', in *The Empire Strikes Back*, Centre for Contemporary Cultural Studies, University of Birmingham, London: Hutchinson.
Chodorow, N. (1978) *The Reproduction of Mothering*, Berkeley: University of California Press.
Craig, C. (1979) 'Simone de Beauvoir's *The Second Sex* in the light of the Hegelian master–slave dialectic and Sartrian existentialism'. Unpublished Ph.D. thesis, University of Edinburgh.
Delmar, R. (1976) 'Looking again at Engels's *Origin of the Family, Private Property and the State*', in J. Mitchell and A. Oakley (eds) *The Rights and Wrongs of Women*, Harmondsworth: Penguin.
Evans, M. (1985) *Simone de Beauvoir: A Feminist Mandarin*, London: Tavistock.
Firestone, S. (1982) *The Dialectic of Sex*, London: Paladin.

Gilbert, S. and Gubar, S. (eds) (1979) *The Madwoman in the Attic*, New Haven: Yale University Press.

Harris, O. (1980) 'The power of signs: gender, culture and the wild in the Bolivian Andes', in C. McCormack and M. Strathern (eds) *Nature, Culture and Gender*, Cambridge: Cambridge University Press.

Irigaray, L. (1977) 'Women's exile', interview with Luce Irigaray, *M/F* no. 1: 62–76.

Jardine, A. (1979) 'Interview with Simone de Beauvoir', *Signs* 5(2): 224–36.

La Fontaine, J. (1972) 'Ritualisation of women's life-crises in Bugisu', in J. La Fontaine (ed.) *The Interpretation of Ritual*, London: Tavistock.

McCormack, C. and Strathern, M. (eds) (1980) *Nature, Culture and Gender*, Cambridge: Cambridge University Press.

Millett, K. (1970) *Sexual Politics*, London: Virago.

Mitchell, J. (1974) *Psychoanalysis and Feminism*, Harmondsworth: Allen Lane.

Oakley, A. (1972) *Sex, Gender and Society*, London: Temple Smith.

Okely, J. (1986) *Simone de Beauvoir – A Re-Reading*, London: Virago/ Pantheon.

Ortner, S. (1974) 'Is female to male as nature is to culture?', in M. Rosaldo and L. Lamphere (eds) *Woman, Culture and Society*, Stanford: Stanford University Press.

Sacks, K. (1974) 'Engels revisited: women, the organisation of production, and private property', in M. Rosaldo and L. Lamphere (eds) *Woman, Culture and Society*, Stanford: Stanford University Press.

Sartre, J.-P. (1938) *La Nausée*, Paris: Gallimard.

——— (1943) *L'Etre et le néant*, Paris: Gallimard.

Sayers, J. (1982) *Biological Politics*, London: Tavistock.

Schwarzer, A. (1984) *Simone de Beauvoir Today: Conversations 1972–1982*, London: Chatto and Windus.

Walters, M. (1979) *The Nude Male*, Harmondsworth: Penguin.

Wilson, E. (1980) *Only Halfway to Paradise: Women in Post-War Britain 1945–1968*, London: Tavistock.

Chapter 10

Defiant moments

Gender, resistance and individuals

This chapter re-examines Phyllis Kaberry's study of Aboriginal women where, in contrast to earlier studies, she is concerned to present women as active subjects rather than submissive objects. Gender complementarity is implied. But a re-analysis of the ethnography reveals gender asymmetry and the ultimate subordination of women. I argue for an alternative approach to the study of individuals and active subjects, focusing on moments of resistance to the conditions of subordination. In some circumstances these may be the ingredients for a mass protest but in others they occur in fragmented form. The atypical also gives insights into structures of power. Two examples are presented from my own experience: an Oxfordshire deserter from the Great War and a Normandy woman dairy farmer. The contexts of their resistance are outlined. The apparent eccentricity of these two individuals has been or will be vindicated in time. But they and others have risked being homogenised, or buried in field notes and lost for history.

I celebrate the work of Phyllis Kaberry – one of our anthropological mothers. To honour her and other women anthropologists is to restore a lost lineage, for social anthropology is a discipline passed on by fictive descent.[1] The descent system is often patrilineal. Whereas the revered male figures of the discipline such as Malinowski and Radcliffe-Brown have academic offspring, female figures such as Mead are strangely barren (Brian Morris, personal communication). It may be no improvement to create a matrilineal, or rather matriarchal, academic descent system, but there are intellectual rewards to be gained from looking again at our intellectual mothers and great-aunts.

An interpretation of women anthropologists in the past will involve both an understanding of the time in which they worked, and also a critique from the present. Some of the questions raised by Kaberry's work fall straight into current debates within both feminist and general anthropology. In the early 1970s, a number of women anthropologists (Rosaldo and Lamphere 1974; Reiter 1975; S. Ardener 1975) and a few men (E. Ardener 1975) asked why it was that women were marginalised in many monographs. Some renewed questions about their subordination. Beyond her ethnographic area, however, it seemed that Kaberry's pioneering contributions had disappeared from the anthropological mainstream in Britain, if not elsewhere.

In the 1930s, Kaberry was innovative in focusing on women, and in the context of their relations with men. In providing detailed ethnographies of women, she reversed an established tradition of ethnographies which purported to be about both sexes but which were really about men. She aimed to describe women's active participation in both Australian Aboriginal and West African societies. In asserting women to be active subjects rather than submissive objects, she effectively by-passed the question of their subordination. A similar position continues in contemporary anthropology. It is still considered important by some anthropologists to counter the labelling of women as mere pawns and objects, but in the process, the anthropologists and their readers may be charmed into the comfortable conclusion that women are equal but different. Such implications are embedded in Kaberry's *Aboriginal Woman: Sacred and Profane* (1939).

SUBSERVIENCE AND SUBORDINATION IN KABERRY'S ACCOUNT OF ABORIGINAL WOMEN

Kaberry commenced her first field research at a specific moment in anthropological history and in the consideration of the subordination of women. The earlier theories of Bachofen and beliefs in matriarchy or an original mother-right had been largely discredited. Women were generally seen as subordinate in societies studied by anthropologists. Engels' argument, that the subordination of women only began with private property and the ownership of cattle and land, could not hold if gathering and hunting societies were shown to have gender hierarchy. The Australian Aborigines, although changed by the horrendous intrusions of white settlers, including missionisation, land theft and genocide, offered examples of gathering and hunting societies. The general anthropological agreement was that women were subordinate in these societies.

The study of the form that subordination took was neither considered of import, nor was subordination seen as problematic. Aboriginal women were so portrayed, as if subordinate once and for all, without signs of resistance. Comparisons with Western anthropologists' own societies were complacent and uncritical in the anthropological texts. The language used to describe Aboriginal women was not of the sort which Western male anthropologists would openly dare to apply to women of their own race and class, although the pejorative metaphors were drawn from Western culture. Kaberry (1939: 9) quoted Ashley Montagu (1937: 23), for whom Aboriginal women were 'no more than "domesticated cows"'. Since in the English-speaking world, the equation of women with cows is a form of abuse, a way of treating them as objects, it is no wonder that Kaberry was to resist the comparison. Earlier, her teacher, Malinowski, whom Kaberry quotes (1939: 9, 15), had claimed that in Australian Aboriginal society 'the relation of a husband to wife is in its economic aspect, that of a master to its slave' (Malinowski 1913: 287). Thus Kaberry was conducting a critical argument with her male anthropological mentors. Those who had done fieldwork had very little material on women (Elkin 1939: xix).

Kaberry was also engaged in a covert debate with a European or white settler view; an external objectification of women and Aborigines which was not only ethnocentric but also potentially racist. This hidden debate makes sense of Kaberry's intermittent and seemingly arbitrary comparisons, in her text, between Aboriginal women and settler (or European) women. Aboriginal women usually come out better. Although these interventions divert us from internal comparisons with Aboriginal men, from considerations of men's relations with women and from generalised discussions of women's subordination, Kaberry's comments are comprehensible if seen as a counter to the male anthropologists' view that Aboriginal women were mere 'beasts of burden', and therefore unlike white women. Kaberry was speaking to a time after the granting of female suffrage, when the subordination of European women had again disappeared from dominant political or academic discourse. By contrast, women in so-called primitive societies were seen as brutalised in what could be read as an early stage in a social evolutionary process preceding Western civilisation. Such stereotyping of the primitive was everywhere a convenient rationale for colonialism or genocide.

Kaberry (1939: 8) commenced her monograph with an outsider's impression of 'the subservience of the women and the imposition on them of the more onerous and monotonous tasks'. Thus the agenda is set. Kaberry is forced into a counter-argument that women's work is neither onerous nor monotonous. The covert argument is with a European tradition which sees the release from manual labour and all external production as the ideal for the wife of the privileged. By contrast, feminist anthropologists of the 1970s and later might seize upon this example from the Aborigines as a counter to the universalising stereotype of women's physiological weakness.

From the outset Kaberry is concerned to humanise Aboriginal woman and to 'envisage her as an active social personality: as a human being' (ibid. 9). Women are interpreted as more autonomous than earlier anthropologists had claimed. Their labour in gathering food, in childcare and domestic production is seen as indispensable. They have rights in land through descent, they participate in a few rites controlled by men and their own ceremonies. Above all, Kaberry argues, they are not subservient. What is submerged in the text is the question of women's subordination, which is confused with the question of subservience. To claim that women are not subservient is to demonstrate that they are active subjects and not passive objects. To claim that women are not subordinate is to demonstrate that in all spheres, such as the economic, political, ritual and sexual, women are not lacking in authority, power and control relative to men (see Okely 1975: 69, and p. 77 above).

As a detailed first-hand account of a gathering and hunting society, Kaberry's study can be seen as an invaluable test of Engels' (1958 [1884]) argument and its subsequent elaborations. Kaberry's monograph gives us ample material for analysis, regardless of the intended forms of her argument. If we look at the economic and political power relations and gender differences embedded in ritual and ideological constructs, her own evidence can be read differently as supporting a thesis of subordination. Kaberry confirmed in detail Malinowski's conclusion, from various sources (Malinowski 1913: 283, 288), that women supplied the major proportion of subsistence through their gathering of wild fruits, honey, etc. Men's contribution of meat through hunting was only intermittent. The society could have survived on the women's produce, but not on meat alone, despite the latter's greater ideological value. This early ethnographic observation should have tempered subsequent notions of 'Man the Hunter', current in the 1960s, but questioned again in the 1970s (Slocum 1975; Friedl 1975).

Feminist anthropologists have argued convincingly that women's participation in external production gives them greater autonomy, in contrast to societies where women are limited entirely to domestic labour and production (Caplan and Bujra 1978). Ironically, Briffault (1927: 436) made a rather similar observation – 'so long as woman remained economically productive, it was impossible for complete patriarchal supremacy to become established' – which was cited by Kaberry (1939: 270) as a flawed argument. The question of the subordination of women is lost in her focus on the indispensability of women's external production. To point to economic necessity is not sufficient to deny subordination or exploitation.

The Aboriginal women's potential control, or lack of control, of the society's surplus and the total demands on their labour need to be examined. First, the food from gathering was invariably consumed within the domestic unit. By contrast, meat was distributed as prestigious surplus by men beyond the domestic unit and thus created and strengthened political power (cf. Friedl 1975). Additionally, the gender division of labour was asymmetrical. Women had a double shift. As well as gathering, women were responsible for the major tasks of domestic production – fetching wood and water, tending the hearth, cooking and child rearing. Kaberry's defensive argument that men's hunting was more physically strenuous is vitiated by the fact that gathering demanded sustained effort and, together with domestic production, was more time-consuming. Kaberry unwittingly draws on the stereotyped and androcentric view that short bursts of physical strength are more valuable than sustained physical stamina. The latter has been ideologically undervalued.

Without the duties of domestic labour, men were thus freed for the time and flexibility required for extra-domestic political activities. Kaberry (1939: 276) does concede that the men had a near monopoly in the political sphere. As is familiar elsewhere, women could *influence* men's decisions, but could not make them in their own right (cf. Devereux 1987: 106). Some of this influence was attempted through ritual. Here, Kaberry made another original contribution in her detailed ethnography of women's ceremonies. But again, the question of subordination cannot be ignored in her material. In what she explicitly labels 'love magic', women aspired to attract or retain potential male lovers or husbands. Energy had to be directed towards relations with individual men in which women were asymmetrical partners.

The husband also had the right to beat his wife. In practice the women were ready to retaliate with force, in spectacular contrast to the more passive conduct demanded of the European bourgeois woman (Kaberry 1939: 142). Again the question of relative submission takes precedence in Kaberry's text over that of subordination. The fact that Aboriginal women put up a fight, and ultimately lost, could alternatively be interpreted as a momentary *resistance* to their fundamental subordination, rather than as evidence of autonomy and complementarity.

Whereas the women's ceremonies documented by Kaberry are preoccupied with influencing specific males, the major ceremonies for men concern a more generalised identity, their masculinity and entry as adults into the society at large. These initiation rites are detached from any relations with specific women. Males are initiated into tribal law and participate in inter-tribal gatherings. By contrast, women are excluded from these ceremonies and the knowledge imparted. Here there is asymmetry.

Kaberry convincingly challenged the commonly held assertion among previous anthropologists that whereas men were linked to both the sacred and the profane, women were only associated with the latter. She demonstrated that women had their own ceremonies or rituals. They also, 'like the men', had 'a direct link with the spiritual forces' (ibid. 191). Through their parents they contracted rights of ownership over certain horde countries (ibid. 217), and had their links with 'Time Long Past'. Again, if we look at these ethnographic facts differently, we see asymmetry rather than complementarity. First, the Kimberley Aborigines practised virilocal post-marital residence. Wives, unlike husbands, had moved out of the territory with which they had spiritual links. Certainly, other studies of Aborigines indicate far greater flexibility in movement and in spiritual affiliation, but in Kaberry's ethnography this is not the case. Kaberry restores some spiritual identity to women, but relative to men, women have reduced spiritual rights and participation. There is veiled irony in Kaberry's observation that the mourning ceremonies held when a woman dies are one of the few occasions when a woman, albeit a dead one, is the object for an inter-tribal meeting (ibid. 216).

Subsequent studies of Aboriginal women have built upon Kaberry's pioneering observations, continuing to demonstrate how women have areas of autonomy (Rohrlich-Leavitt *et al.* 1975; Berndt 1981). More elaborate women's rituals, expressing their spiritual attachment to land and having wider impact than love magic, have been recorded (Bell 1983). Anthropologists have been compelled to examine women's participation and spiritual powers. But despite the claims of these later anthropologists, there is still evidence in these texts of women's ultimate subordination to men.

My intention, however, is to provide neither an update nor a definitive overview of the research and literature on Aboriginal gender relations since 1939. I am concerned, rather, to highlight the inconsistency between Kaberry's argument and the material which she presents in her text to substantiate it. A focus, thought necessary at the time, on women as active subjects rather than as passive objects conflates lack of subservience with absence of subordination, a conflation that is still apparent in some recent anthropological discussions of gender relations. There are indeed implications for an analysis of gender relations in other ethnographic areas both in Kaberry's time and today, as is shown by the examples I present.

SUBORDINATION AND RESISTANCE

Here I find myself thrown into a continuing controversy. Whereas the majority of anthropologists would still reject the belief in any previous era of matriarchy, some have held on to Engels' line (Leacock 1982). To me the most fruitful enquiries are those directed towards the enormous variations in the extent of women's subordination or relative autonomy, as well as towards the multiplicity of gender constructions. For some, the controversy still lies in the extent to which it can be concluded that the idea of subordination is merely a Eurocentric imposition (Keesing 1987; Errington and Gewertz 1987). It is argued that since the people do not recognise subordination, it therefore does not exist. If we were to adopt this line, we might as well abandon any attempt at anthropological analysis. Indigenous interpretations are significant; the observation that people appear content and do not see themselves as victims of domination cannot however be conclusive proof of its absence. In the last instance the anthropologist has to attempt to formulate more objective criteria. This includes examining examples of resistance which reveal the cracks in contentment.

To argue (as does Weiner 1976) that women's alternative exchanges and cosmology not only add value and self-esteem, but also cancel out men's relative political and economic power, is mystificatory. In foregrounding hitherto unstudied women's ceremonies or contributions, an overall view of subordination may be submerged. Such studies are concerned, as was Kaberry's fifty years ago, to prove that women are not mere pawns but active agents. In so doing, Weiner (1976: 11) goes so far as to confuse *activity* with equality. Yet women may be obliged, actively and not just passively, to collude with patriarchal formations (Kandiyoti 1988). The danger is that the Western observer, imbued with an ideology which associates the feminine with passivity, is so astonished at finding individual women elsewhere to be self-possessed that she or he confuses individual agency with Western notions of freedom and equality.

Given contexts where persons or groups are ultimately subordinate, we need to know more about their necessary complicity in some cases and potential or actual resistance in others. Here we may find multiple perspectives. It also depends on the occasion; who is listened to, who is doing the interpreting and where. Thus Omvedt (1978) has captured the normally concealed discontents among Indian women and Huizer (1978) has captured both peasants' discontents and the reasons for their lack of organised resistance. Since Kaberry did not look at women as subordinate, she did not analyse their potential or day-to-day resistance. Given the facts of subordination, it is the phenomenon of intermittent resistance that I now wish to address.

In the early 1970s anthropologists restated the character of women's subordination. The gender literature in Britain was inspired in part by the anthropological seminar on women initiated at Oxford in 1972–3 which continues today, and by the London Women's Anthropology Conference in 1973. At one such seminar in 1974, attended by Kaberry, I outlined the extent of Gypsy women's subordination to Gypsy men, but also asked how women in daily practice might be found to resist that subordination. I suggested we had to look in the 'crevices of . . . verbalised activities' (Okely 1975: 70 and chapter 4, this volume). Specific incidents, anecdotes, individual acts or in some cases clusters of women revealed an awareness, albeit fragmented, of their ultimately subordinate position. In some contexts they resolved, if only in imagination, problems of internal subordination, through their relations with the wider non-Gypsy society. Here I was pursuing an illuminating suggestion by de Beauvoir (1949), that we should examine the ways in which women evade subordination, as well as how they are 'apprenticed' in these conditions (Okely 1975: 84). This was tucked away in a footnote, although it formed a key to the text. My concern was in no way to suggest that Gypsy women ceased to be subordinate. I was concerned with how they resolved it and attempted to subvert or defy it in devious ways. I want now to pursue this fragmented,[2] momentary resistance.

In looking at resistance I am interested here in something other than organised protest, or sustained mass movements viewed over time. Instead I shall focus on the forms in which it may be fragmented and therefore less visible; namely, moments where resistance crystallises in isolated individual acts or gestures.[3] They may be subtly woven into daily practice. Comparable acts have sometimes become signals for mass protest.

My focus fits with other concerns of Kaberry – not only gender, but also the treatment of individuals in theoretical analysis. She argued against anthropologists such as Radcliffe-Brown, in whose texts she noted that 'A few individuals may make a brief appearance in a preface . . . but thereafter they become ciphers . . . they occupy statuses and carry out activities which maintain the social system' (Kaberry 1957: 88). Kaberry did indeed note the differences in individual women's responses, depending on kinship ties, age, experience and temperament (Kaberry 1939: 275). Nevertheless, these women were portrayed as maintaining a social system which, I have argued, reveals women's subordination. Kaberry caught a glimpse of the resentment felt by an individual woman to the routine of foraging: 'I never heard the women grumble, except in one instance, when I sympathetically brought the subject round to this point, and my informant was too human to resist the temptation' (ibid. 23). In this instance, Kaberry had used in effect the questioning technique later advocated by Omvedt (1978), which elicits a covert resistance, but instead of pursuing this alternative perspective, she dismissed it as 'not a permanent attitude'. Because it was not displayed as 'an obvious sullenness, weariness, possibly timidity and chronic resentment' (ibid. 23), this moment was considered insignificant for theorising as potential resistance.

I focus on individuals, or more specifically on individual moments, *not* out of a desire or need to ignore the wider whole; the individual always carries the cultural and social. However, my individuals are in no way selected as simple representatives of their societies. Sociologists, especially, have been bedevilled by the search for the *typical*. When individuals are treated as worthy of whole texts and dialogues, the old positivistic theories may lurk behind the choice. Shostak (1981) is repeatedly obliged to justify her study of Nisa in terms of her typicality as a !Kung woman, worrying that Nisa's story might be 'idiosyncratic'. Instead it would have been illuminating to learn why and to what extent Nisa *resisted* homogenisation. This does not mean that individual manipulation could on its own transform wider structures.

My criteria for selecting the individuals on which I shall focus includes their very ordinariness as well as their defiant acts. To social scientists, they would appear articulate, but they risk being homogenised in specific traditions, both of them rural, and being excluded from a generalising text. To conventional (rather than oral) historians they might be lost because neither have written their lives. Archival sources are so often those of the powerful, as the social historian Samuel reminds us (1975: xii).

A renewed focus on individual voices and moments has arisen for a number of theoretical reasons. Some have justified recording the specific details of the individual's voice, in humanistic terms (Plummer 1983). To eradicate the individual is seen as a betrayal. This argument has been interpreted, especially by sociologists, as a call for the kind of anecdote conventionally associated by some social scientists with literary traditions, on the grounds of an illiterate misconception that literature is mere melodrama and the stuff of emotions. Yet literature can also be clinically detached. The study of one individual, as in Shostak's work, is also mistakenly associated with the maudlin search for elusive inner feelings of other cultures ('how does it feel?'). The humanistic plea has, in the extreme case, been associated with the rejection of all generalisable theory. Here power relations and history tend to be ignored.

The Durkheimian functionalist tradition relegated the study of the individual to psychology. As with the social scientists' stereotype of literature, there is still today a lingering tendency to link the study of the individual with the arena of emotions. Kaberry, by contrast, did not restrict the study of individuals to that of emotions in her critique of Radcliffe-Brown's structural functionalism. Kaberry argued that Aboriginal women cannot be reduced to automata for reproducing determining structures. My argument with Kaberry is that she minimised the impact of the determining structures which in the last instance ensured women's subordination. Some actions can be interpreted as momentary resistance to those structures rather than as proof of equality.

Yet another interest in individual or multiple voices comes from the scepticism of the *author*, rather than of the determining structures, as all-powerful authority. This has indeed been a preoccupation in contemporary anthropological debates (e.g. Clifford and Marcus 1986), influenced by Bakhtin's (1981) decentring of the author in a quest for a dialogue or multiple voices. Bakhtin's carnivalesque, like Turner's liminal persons, reveals crucial inversions from the margins. I have seen this also among Gypsies (Okely 1983) and suggest that atypical individuals, in addition to marginalised groups and seemingly peripheral incidents, rather like Derrida's footnotes, can be studied for the critical, alternative perspectives they offer on power. Atypical individuals risk being dismissed as eccentrics, yet they are so defined by the structures which they resist (cf. Marcus 1992). Marginal voices, like the court jester, both challenge the centre and also show its form. Thus my rationale for thinking about individual moments, whether as persons or as incidents, goes beyond a humanistic rescue operation and beyond what is naively interpreted as mere entertainment.

Certainly, an exclusive focus on individuals can *also* be a betrayal, as in the current political rhetoric (in Britain) that there is no society, only individuals. It is no paradox that this ideology emanates from an increasingly powerful state. I am not proposing that individuals be seen as self-contained or unitary. Instead, we could look at *aspects* of individuals or specific moments in their lives. Key incidents or actions may be momentarily located in persons, and then disappear in history.

Through careful examination and in the telling, we can discover that specific moments in individual lives inform us about both dominance and points of resistance. To retain some of the specificities in analysis and writing is another way towards a more total knowledge, if we allow ourselves to surrender to it. The holistic approach of which anthropologists are so proud should embrace passing moments, whether in defiance or conformity. The individual moment also has its hidden structures, unique in combination yet always culturally and historically shaped (cf. Samuel 1975: xix).

TWO CASE STUDIES

I take two examples of fragmented defiance located in individuals at specific moments of their life cycles and in history. The individuals I narrate have both resisted at specific moments in their lives. They are both exceptional, partly through these moments. They were neither born with nor acquired privilege. As to whether their distinctiveness owes anything to the ideology of Western individualism, I remain sceptical. There are, of course, distinctive individuals in non-Western cultures too, which do not share this ideology (cf. Spencer 1992).

I knew these two individuals over a number of years and lived in their localities. My knowledge of the first is grounded in a friendship which began in 1965 and continued intermittently until his death a decade later. During two of those years I lived in adjoining villages. I did not come as a stranger with clip board, and it was not as an anthropological fieldworker that I came to know him. Through him, however, I was drawn into studying another facet of my own society. I became acquainted with the second individual whilst engaged in long-term fieldwork, and my encounter with her made me refocus my entire study.

HAROLD BUSBY

Just as Kaberry argued that women ultimately could not be studied separately from their relations with men, so feminist anthropology asks that masculinity also be studied as part of the construction of gender. Women were initially given specific focus by feminist anthropologists because they had been merged with men. At the same time, it was argued that men and masculinity needed to be separated out from the generic 'man'. This had rarely been done and usually only in the context of analysing initiation rites. Harold Busby, whom I have chosen as my first example, is a person who at a key moment defied the demands of masculinity, in the equivalent of an initiation rite comparable to those studied elsewhere by anthropologists. He refused to be a warrior like the majority of his generation, class and nation, and deserted after being conscripted to fight in the First World War. Other men who resisted through hysterical symptoms on the battle front were brought back to what was specifically identified as 'masculine normality' through various psychiatric techniques (Showalter 1985).[4]

I choose Harold Busby also because he risks being lost to history. Yet he was an inhabitant of what could also be an 'ethnographic region' for native anthropologists: Oxfordshire and the 'Home Counties'. Once a gardener, labourer and chauffeur, he was a resident of Lower Heyford, a few miles from the centre of Oxford. A few relics were bequeathed to the Bodleian Library by his neighbour: a clothes brush and some photographs. The objects are meaningless unless their context is explained. Here I venture also onto territory held confidently by historians, examining the powerless unrecorded

Figure 10.1 Harold Busby.

in many official documents. I am, as Samuel (1975: xix) has suggested for a certain type of social history, travelling 'on foot instead of in armoured car'. Indeed that is what anthropologists normally do.

I focus on an individual in the knowledge that historians have given us a wealth of material to place him in context. To straddle history and social anthropology is again to be in accord with Kaberry who, at a lecture in Oxford in 1968, said that if she had not become an anthropologist she would have become a historian (Kaberry 1968). Her research in Africa entailed scrupulous attention to historical records and to oral history.

I describe a man from a seemingly rural backwater,[5] whose heroic act of anti-heroism, whose defiant views and beliefs – however isolated and fragmented – teach us something and inspire. Much of his later life was seen as querulous and eccentric, but his entire life was marked by his defiance of 1916. He was also a self-taught intellectual, eager for knowledge, and a musician striving for harmony.

Of the First World War, Hobsbawm (1987: 310–11) notes that 'no government of a great power before 1914 wanted either a general European war or even . . . a limited military conflict with another European great power'. Moreover, the British had to rely on volunteers. Governments and the opponents of war were 'taken utterly by surprise . . . by the extraordinary wave of patriotic enthusiasm' (ibid. 325). In Britain 750,000 volunteered in the first two months, and another million in the next eight. It was seen as a release, especially by young middle-class men. The initial euphoria is echoed in an international anthology of writers and poets, all killed in the war (Cross 1988). Almost to a man they were imbued with nationalistic fervour. These lost writers 'discovered values they admired', namely manliness and comradeship (ibid. 381). To enlist was to find and forge a masculine identity. Here we find the multiple yet strangely uniform voices of the educated, artistic elite of Europe. By contrast, as Williamson (1989: 12) remarks in a recent review:

> More needs to be known about the common soldier – the product of state schools . . . . Here academic study has been slow . . . . While labour history has produced much valuable work on the 'industrial heroes' of the period, the war heroes and their families are less familiar.

Even less is known about other types of heroes, such as Harold Busby, who resisted. Another example is Percy Topliss, who led a mutiny in northern France about which information is largely inaccessible and still provokes controversy.

Williamson, like other commentators, finds astounding 'the acceptance of the war by the ordinary volunteer or conscript and tolerance of the trenches' and asks what it did 'to their patriotism, their religion, their views about authority, their politics and social or class conceptions'. While believing that popular anthologies offer 'human interest', Williamson does not think they can 'transcend the sources to enable understanding to advance significantly' (ibid. 12). His opinion reflects the view I outlined above, which associates an interest in the individual voice only with a humane salvage operation.

Doubtless, common themes and abstract generalisations could be extrapolated from an anthology. Here again, however, the individual exception, testimony and resistance might be passed over. The understanding which Williamson calls for is only complete if it includes the moments of defiance; elusive and fragile, yet part of the totality of that historical experience. Paradoxically, we accept the uniqueness of perceptions when encountered in an individual published poet, whose name we reify because the words resonate with shared cultural values or some imagined possibility.

Harold Busby's acts of defiance and their narration cannot be appreciated simply as aesthetic artefacts. The fragments of written testimony, including some poems, cannot be extracted from his life and subjected to the cultural criteria applied to the poetry of the educated elite of his generation. Busby's poem of his desertion is a narrative, exact and in rhyming couplets. Without readers knowing the background to his story, this deserter's tale risks being trivialised. He was not a professional poet, as are those represented in the war anthologies. He resorted to verse at significant junctures. In thinking about how to present the poem, I realised that I had been trapped by my own education and culture. I was being ethnocentric in my own land; a snare just as much for anthropologists of Europe as of exotica. Elsewhere, anthropologists are only too delighted to record indigenous texts as ways into understanding the culture, whether or not according to indigenous aesthetic criteria.

Busby's aesthetic criteria were very different from the emergent modernism which the elite intellectuals and artists embraced before the First World War. His were rooted in a tradition against which the privileged elite were rebelling. For Harold Busby, whose formal education at Kiddington village school ended by about twelve, knowledge and the arts were firmly based in reason, science and realism, and were consolidated through years of self-education. His favourite poet was Longfellow. He recited Tennyson and Swinburne. He quoted Ibsen, Shaw and Tom Paine. He read Ingersol probably at the same time that Malinowski was doing so in the Trobriands, and he read other books on science and astronomy. A favourite composer was Haydn, whose *Creation* he conducted in the village hall with professionals, bussed in from Oxford at his own expense, to perform with his choir and orchestra. He was selected to play with professional musicians in the Sheldonian. He disliked atonal music, and although a vehement atheist, he loved Victorian hymns. The paintings he made in his mid-sixties were rigidly naturalist. He defined himself as both atheist and communist. Having left school, he worked at stone breaking. His father was a skilled labourer. His musical education began thanks to his father's violin. Self-taught at first, he gathered a number of boys into a group. After hearing a performance at a village fete, a lady from Oxford arranged for a teacher from Woodstock to give them some weekly lessons. At the age of fourteen, Busby paid for more lessons.

His religious scepticism and political interests found a vocabulary when he moved as a gardener to London. Hyde Park was the educational forum not only for urban workers but also for rural migrants. He kept his political views hidden from his employers, but had already made a name for himself as an atheist in the Oxfordshire villages. His neighbours were among those who voluntarily enlisted in 1914.

> They volunteered like mad . . . . They thought 'oh let's all join, the bloody war will be over before we get trained and we'll have a holiday'. They were fed up with all their work on the farm . . . I joined up because I had to.

He faced compulsory conscription in 1916. The calls for God and country were meaningless. But there was no acceptable way in which he could declare himself a conscientious objector, a category open for the middle class and possibly the urban worker. In his neighbourhood, Busby said, conscientious objection would bring total shame on his family. In any case, he was not a pacifist but objected to *this* war. Once enlisted, he attracted the ears of his fellow conscripts:

> The first night I was in barracks and we hadn't been there very long before I started up, and I kept them going until 2 o'clock. And there was . . . a room full. About 30 of them . . . and I let them have it full blast about religion and the war and everything else . . . well everywhere I went I wasn't afraid of getting the sack, don't you see. I wasn't afraid of being told off for doing something I ought not. I didn't care a damn what happened to me.

One evening on the Dover cliffs he wrote a poem outlining his religious scepticism. It reads as a lone voice in agonised argument. Unlike the educated modernist elite, he had no access to atheist circles. He met a number of like minds in the army but found 'they kept moving us around . . . they weren't allowed to congregate'. Instead of defining himself as a conscientious objector at the outset, the more honourable but dangerous, irrevocable act for Busby, the rural worker, was to desert and leave Europe. When a man said he could buy him a ticket to America, Busby gave him most of his savings. The boat he eventually boarded was in fact set for the Caribbean. Cheated, he had to work some of his passage and eventually he landed at Panama. He travelled to New Orleans and sent word to a sister. He was informed that so great was the shame of desertion in the Oxfordshire villages that a brother-in-law would hand him over to the authorities if he returned.

Letters from his sister revealed his mother's despair. She would lean out of her window at night and call his name. Finally, he decided that the tropics and a foreign land were not for him. No nationalist, he loved his native Oxfordshire and worked his passage home shovelling coal in the bowels of a steamer. He gave himself up and was arrested at Liverpool.

Harold Busby's poem

> I didn't take kindly to the army life.
> It seemed to me nothing but care and strife
> and I said to myself you will have to stick it.
> Yet I had faint hopes that I would work my ticket.
> As time went on my hopes had fled
> but others had risen so again I said.
> I'll keep up courage I still have time
> to make other plans so you'll see to the crime.

Figure 10.2 Harold Busby (right) as a younger man after rabbit hunting.

I set about these with a little exertion
as my mind you see was set on desertion
and I found a friend in the same state of mind
but he proved at last to be very unkind.
With plans all complete I then took a trip
to London and there I awaited a ship.
The day came at last when she was to sail
and I boarded this steamer Royal Mail.
As we went down the Thames I thought all goes well.
But it didn't do so as I've yet to tell.
For on reaching the Channel or not far from it
I hung over the side and commenced to vomit.

This ship as I thought to America bound
went to the West Indies and soon it was found.
I had been deceived by this so-called friend
and my chances I thought were now at an end.
The days they all are much too slow to suit me
for when not sea-sick I was sick of the sea.
My associates too I wish I could shun.
It was an unpleasant job this task I'd begun.
As bad as things were something seemed to say
don't despond don't give in
Perhaps one day something may happen.
Your luck it may change.
From then future plans I commenced to arrange.
The first island we came to was Barbados.
We called and there a few passengers left us.
We were soon moving on towards Trinidad
and this place was only a glimpse that I had.
At the two places mentioned short was our stay
and no matter we called and went on our way.
Our course was north-west and it took five days more
before landing safely on Jamaica's shore.
To get on the land was a treat to me
though I didn't admire its scenery.
Disappointment undoubtedly was my fate
my expectation was much too great.
It didn't take long for me to decide
it was not a fit place for me to reside.
When one of our calls I heard was Colon,
I thought it was the best place I could fix upon.
Now a stay in Colon I thought at first sight
was a place that I sought, it looked alright.
But it proved after some investigation
not nearly up to my expectation.
To desert the ship I then journeyed by train
and in Panama was content to remain
until she left port. That I learned by the news
then I took the train back midst tropical views.
'Twas here in this district, the Canal zone
that my spirits fell when I thought of home.
I pictured other countries just as good
but it seemed to myself no one understood.
Rather more than a week was all I spent here
and it seems sufficient to make it quite clear
that a tropical country would not suit me.

I soon got a ship and was back at sea.
This time I was under a different flag.
It was the stars and stripes though I didn't brag.
Although I could see it was beyond all doubt,
my original plan was to be carried out.
From Bocas we took a load of bananas.
And in a few days we had reached Havana
where we then took on board additional fruit
and lots of passengers for the States en route.
Our next call or rather our destination
could afford me at least one consolation.
For on leaving England it was my ambition
to reach the States under any condition.
We arrived in port, I received some pay
and in New Orleans had a fortnight's stay.
But having no wish any further to roam
I made all arrangements for getting back home.
My conclusions perhaps too hasty appear
but please bear in mind that to me home was dear.
How I forsake it the land I loved best.
This question was settled without further test.
During all this time it had been my remorse.
Yet by going home I was aware of course
that my troubles weren't over but I should find
the contentment desired, that peace of mind.
The perils at sea were now worse than ever.
With submarines, radars and winter weather.
So all of these risks I was willing to take
rather than England, home and friends forsake.
The homeward bound journey was not very dull
until leaving Norfolk where we called for coal
and then I assure you we had a rough time
much too rough to express in this little rhyme.
The weather was bad nearly all of the way
and it made me say things well I hoped not to say.
But when land was sighted as you may suppose
the feeling of joy within me arose.
The land I refer to was the Emerald Isle
at its farthest point west so it will take a while
to reach Liverpool for that's where we were bound
and eventually we gained quite safe and sound.
It was Sunday morning we arrived in port
and I feared the next day before a court.

> They handed me over not against my will
> to be taken by escort back to Bexhill.
> What would happen next I could give a good guess
> and though bad it seemed I am bound to confess
> I was glad to get back for it seemed like home
> when compared with the life from which I had just come.
> For an RCM I had some time to wait
> my stories are many I've had to relate.
> I was three months adrift to the very day
> and it was a very expensive holiday.
> My sentence was read it was four months detention.
> It may seem a lot but here I must mention.
> I did 13 days then was sent out to France
> I suppose with the rest must take my chance.

At his court martial he took full responsibility for his actions, refusing to take the line that he had been manipulated by others:

> One of them says 'Couldn't you make up a story about how you was persuaded to go by somebody?' I said no I had to go on my own. I said I couldn't put the blame on anybody. I was to blame . . . I wanted to be kept there you see. . . . I thought I was well away in Wandsworth. I thought I was well safe as houses.

Sentenced to only three months in Wandsworth gaol, he had hoped to spend the rest of the war there, as if his cell were a private study for avid reading.

Paradoxically his independent mind brought an early pardon. A well-meaning archdeacon whose attention he had attracted at church sent him a book through the prison governor, then brought pressure on the authorities and after only a few weeks he was released. He was told in all magnanimity that as soon as his feet were on the boat for France he was a 'free man'.

> Of course after I was in France . . . I let rip in my old style and I had quite a few decent people tack on to me when they knew what I had to talk about.

While Harold Busby's enquiring mind sent him from Wandsworth earlier than hoped, it also saved him from the trenches. When one officer gave his name as Paine, Busby asked 'Any relation to Tom?' When the officer was asked to select some men for the big guns, safely behind the lines, he included Busby. He did indeed receive injuries but returned with sufficient wounds to be discharged without being totally disabled. The injuries he received in the war worsened in old age. When his damaged shoulder forced him to give up the violin in his sixties, he took up the cello. Although his deteriorating hearing made a free-flowing dialogue increasingly difficult, the unexpected consequence of my producing a tape-recorder was a sudden clarity in his monologues. The repetitious snippets of our everyday exchanges diminished as he spoke his concentrated testimony.

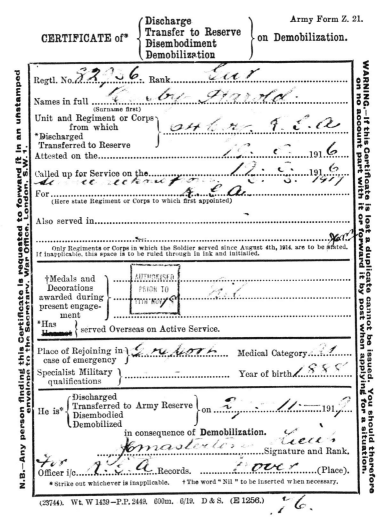

Figure 10.3 Harold Busby's demobilisation certificate. His period of desertion and imprisonment is concealed in the text.

He knew it was his only chance to live on beyond his death. And the stories he chose for special focus were about these moments of defiance. Necessarily, I pass over most of his life and the details of his death, and conclude my tribute to Busby with a piece he wrote in his seventies (figure 10.4). Estranged for years from his wife, he lived alone. He joked about putting the text as an advert in the local post office. Written before the Women's Movement, it

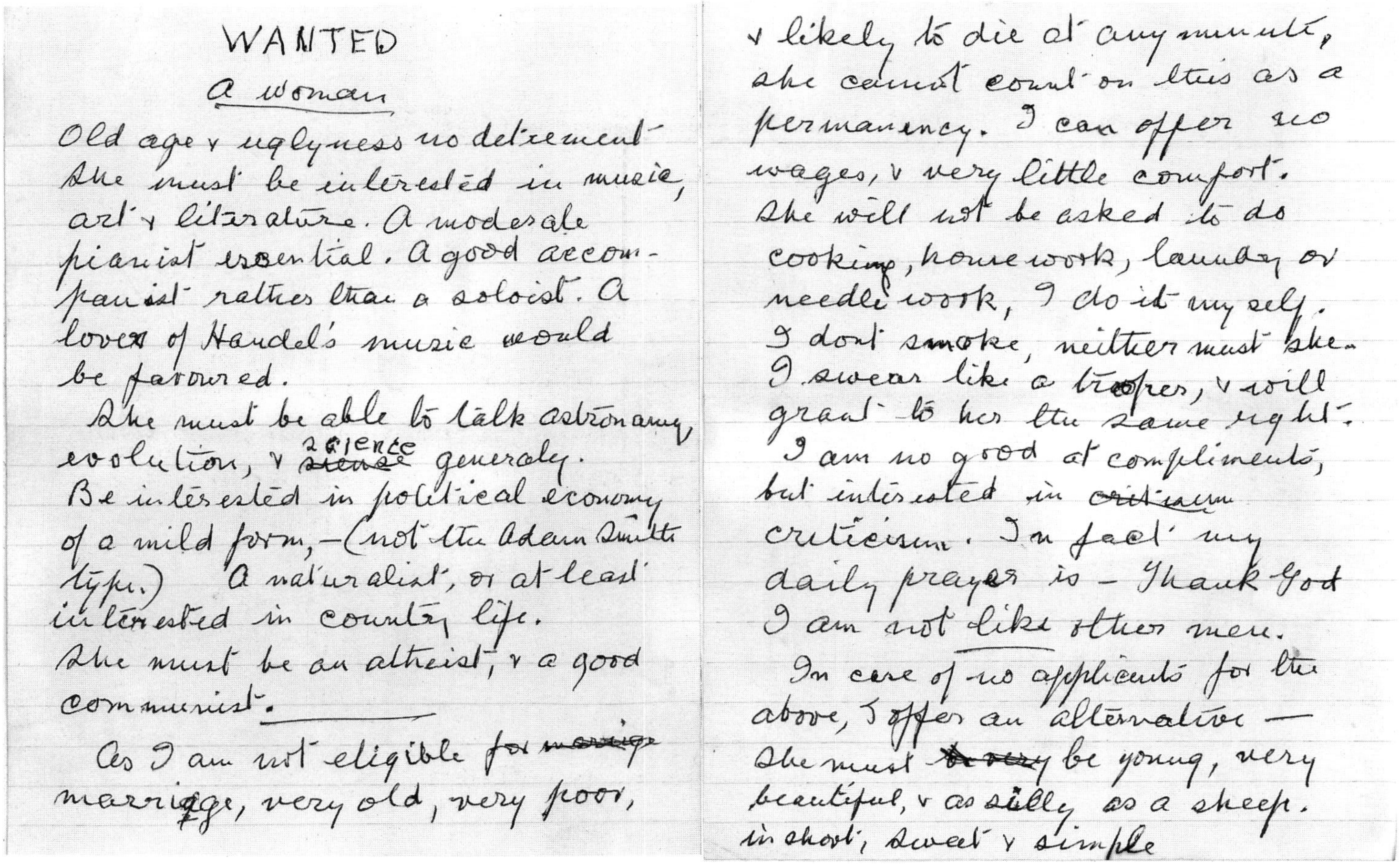

WANTED
<u>A woman</u>

Old age & ugliness no detriment.
She must be interested in music,
art, & literature. A moderate
pianist essential. A good accompanist rather than a soloist. A
lover of Handel's music would
be favoured.
She must be able to talk astronomy,
evolution, & science generally.
Be interested in political economy
of a mild form — (not the Adam Smith
type.) A naturalist, or at least'
interested in country life.
She must be an atheist, & a good
communist.

As I am not eligible for ~~marriage~~
marriage, very old, very poor,
& likely to die at' any minute,
she cannot count on this as a
permanency. I can offer no
wages, & very little comfort.
She will not be asked to do
cooking, housework, laundry or
needlework, I do it myself.
I don't smoke, neither must' she.
I swear like a trooper, & will
grant' to her the same right.
I am no good at compliments,
but interested in criticism —
criticism. In fact' my
daily prayer is — thank God
I am not' like other men.

In case of no applicants for the
above, I offer an alternative —
She must ~~be very~~ be young, very
beautiful, & silly, do a sheep,
in short, sweet & simple.

Figure 10.4 WANTED: A woman

shows again a defiance of gender conventions – concerning a woman's age, intelligence, domestic labour and physical appearance. Like his resistance to fulfilling a masculine ideal through becoming a soldier, there is a resistance to the very gender ideals which remain with us today.

WANTED

A Woman

Old age & uglyness no detrement. She must be interested in music, art & literature. A moderate pianist essential. A good accompanist rather than a soloist. A lover of Handel's music would be favoured.

She must be able to talk astronamy evolution, & science generaly. Be interested in political economy of a mild form. – (not the Adam Smith type). A naturalist, or at least interested in country life. She must be an atheist, & a good communist.

As I am not eligible for marriage, very old, very poor, & likely to die at any minute, she cannot count on this as a permanency. I can offer no wages, v. little comfort. She will not be asked to do cooking, housework, laundry or needlework, I do it myself. I don't smoke, neither must she. I swear like a trooper, & will grant to her the same right. I am no good at compliments, but interested in criticism. In fact my daily prayer is – Thank God I am not *like* other men.

In case of no applicants for the above, I offer an alternative – she must be young, very beautiful, & silly as a sheep. In short, sweet & simple. (Original spelling retained)

Figure 10.5 Harold Busby canoeing down the Oxford Canal in the late 1960s.

JACQUELINE GRÉGOIRE

My second example of resistance concerns a woman in Normandy, France:[6] Jacqueline Grégoire, who has worked most of her life with dairy cows, those domesticated creatures used as a metaphor by Ashley Montagu. She has become central to my study of ageing and the aged in a rural locality. In order to understand the life's labour of the retired elderly in hospices and homes, it was important to see a small tenant farm being worked in ways similar to those to which my elderly informants were accustomed. Madame Grégoire hand-milks thirteen cows twice a day. From the perspective of some younger farmers and agriculturists, and in terms of the common agricultural policy, she is a last eccentric, engaged in monotonous and onerous labour which will disappear with technological progress. At 58, she is the last in the locality to carry on her skills. The milk quota has encouraged farmers to give up their cows. They receive financial reward for accepting a ban on having dairy cattle on their pastures. Others have been able to amalgamate farms and have received loans for investing in large mechanical dairy parlours. The cows are given chemical concentrates to increase their yield. At one farm they wear special collars to trigger the concentrates in individually computerised quantities. Each has a number on the computer printout.

By contrast, Madame Grégoire names each of her thirteen cows and knows each animal's individual idiosyncrasies. 'Mère No-No' is gentle, so I was given her for learning how to milk. Others will incline to kick, and need an iron bar on their haunch when milking. After centuries of breeding, cows are not as bovine as anthropologists would believe. Even Mère No-No, with her sweet temperament, needed to be introduced to me with voice and gaze before I could confidently pull at her teats.

Madame Grégoire refuses to treat her cows as mere objects. She will not give them concentrates, rejecting a technological intervention which would increase the yield but shorten the cow's productive life. She is outraged by the experimental use of hormones and by genetic engineering which would produce more calves. The cows are fed from rich and varied hay, untreated by chemicals which she insists would affect the quality and purity of the milk. While all around her farms are changing, she resists as far as possible the cycle of dependence which investment in milking machinery would bring. Even a small hand-held machine would increase electricity and water bills. Instead, she uses her own bodily power. To walk round her farm, to see its workings and listen to her theories, is to perceive an uncanny resemblance with the metropolitan-based green movements. She has an entirely coherent ecology. Her ducks and hens roam around the yard, free range. No batteries, no salmonella risks there. In winter the cattle byre is cleaned out daily, the dung mixed with straw and used as manure for crops and the organic vegetable garden. This method, and the ample space for the cows to graze, means that there is no risk of concentrated slurry polluting the rivers and water supply. Her apple trees are unsprayed. The variety blends well for the house cider and the stronger *eau-de-vie*. Above all, the milk has a rich, unique taste now lost from supermarket cartons. To drink the milk is to experience a magical involvement with the landscape, its cows and a woman's labour. Madame Grégoire and her neighbours take and savour what they require. The bulk is collected and blended with the others' milk which she sees as chemically tainted.

Madame Grégoire learned to milk as a child. In one context her years of labour as a small farmer with her husband can be seen as ones of exploitation and subordination. In the area, younger non-farming women characterise the past as one where men hung around at markets, while their slave wives were locked in the daily milking routine. Like the Aboriginal women, they were also mainly responsible for domestic production. The absentee landowners lived off the rents from these dozens of farms. This is and was no pastoral idyll.

In Madame Grégoire's case the gender division is modified. Her husband's physical frailty precludes heavy labour in the yard, so he now takes responsibility for tending the log-fired stove, cooking and housework. Her unmarried son, a garage mechanic, helps in the yard. He would have liked to continue the farm but one of so few hectares is no longer viable. The son could not take on the capital loans for expansion and technical investment. The landowner, now confronted with the low profitability of small farms, has recently sold the property to the family. The three adult offspring have bought portions. But its future as a dairy farm is finished. The cows will be there only as long as Madame Grégoire is able to work. Meanwhile, hand-milking takes up her mornings and later afternoons. She was proud to tell me that since her youth she has only missed milking twice, through illness and when she gave birth. The best time to record her speech is when she is perched on her three-legged stool in the stable. Our conversation is backed by the rhythm of the squirting milk. At first it sounds like hail in the empty bucket, then it softens. The last slow drops fall onto the creamy foam at the top of the bucket. These rhythmic sounds on the tape are sure and defiant. For these moments she is resisting history. Her skills and views on the treatment of animals, food production and agriculture are being eroded at the rural margins.

But they are vindicated by many at the metropolitan centre. She has read no leaflets from Friends of the Earth. Her articulate, coherent views come from practice and a critical resistance. Unlike members of the Green Movement, most of whom are metropolitan consumers, she, as small-scale producer, works in relative isolation. Her contemporaries have retired or have been obliged to adopt mechanical techniques.

It seems at first that I have interpreted Madame Grégoire's actions much in the style of Kaberry. From the outside she and her cows could be dismissed as domesticated slave and beasts of burden. Yet Madame Grégoire takes pride and pleasure in her productive labour. She has found areas for creative autonomy. It should not, however, be concluded that her lack of subservience means absence of subordination. The implications of Kaberry's argument hold no more for the traditional French peasant woman than they do for Aboriginal women. Women's productive yet different participation in a gender division of labour is not evidence of equality. Despite the conclusions of a brilliantly detailed historical study (Segalen 1980), an alternative reading reveals that relations between French peasant women and men are marked by political, economic and ritual asymmetry, but the form of that subordination changes.

We need to consider the historical moment of Madame Grégoire's defiance. Hand-milking, as it was in her youth, can be seen differently. It was more of an imposition. A number of older women I spoke to disliked milking but had no alternative. Over time, Madame Grégoire was 'apprenticed', in de Beauvoir's terms (Okely 1975, chapter 4, this volume). Today the alternatives are even fewer. Her granddaughters, like other young persons in the locality, face unemployment with the increasing amalgamation of farms and agri-business. Urban employment is not on offer. At the same time the food produced by agribusiness and the changes in the landscape are not convincing improvements. Thus what was once routine is now experienced as a coherent view of culture and nature, under threat. To hold that view is to be subversive towards the new orthodoxy.

Kaberry was acutely aware of gender implications in discussing develop-ment plans and women, as for example in the Cameroons (Kaberry 1952: 154). Women risk losing what economic power they had. In Normandy, the transition from hand to machine milking has transformed the division of labour. Women have been deskilled, and men now manage the cows with and as machines. Agricultural development marginalises women in dairy and agricultural production (cf. Segalen 1980). Madame Grégoire sees that.[7]

Like Harold Busby's resistance to the First World War, Jacqueline Grégoire's fragmented defence of green farming techniques will be vindicated by history. Later it may be asked, as it was of volunteers to the First World War, how could so many have appeared to submit to self-destruction? In both instances, the people concerned lacked the power to do otherwise. In some cases individuals at specific moments have the knowledge which history might later vindicate, or which in other contexts may form the basis for organised, group resistance and change. Absent from the archives but scattered in our field notes, there are fragments of resistance. It is not that the atypical individuals should be seen as unitary isolates. Only at certain moments may they show difference and defiance. These moments are fragile and often submerged from view. We should capture them where we can.

To conclude: I have argued that in demonstrating that Aboriginal women are active subjects rather than passive objects, Kaberry was engaged in a critique of potentially derogatory images of women. She was diverted, however, from the question of subordination. Her text, and others even today

Figure 10.6 Madame Grégoire hand-milking.
Source: Alan Campbell.

in discussions of gender relations elsewhere, can be misread as evidence of women having power and control equivalent to that of men. Although Kaberry argued against the treatment of individuals as ciphers supporting the social system, she did not systematically examine examples of individual resistance to that system. In this chapter, I have presented an alternative theoretical and methodological focus on persons as active subjects, by examining specific individuals' momentary resistance to systems of subordination. Resistance may be fragmented and less visible than that usually associated with collective action and organised mass movements. Using the examples of a man and a woman who, at specific times in their lives, have been regarded as atypical or idiosyncratic individuals, I have explored moments when their actions can be interpreted as resistance. In both cases there are gender, as well as class, rural and other implications. The one resisted becoming a soldier, a masculine identity, the other resisted the deskilling of her feminine labour. The one also resisted nationalistic, class and religious ideals, the other resisted the mechanisation of agriculture, a more exploitative treatment of animals and what she saw as an ecological disaster. Their resistance came only at specific times in their life cycles and coinciding with wider historical events or changes. It is precisely because they do not appear to be 'typical' members of their community, especially in their defiant moments, that they risk being lost from general monographs. Yet their fragmented resistance informs us of the power of structures of subordination.

NOTES

This chapter is a revised version of the text originally presented as the Phyllis Kaberry Memorial Lecture organised by the Centre for Cross Cultural Research on Women, at the Taylor Institute, Oxford, on 24 May 1989. I am grateful to Alan Abramson for comments during preparation of this text.

1 Anthropologists, unlike sociologists, are likely to be asked with whom or under whom they are working, and in this respect I am proud to declare my link with my supervisor Godfrey Lienhardt.
2 There was a hidden fragmented resistance in the 1950s among the hundreds of women who read de Beauvoir (see Okely 1986). Only later did it crystallise in the Women's Liberation Movement.
3 In an extensive study of resistance among peasants, Scott (1985) has considered contexts where it is kept from public view. In his opinion the term should not be reserved for collective or organised action.
4 In this the anthropologist W. H. R. Rivers colluded (Showalter 1985: 167–94).
5 Elsewhere Howkins (1985) reveals hitherto undocumented rural resistance which was ungeneralised. Apparently 'stable' relationships concealed antagonisms (ibid. 18).
6 Fieldwork in France (1985–6, 1987, 1988) was financed by the Economic and Social Research Council (grant no. G01250006) and the Fuller Fund, the Department of Sociology, University of Essex.
7 In the course of the original lecture, I pointed out how a defiant gesture was completed in Normandy. Two hours previously Madame Grégoire had brought in the cows from the meadows. By the end of the lecture in Oxford, she had finished milking them. She was to do the same again twice the next day. In fact the present tense used earlier has become the ethnographic present. Madame Grégoire disposed of all her cows at the end of the year.

REFERENCES

Ardener, E. (1975) 'Belief and the problem of women', in S. Ardener (ed.) *Perceiving Women*, London: Malaby Press.
Ardener, S. (ed.) (1975) *Perceiving Women*, London: Malaby Press.
Bakhtin, M. (1981) *The Dialogic Imagination*, M. Holquist (ed.), Austin: University of Texas Press.
Beauvoir, S. de (1949) *Le Deuxième sexe*, Paris: Gallimard.
Bell, D. (1983) *Daughters of the Dreaming*, Melbourne: McPhee Gribble.

Berndt, C. (1981) 'Interpretations and "facts" in Aboriginal Australia', in F. Dahlberg (ed.) *Woman the Gatherer*, New Haven: Yale University Press.

Briffault, R. (1927) *The Mothers: The Matriarchal Theory of Social Origins*, New York: Macmillan.

Caplan, P. and Bujra, J. (eds) (1978) *Women United, Women Divided*, London: Tavistock.

Clifford, J. and Marcus, G. (eds) (1986) *Writing Culture*, Berkeley: University of California Press.

Cross, T. (ed.) (1988) *The Lost Voices of World War I*, London: Bloomsbury.

Devereux, L. (1987) 'Gender difference and the relations of inequality in Zinacanta', in M. Strathern (ed.) *Dealing with Inequality*, Cambridge: Cambridge University Press.

Elkin, A.P. (1939) Introduction to P. Kaberry, *Aboriginal Woman: Sacred and Profane*, London: Routledge and Kegan Paul.

Engels, F. (1958 [1884]) *The Origin of the Family, Private Property, and the State*, Oxford: Blackwell.

Errington, F. and Gewertz, D. (1987) 'The remarriage of Yebiwali: a study of dominance and false consciousness in a non-Western society', in M. Strathern (ed.) *Dealing with Inequality*, Cambridge: Cambridge University Press.

Friedl, E. (1975) *Women and Men: An Anthropologist's View*, New York: Holt, Rinehart and Winston.

Hobsbawm, E. (1987) *The Age of Empire 1875–1914*, London: Weidenfeld and Nicolson.

Howkins, A. (1985) *Poor Labouring Men: Rural Radicalism in Norfolk 1870–1923*. London: Routledge and Kegan Paul.

Huizer, G. (1978) 'Research-through-action: some practical experiences with peasant organisations', in G. Huizer and B. Mannheim (eds) *The Politics of Anthropology*, The Hague: Mouton.

Kaberry, P. (1939) *Aboriginal Woman: Sacred and Profane*, London: Routledge and Kegan Paul.

—— (1952) *Women of the Grassfields*, London: HMSO Colonial Office.

—— (1957) 'Malinowski's contribution to field-work methods and writing of ethnography', in R. Firth (ed.) *Man and Culture*, London: Routledge and Kegan Paul.

—— (1968) 'Historians who provide cautionary tails for anthropologists (male and female)'. Fragment of paper given at Evans-Pritchard's Seminar, Oxford: LSE Archives.

Kandiyoti, D. (1988) 'Bargaining with patriarchy', *Gender and Society* 2, 3: 274–90.

Keesing, R. (1987) 'Ta'a geni: women's perspectives on Kwaio society', in M. Strathern (ed.) *Dealing with Inequality*, Cambridge: Cambridge University Press.

Leacock, E. (1982) *Myths of Male Dominance*, New York: Monthly Review Press.

Malinowski, B. (1913) *The Family Among the Australian Aborigines*, London: University of London Press.

Marcus, J. (1992) 'Racism, terror and the production of Australian auto/biographies', in J. Okely and H. Callaway (eds) *Anthropology and Autobiography*, London: Routledge.

Montagu, Ashley M.F. (1937) *Coming into Being among the Australian Aborigines*, London: Routledge.

Okely, J. (1975) 'Gypsy women: models in conflict', in S. Ardener (ed.) *Perceiving Women*, London: Malaby Press.

—— (1983) *The Traveller-Gypsies*, Cambridge: Cambridge University Press.

—— (1986) *Simone de Beauvoir: A Re-reading*, London: Virago/New York: Pantheon.

Okely, J. and Callaway, H. (eds) (1992) *Anthropology and Autobiography*, London: Routledge.

Omvedt, G. (1978) 'On the participant study of women's movements: methodological, definitional and action considerations', in G. Huizer and B. Mannheim (eds) *The Politics of Anthropology*, The Hague: Mouton.

Plummer, K. (1983) *Documents of Life*, London: Allen and Unwin.

Reiter, R. (ed.) (1975) *Toward an Anthropology of Women*, New York: Monthly Review Press.

Rohrlich-Leavitt, R., Sykes, B. and Weatherford, E. (1975) 'Aboriginal woman: male and female anthropological perspectives', in R. Reiter (ed.) *Toward an Anthropology of Women*, New York: Monthly Review Press.

Rosaldo, M. and Lamphere, L. (eds) (1974) *Woman, Culture and Society*, Stanford: Stanford University Press.

Samuel, R. (1975) Introduction to R. Samuel (ed.) *Village Life and Labour*, London: Routledge and Kegan Paul.

Scott, J. (1985) *Weapons of the Weak: Everyday Forms of Peasant Resistance*, New Haven: Yale University Press.

Segalen, M. (1980) *Mari et femme dans la société paysanne*, Paris: Flammarion.

Shostak, M. (1981) *Nisa: The Life and Words of a !Kung Woman*, Cambridge: Harvard University Press.

Showalter, E. (1985) *The Female Malady: Women, Madness and English Culture*, London: Virago.

Slocum, S. (1975) 'Woman the gatherer: male bias in anthropology', in R. Reiter (ed.) *Toward an Anthropology of Women*, New York: Monthly Review Press.

Spencer, P. (1992) 'Automythologies and the reconstruction of ageing', in J.Okely and H. Callaway (eds) *Anthropology and Autobiography*, London: Routledge.

Weiner, A. (1976) *Women of Value, Men of Renown*, Austin: University of Texas Press.

Williamson, P. (1989) 'Something of importance', *London Review of Books* 2 (Feb.), 11–12.

Reference index

(Numbers in italic refer to photographs)

Subject index